REVI

"*Ecosystems as Models for Restoring our Economies* appeals to a broad range of people across ages, values, and political beliefs, and will change the way we live our lives. I'll be sending this book to many people in my life moving forward, and believe it should be required reading for high schools, colleges, and any other educational program."
  ~ **Morgan Day, urban planning and sustainability writer**

"Giordanengo provides a comprehensive synthesis of ecological foundations and economic structure, sorely lacking in our quest to develop sustainable economies in the face of growing economic and environmental turmoil. From the roots of ecological restoration, this book delivers a clear path to restoring the American economy, in a way that speaks in a universal language to policy makers, business owners, academics and the general public. The identification of three drivers of highly resilient and productive economies and ecosystems—diversity, energy, and trade—is perhaps the most important insight to resolving growing tensions between society, nature, and the global market economy. This book provides hopes for species, ecosystems and the planet."
  ~ **Kingsley Dixon, vice chair of the global board of directors, Society for Ecological Restoration.**

"If you care about the environment; you will not want to miss reading this book."
  ~ **Don Hijar, life-long conservationist, and owner of Pawnee Buttes Seed Company**

"Entrepreneurs play a critical role in the ecosystem, and in the endurance and restoration of a thriving economy. *Ecosystems as Models for Restoring our Economies*, Giordanengo's masterpiece book, distills nature's most important principles with basic economic theory in a logical and seamless narrative. Your first takeaway might be—why haven't we looked at the earth's ecosystems before —for the answers to a sustainable economy? As a reader, you will be drawn to new clues and conclusions."
  ~ **Patty Alper, author of Teach to Work, president of the Alper Portfolio Group Ltd.**

"As an ecologist and ecosystem restorationist John Giordanengo, like myself, has spent decades pondering the plight of humanity while simultaneously working with natural plant communities that have been able to survive every disturbance imaginable. There are predictable strategies used by nature, in order to survive in a world of unpredictable disturbances. Giordanengo points out that it is the built-in strategy of natural systems to increase energy capture, increase diversity, and to maximize the recycling of nutrients within the system beginning at the local level. The in-depth work of this book reveals our economy has become "upside down" compared to ecosystems. The human economy has grown "out" to the limits of our biosphere. It is time, as Giordanengo asserts, to mimic nature and to grow IN."

    ~ **Mark Shepard, author of Restoration Agriculture**

"Finding the 'win-win-win' solution that optimizes economics, environmental sustainability, and human well-being is an essential and urgent task facing all of us. Giordanengo approaches this problem with his unique background of scientist, NGO leader, and business owner. He makes credible arguments and presents credible scenarios to solve the crisis, offering empirical solutions that resonate and build up from the local to global scales. John writes with a level of clarity not common to his colleagues and has created a treatise well worth reading."

    ~ **Tim Seastedt, professor emeritus, University of Colorado, Boulder**

"Biomimicry has helped ranchers like us develop rapid rotational grazing and other practices that help the environment as well as the bottom line. Can the lessons of ecosystem science be applied to entire economies? That is the critical question addressed by John Giordanengo in this insightful book. It is time for economic policy makers to collaborate with environmentalists and ecologists, to develop creative solutions for restoring both the planet and its human communities."

    ~ **David M. Jessup, co-owner of Sylvan Dale Ranch,**
    author of *Mariano's Crossing* and other award-winning novels.

ECOSYSTEMS

—— as models for restoring our ——

ECONOMIES

John H. Giordanengo

Ecosystems as Models for Restoring our Economies

Printed in Colorado, USA by Morrell Printing Solutions
Second Printing, with editorial and technical revisions: 2022

ISBN: 978-1-7379515-0-6

Published by: AloTerra Restoration Services, Fort Collins, CO, USA.

Cover Art by Zara Danyal and Lotus Design, LLC
Interior Design by Strijek Design and Lotus Design, LLC

Recycled Paper Note: Printed on 100% post-consumer recycled content, unless attained through Amazon.

Digital Copies and Speaking Engagements
To catch the author at a speaking engagement, for additional info, or to acquire a digital copy of this book, visit www.growingin.org

AloTerra

ACKNOWLEDGEMENTS

This book could not have been completed in isolation. I wish to thank the following individuals for their support. My brother, Richard Giordanengo, has provided broad cultural and intellectual insights for understanding the restoration of the American economy, which helped shape part III. Thanks to Mike Larsen and Linda Nelson, for our shared stories of ecology, business, systems thinking, and economics on their restored prairie in SE Minnesota, which had more influence on Part III of this book than they likely realize. I am further grateful to Tripp and Missy Hughes, who shared insights into some of Wisconsin's most important industries. Editors and reviewers: Amy Hahn, Pam Joern, Orvel Ray Wilson, Dean Birkenkamp, Dan Gould, Kevin Gurney, Joanna Zea, Mark Shepard, Brandon Lewis, Jody Berman, Apollo Madayag, Pete Eberle, Sarah Paige Ryan, Carmen Smith, Preston Bishir, and others. Of course, I am grateful for the eternal patience and support of my wife, Cheryl Giordanengo, with whom I was fortunate to discuss the more personal details of this book. Countless others, from San Francisco, CA to Washington, DC, have shared their passion for economic and ecological restoration, all of which influenced the content of this book. Thank you!

AUTHOR'S NOTES

I use the word American throughout this book to refer to people who live in the United States of America. From thirty years of travel and work throughout Latin America, I have discovered what many others have come to believe, that citizens of these diverse countries prefer to be associated with their nation of origin: Colombia, Guatemala, Mexico, Costa Rica, etc. It is out of respect and deep appreciation for these diverse cultures that I do not lump them into the one word, American.

100% of profit from the sale of this book is used to support agricultural restoration.

CONTENTS

Part II: The Foundations of a Self-Regulating (Sustainable) Economy

Part III: A Roadmap for Economic Restoration

INTRODUCTION

At the onset of the 2007 Great Recession, professor Simon Johnson of MIT revealed a powerful metaphor at the annual meeting of the American Economic Association. Highlighting the failure of existing economic models, Johnson noted that sustained progress in health and sanitation came only after society had discovered how the body worked, and the nature of diseases that threaten it—known as the germ theory of disease (Wessel, 2007). Economics, Johnson professed, has failed to make meaningful progress, for it has yet to discover its own "germ theory."

The model of global market capitalism, while growing unprecedented levels of wealth for some, is built upon a faulty structure. This faulty structure is akin to a disease, placing every human at risk of supply chain disruptions, turbulent energy markets, political uncertainty among trading partners, and a litany of social and environmental maladies. Hanging in the balance is the security, health, and prosperity of people across the world, the wholeness of our communities, and the ecosystems upon which we rely.

It is no surprise that protests against globalization have intensified over the last half century. A deeper wave of concern arose in the aftermath of the COVID-19 pandemic, as an increasing mass of humanity began questioning the logic of an economy built on eternal global market expansion. Of course, the virus did not cause the subsequent economic calamity. The virus merely highlighted the cracks in our economic foundations. More cracks were illuminated by the recent Russia-Ukraine conflict, and resulting spikes in the cost of energy, fertilizer, and other essential goods for communities across the globe.

Such moments remind us not only that the structure of our economy is deeply flawed, but that at our core we are social beings. We thrive by nourishing the interpersonal bonds between us, and yearn for purpose within our community. The structure of our economy determines whether or not such purpose may be fulfilled, and governs the richness of our relationships. This includes the amount of time we spend with smartphones rather than with those we love; how motivated we are to work, pay taxes, or feed and clothe our neighbors; or whether we will ever know the people responsible for feeding and clothing us. Trite as it may seem, the structure of our economy determines not only how well our needs of today are met, but how well our needs will be met in the age of economic turmoil lying ahead.

Ecosystems as Models for Restoring our Economies peels back those layers of the economy that are the focus of policy, traditional theory, and social science to reveal the structure around which the system is built. That structure has been misunderstood—or completely ignored—by economists, politicians, and activists alike since the founding of capitalism. As capitalism has grown into a truly global system, monumental efforts have been waged by dozens of nations and untold numbers of individuals and organizations over the past century, aimed at resolving our most important social, environmental, and economic challenges. Painful as it may seem, we must question if our most critical problems can be resolved without first resolving the economic flaws responsible for their creation.

My efforts to synthesize the principles of ecology and economics grew out of a passion for preserving the integrity of earth's ecosystems, and the health of our communities. I was studying business and ecology at San Diego State University in the early 90s when the relationship between ecosystems and economies first began to materialize in my thoughts. Yet the strength of the relationship, and where the overlap existed between these seemingly disparate systems, remained only questions in my mind. I had no clue what the foundational components of an ecosystem were, let alone of an economy.

It was the era of exploding consumerism when I, like so many conservationists, activists, politicians, and economists, began questioning how our economies could thrive without undermining the ecosystems and social systems on which they depend. I was working in the recycling and composting industry, and began volunteering to restore riverside forests and wetlands in the Seattle area. That experience inspired me to pursue a graduate degree in restoration ecology in Colorado.

I spent the next two decades restoring highly disturbed landscapes across the arid west while expanding my search for the relationships between ecosystems and economies. Nudged by the Great Recession, I broadened the research for this book, including an exploration of those foundational (i.e., governing) components responsible for sustaining the productivity, health, and resilience of ecosystems and economies.

Part I of this book explores the history of capitalism, and the complex structure and properties of ecosystems and economies, through the lens of systems thinking. These two global systems are not only governed by the same foundational components, but they are tightly interwoven within the same space—earth—to a degree that the health of one has profound impacts on the health of the other. Part II outlines three foundational components of economies and ecosystems, key drivers of their resilience and sustained productivity. These components have been grossly mismanaged since the birth of capitalism.

My career has been built on the knowledge of restoring damaged ecosystems, which provides the framework for Part III—a roadmap for restoring our economies. The science behind ecological restoration indicates that economic restoration should begin with key industries, while basic theories such as evolution and ecological succession provide guidance for the process of economic restoration. The natural distribution and functioning of ecosystems across the earth also offer answers to questions such as: What is the right scale for an economy to be functioning? How local is too local? How big is too big?

I have witnessed, countless times, how the simple act of digging in the soil and planting plants to restore an ecosystem nurtures a vibrant connection between humans, their community, and the natural landscapes surrounding us. Those connections form essential bonds for the fabric of life. So too may humans heal from the practice of economic restoration. In the process of restoring our economies, a more resilient economy is born, enriching our communities while at the same time arming them against a future of global and national economic turmoil. An economy that delivers produce, toilet paper, semiconductor chips, fertilizer, and medicine regardless of international politics, the price of oil, or the availability of government bailouts.

The public will to restore our economies is here, along with the necessary human, financial, and natural resources to achieve meaningful restoration. What humanity has lacked for centuries is a full understanding of the actual structure of sustainable economy, and the knowledge of how to restore such a complex self-regulating system. It is my hope that this book provides a portion of that knowledge, while stimulating meaningful dialogue and, of course, action.

PART I

The Model of a
Self-Regulating (Sustainable)
Economy

And the challenge of capitalism to build it

ONE

THE CHALLENGES OF CAPITALISM IN A POORLY STRUCTURED ECONOMY

You might have opened this book because you question whether the global market economy can sustain the needs of earth's eight billion-plus humans, let alone the remainder of life on earth. And if you cannot put your finger on the root of the problem, you're not alone. The actual structure of any economy is so elusive that even economists struggle to understand past downturns, let alone predict future failures. Unresolved questions remain about the root cause of the Great Depression, the failures of past monetary policy, and other economic crises across the globe. Such academic challenges stem from the fact that most economists and policy makers are trained as linear thinkers, while an economy exists in a highly complex and nonlinear world. That said, most ecologists also struggle to understand the core structure of ecosystems.

Laying the Groundwork to Resolve Social and Environmental Challenges

Until the structure and the foundations of our economies are known and restored, resolving humanity's most pressing social, economic, and environmental challenges will remain a struggle. Is the root of the problem simply globalization? Or is it capitalism? Or is shoddy economic policy to blame? Maybe it's plain greed, which has defined humanity since the days we stopped swinging from trees.

There is far more finger-pointing than answers, in part because the inner workings of global market capitalism—the realm of immense profit and power that drives our daily decisions—remain quite murky. Blaming technology would be equally frivolous. Rather, ecology, economics, capitalism, and technology are more allies than enemies in resolving the innumerable cases of social and environmental degradation across the globe. And they will be allies in resolving our economic woes, from ever-decreasing real wages to ever-increasing social tensions, and a fundamental inability to sustain key production needs in the face of growing global and national turmoil.

To lay the groundwork for solutions to our economic challenges, consider the classic rancher-environmentalist battle. Cattle have been ridiculed as scourges of America's arid west, obliterating grasslands and destroying watersheds for over a century. Angry at the destruction, the public points a finger at the cattle, while they sit in the meadow, staring blankly back, chewing their cud. Yet the wise rancher and the savvy ecologist, while studying the influence of grazing on biodiversity in the prairie, have discovered something in common. The cattle are not the problem.

By resting the land from grazing in certain years, varying a herd's numbers over time, and altering which pasture is grazed in what season, a well-managed herd can increase the diversity and productivity of the system. And in doing so, the grazing cattle, bison, or elk can increase the quality and quantity of fodder not just for themselves, but for pollinators, grouse, antelope, and other wildlife. In turn, healthier watersheds improve fisheries and water quality for downstream communities, and other socio-economic benefits materialize. The ecologist, the rancher, and the economist would agree that, with improved grazing management, we can feed ourselves while enhancing the diversity and productive capacity of our agricultural landscapes.

To resolve our greater economic challenges, we must drive at the heart of the problem rather than addressing the symptoms. We must further understand some critical details and misconceptions about productivity.

The Critical Distinction Between a Nation's Productive Capacity and its Productivity

The term *productive capacity* deserves a clear definition, as that capacity is far more important to a nation's economic, environmental, and social health than is its productivity. A nation's productive capacity determines its ability to produce goods and services now and, more importantly, in the future. Productive capacity is raised by:

- the efficiency with which a country or business can produce goods or services (e.g., producing a bushel of wheat with the fewest inputs);

- labor, including the quantity and skill of that labor;

- entrepreneurship;

- capital stock, such as factories and machines used in production, and the energy to power that stock;

- a stable and secure supply of natural capital (e.g., ore, timber, water, fertile soils);

- the state of technology, including physical infrastructure, high-speed internet, computing power, etc.; and

- political stability, law and order, and security of personal capital (i.e., lack of corruption), all of which influence capital investment, financial risks, and strategic planning.

Of these variables, *efficiency of production* stands at the center, influenced predictably by the others. Yet there is a deeper influence on a nation's efficiency of production, and hence its productive capacity: the management of an economy's foundational components. For instance, cheap imports (trade component) and low-cost fossil fuels (energy component) may generate financial efficiencies for an industry or nation, but at the expense of resource-use efficiency. In other words, *financially* efficient means of production (e.g., inexpensive energy, cheap water, low labor and land costs in export countries, etc.) often mask resource inefficiencies and degradation of key system components, such as declining social conditions, tenuous trade ties, dwindling soil fertility, volatile and/or uncertain future energy supplies, polluted air and water, etc. Higher productivity may stem from such inefficiencies, but in the process a nation's productive capacity declines.

A country's *productivity* is its current rate of output relative to the quantity of inputs, and should take into account the efficient use of resources. Instead, most nations champion economic policies aimed at the highest possible productivity, while ignoring a critical question: Can that productivity be sustained without jeopardizing the nation's productive capacity? For instance, US policy has stimulated the production of more corn per acre than in any previous time in history. But there's a catch. The very methods that produce high yields also degrade the soil's natural fertility, which translates to a diminished productive capacity. America's ability to produce food in the future has been jeopardized.

Countless economic, environmental, and societal byproducts result from policies that stimulate a nation's productivity at the expense of its productive capacity. This includes high rates of unemployment across entire regions, stagnant real wages, economic volatility at state and federal levels, environmental degradation, and weak profitability in many sectors, which will be explored later. Put simply, excessive rates of productivity can degrade the health and wellness of a nation's workers, as well as its land and natural capital, while posing threats to political stability—the building blocks of a nation's productive capacity. Ultimately, such an economic system threatens the benefits of capitalism itself, while degrading a nation's ability to survive future economic turmoil. Turmoil comes in the form of volatile energy markets, political and social unrest, quickly changing climatic shifts and the impacts thereof, supply chain disruptions between trading partners, etc.

The Benefits and Challenges of Capitalism

Capitalism is one of many economic systems that have been experimented with throughout history, and like communism or socialism, it is simply a means by which a country manages the ownership and distribution of capital. However, capitalism requires a nation's capital—its financial resources, equipment, factories, materials, and other factors of production—be privately owned rather than owned by the state.

There is little doubt that capitalism has brought innumerable benefits, or at least significant changes, to hundreds of countries and billions of people around the world. This includes modern medicine, a greater quantity of calories produced than ever before, broader and denser transportation networks, high tech entertainment, a greater diversity of services, lower costs for basic goods, higher standards of living, labor-saving devices, etc. But we must question if such changes translate to greater economic resilience and stability for the impacted economies and their citizens. Are the benefits of capitalism equally desired, let alone equally distributed, among citizens of nations that subscribe to a global market economy? If the benefits of capitalism are equally desired, can the current global market economy sustain them?

We must also question if such benefits are best derived by exercising capitalism at a global or a smaller scale. Could a capitalist country attain greater resilience and stability, achieve the most efficient allocation of resources, and better meet the needs of its citizens without tethering itself to the global market economy? Or is there an alternate model, capable of sustaining the needs of the greatest number of participants, without jeopardizing the social and ecological systems upon which they depend? The terms *sustainable* and *self-regulating* are used interchangeably throughout this book to represent such an economic system, for a sustainable economy, by definition, cannot result from a system that requires continual external resource transfers.

I recognize there is an abundance of social and environmental justice advocates that believe capitalism is the root obstacle to their progress. Before storming the barricades of capitalism, however, we should consider whether capitalism might actually be a key ingredient in restoring a self-regulating (i.e., sustainable) economy. In the process, it is essential we tease apart capitalism from the economic structure in which it exists.

Is Capitalism the Scapegoat of a Poorly Structured Economy?

While capitalism plays an important role in maintaining a nation's productive capacity, and distributing resources efficiently, we must be mindful of two key precepts. First, capitalism cannot function properly unless the parties engaged in transactions have an unrestrained ability to determine the fair and reasonable prices at which goods and services are exchanged. The opposite condition, communism, has been tested. In a communist nation, the government decides the best price for a good, or how many units of cheese or other goods to produce. As a result, there is a chronic lack of consistency between supply and demand, and hence the efficiency of production is diminished. Socialist models produce similar inefficiencies, as production decisions are influenced more by policy than consumer behavior.

Even in "capitalist" countries such as the US, government decisions to subsidize and bail out industries lead to gross inefficiencies, which decrease the productive capacity of affected industries. Several cases will be provided later.

The second precept is that a successful capitalist nation must provide a strong code of laws and policies to protect capital, land, and other assets. From such protection, the profits and capital of any individual or business have minimal risk of being unjustly taken. While cronyism, fraud, corruption, and similar market interferences pose great risk to personal wealth and capital, save the small fraction of those in power. It was such a condition, coupled with the absence of laws to protect capital, that spelled disaster for Russia as it made the leap from communism to capitalism in the 1990s (Stiglitz, 2002).

On the surface, it appears the US has fared better than Russia under capitalism. However, whether it be from cronyism, fraud, or other means, the wealth gap in America has risen sharply over the past half century, while real wages have remained flat (Desilver, 2018; Gould, 2020; US Congressional Research Service, 2020). *Real wages* are wages after accounting for inflation and are equivalent to a worker's purchasing power.

Flat wages can result from a country's increasing cost of goods and services, as represented by measures such as the Consumer Price Index—a typical "basket" of goods. In America, the same basket of goods and services that cost US $1 in 1960 would cost $8.75 in 2020 (Bureau of Labor Statistics, 2020).

For a waiter or a factory worker to pay the rent, fill their tank with gas, or buy groceries in 2020, their wages would need to be about eight times higher than they were in 1960. In fact, median income in 2020, across all occupations, was about eight times higher than it was in 1960 (US Census Bureau, 2020). However, half of US workers earn less than the median income level, with a significant portion earning less than US $15.00 per hour.

Flat wages in the US become more startling when compared to the tremendous growth in per capita GDP over the same period (Figure 1). In translation, a small percentage of Americans are navigating the tax implications of mind-boggling levels of wealth while an increasing number of middle- and lower-class Americans struggle to pay for food, medical bills, rent, and basic goods. If the majority of those goods had not been supplied by cheap overseas manufacturers, it's likely that real wages would have actually declined significantly since the 1960s.

How did this occur, given the intense efforts of the US to provide bailouts to failing corporations, give billions in subsidies to farmers, wage monetary policies with surgical precision, negotiate global trade policies in its favor, and increase its labor productivity? As the Nobel Memorial Prize economist Joseph Stiglitz highlights in *The Great Divide* (Stiglitz, 2015b), it is because government interventions such as subsidies, global trade pacts, export-oriented policies, and corporate bailouts are not intended to benefit the working class. They are intended to promote a global market economy, to benefit global market capitalists.

One recent example is US lumber prices, which increased about four-fold in 2021 due to global supply chain disruptions. The price tag for a home increased commensurately, further raising the cost of living for the average American. Raising the supply of timber would typically reduce the cost of timber. Despite the recent trade policy negotiated between the US, Mexico, and Canada (USMCA)—which should favor the trade of products between these countries—enough lumber was exported from North America in 2021 to build about 37,000 houses (Ekstrom, 2021). Historically high inflation followed in 2022, placing additional pressure on real wages, which declined more than two percent (Bureau of Labor Statistics 2022). Americans will be lucky if their real wages don't continue to deflate in coming decades.

The Shortfalls of Socialism, Communism, and Capitalism in a Poorly Structured Economy

It is easy to point up at the economic stage of props and pundits, and blame capitalism for the insidious marketing campaigns bombarding us daily with images of a lifestyle we must possess to be happy. It is tempting to blame capitalism for the increasing mass of humanity that has at its disposal a vast sea of cheap consumer products, yet is left forever wanting. Or we can see, smell, and hear the economy buzzing around us, but we feel no community, nor any sense of purpose within it. We point a finger up at capitalism, or *the economy*.

The finger-pointing is getting old. Centuries of reactionary philosophies and policies have struggled to explain the failures of previous economic paradigms. Karl Marx's treatises on communism and socialism were a reaction to Adam Smith's free-market system that dominated Europe throughout the Industrial Revolution. Marx did have ample ammunition. The working conditions in Europe at the time were truly horrid, inciting him to produce his *Communist Manifesto* and *Das Kapital*. Marx's communist and socialist tendencies aside, his extensive documentation of the social working conditions during the Industrial Revolution serve as an enduring account of the realities of the era.

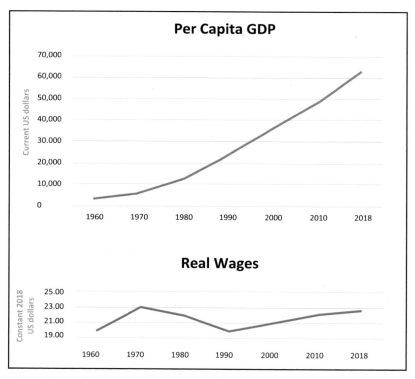

Figure 1. Per Capita GDP and real wages in America, 1964-2018. Data from the Pew Research Center (Desilver, 2018) and The World Bank (2020).

Communist and socialist philosophies swept across Europe in the first half of the 20th century, yet failed to meet basic human needs, alleviate environmental degradation, attain a resilient economy, or attain and sustain a high productive capacity, etc. If anything, social and environmental conditions only worsened under communism and socialism. The financial failures and social-environmental atrocities have stemmed, at least in part, from the fact that communist and socialist governments have operated without understanding the fundamental structure of complex self-regulating systems. And after 700 years of expansion, so too have capitalist governments, their citizenry, politicians, business leaders, and others who comprise the system.

A Brief History of Capitalism: From Northern Italian city-states to a global market economy

Excellent bodies of work exist for readers to better understand the history of capitalism, including *The Long Twentieth Century: Money, Power, and the Origins of our Time; The Age of Turbulence; Power and Profit: The Merchant in Medieval Europe*; and *The Wealth of Nations*. Further perspective may be gained by the career works of Karl Marx, Alfred Marshall, Joseph Schumpeter, John Maynard Keynes, Fernand Braudel, Milton Friedman, Herman Daly, Joseph Stiglitz, and many others. I encourage readers to study these works directly. The purpose of this section is to merely provide context for the remaining chapters.

During his tenure as an economist at John Hopkins University, Giovanni Arrighi detailed the evolution of capitalism in his world-renowned book, *The Long Twentieth Century*. Upon those rich pages of history, Arrighi describes capitalism's evolution through four major epochs spanning nearly 700 years.

Arrighi believed the roots of capitalism could be traced back to a budding system of trade among European merchants. It was amidst the rivalry of Italy's medieval city-states—Florence, Sienna, Lucca, Genoa, Milan, Venice—that a shrewd body of merchants realized a truism most businesses and consumers take for granted today. Profit could be made simply by shipping goods from areas where production was cheap to communities where consumers would pay a premium.

But there was a problem. Great risk remained in trade beyond a country's borders. Therefore, most trade remained local (Spufford, 2002), such as the vast network of regional fairs across Europe in the late medieval period. The assurance merchants needed to gain confidence in global trade was eventually secured by a system of laws, policies, and standardized business practices.

Double entry bookkeeping, marine insurance, holding companies, sophisticated international banking, and other essential shifts propelled capitalism forward. Alongside the birth of capitalism, the corporation was born, simply to broker the trade of goods across economic borders.

Mercantile Capitalism

Over time, global trade grew increasingly complex as it evolved into the first formal capitalist system, *mercantile capitalism*, which defined European commerce the day Columbus set sail for the Americas. The Dutch East India Trading Company and similar companies came to dominate sea routes, profiting from Europe's insatiable appetite for exotic spices from distant lands.

Centered around the banking savvy of Genoa, mercantile capitalism endured nearly three centuries. Eventually, the Dutch, learning from the successes and failures of Genoa, gained the upper hand in global finance and the control of capital. Yet the reign of the Dutch over mercantile capitalism would be even shorter, challenged by a titanic industrial shift that could not be derailed.

The slow blossoming of the Industrial Revolution stoked fundamental shifts not only in the means of production, but in the global financial systems required to manage the novel industrial system. Fueled by vast coal reserves in England and elsewhere, scales of production far exceeded what was possible by wind, sail, and brawn. Raw productivity grew near exponentially, alongside a great extinction of skilled artisans and journeymen. Still, their continued mastery of global finance allowed the Dutch to maintain a grip on global capital through the early decades of the revolution.

Concentrations of wealth grew throughout Europe, but not without building tensions between global trading partners and colonies. This included the budding American states, whose cheap cotton and tobacco was in high demand throughout Europe. Besides an untold number of slave revolts, and the continual raiding and pillaging by pirates, dozens of wars and battles defined life across an expanding network of global trade routes.

Atop a climax of global tension, the American, French, Haitian, and other revolutions fueled a socio-economic backlash that would forever change the course of capitalism. A truly global political upheaval had materialized, as mercantile capitalism surrendered to the full power of the Industrial Revolution in the last decades of the 1700s. The torch of global capitalism was finally ripped away from the Dutch, by a country who would rebrand capitalism in its favor.

Classical Capitalism

Classical capitalism, also called industrial capitalism, produced an even greater expansion of global markets. It was Great Britain who came to wield this new capitalist power to its greatest potential. Ample coal reserves gave Great Britain control over the seas, and with that the reins of global production and distribution. The center of global finance shifted from Amsterdam to London.

Despite (or due to) the great concentration of wealth that followed, Britain's control of global capital was even shorter than that of the Dutch, which was briefer than Genoa's. Another shift in the tides of capitalism began to materialize just as the Industrial Revolution ran its course. As Americans were exploring tribal lands on horseback, its bustling east coast commercial centers began to assimilate the lessons of Britain's industrial progress. And from such knowledge, America reached for the torch of global capitalism.

Back across the Atlantic, Adam Smith, the "father" of classical economics, was challenging a common belief that the world's wealth was constant. *If wealth was constant*, Smith argued, the only means for a country to increase its wealth would be at the expense of another (Smith, 2019, originally published in 1776). In the very year Adam Smith published this hypothesis in *An Inquiry into the Nature and Causes of the Wealth of Nations* (a.k.a., *The Wealth of Nations*), the United States of America gained independence from Great Britain.

In *The Wealth of Nations*, Adam Smith professed free markets were self-regulating, and should not be interfered with by the state. To put Adam Smith's concerns in context, the Industrial Revolution was an age when monopolies defined industry, and a political web of tariffs, bounties, and other government interferences with free trade defined the economic realities of Britain's trading partners. Such interferences, Smith and other economists believed, ultimately jeopardize the wealth of a nation.

As the philosophies of Smith and his colleagues gained favor, *laissez-faire* policies—those against government interference—further stimulated global trade across Europe and America, alongside a daring financial shift. Private (not public) financial institutions began assuming a lead role in the inner workings of the global market economy, to facilitate the considerable variation in currency values among a growing number of nations, and to more effectively manage the ever-increasing demand for global capital. Another monstrous accumulation of wealth, until the balance of power would once again shift. A global depression struck in the final decades of the 1800s, sparking tensions that would erupt into the first world war humanity bore witness to. The allied nations claimed victory, and swiftly erected trade barriers across the world to protect the wealth each nation had built.

Protectionist policies coincided with global changes in the gold standard, among other shifts, and the global market economy would expand once again. This time in the favor of the US. But the boom would be brief. Even while partiers rattled the dancehalls of America and Europe in the 1920s, economic failure was imminent. The wisest of investors would not foresee the decline, save one man. "Sooner or later a crash is coming, and it may be terrific!" proclaimed Roger Babson just weeks before the Great Depression (Galbraith, 2009). "Factories will shut down…Men will be thrown out of work" he warned, only to be ridiculed by the tycoons of Wall Street. In hindsight, the looming depression was evident as early as 1927, when rural banks began failing and flour mills began filing for bankruptcy in farm communities across the Midwest (Schauer, 1962).

Keynesian Capitalism

The Great Depression of '29 squelched the notion that absolute free markets and unfettered competition between firms and nations was in the best interest of all trading partners. From the depths of despair, a new brand of state intervention in the economy emerged, epitomized by the New Deal and other federal actions to rebuild the US economy in a post-depression world.

So potent were the philosophies of economist John Keynes during this new epoch that it is referred to as *Keynesian capitalism*. Keynes believed the market economy was suffering from low demand for goods, and so he advocated for low interest rates and easy credit. In his defining work, *The General Theory of Employment, Interest and Money*, Keynes (2017) argued government action was necessary to stabilize the US economy long enough to spur consumer confidence, which would put an end to rampant poverty.

Massive military-industrial spending during and after WWII stoked unprecedented growth in the US economy, placing America firmly atop the list of greatest economic powers on earth. America's global capitalist victory would not endure. From his analysis of historic economic crises, Giovanni Arrighi believed America's reign over the global market economy endured no more than 80 years. That reign terminated, according to Arrighi and others, with the 1970s oil crisis and subsequent recession.

Global Market Capitalism

Emerging from the recession was a system many economists have come to recognize as true *global market capitalism*, or simply globalization. Dominating our lives today, global market capitalism exists as a vast network of central banks and multilateral trade agreements. The United Nations, the International Monetary Fund, the World Bank, the Group of 20, and the World Trade Organization are key players in the global control of money and capital. They comprise what is referred to as the *transnational state*, tasked with combating the volatile nature of a global market economy.

The transnational state also includes global corporations whose best interests lie not in the success of the countries that gave them birth, but rather in the accumulation of capital for stakeholders, no matter the country of their birth. This includes the modern network of national banks, quickly and conveniently transferring money throughout the globe via the SWIFT banking system. Financial institutions rely on the SWIFT banking system also to facilitate mergers and acquisitions, manage assets, support stock exchanges, etc.

The SWIFT system is so influential that the US and its allies threated to remove Russia from SWIFT in 2022, should Russia invade Ukraine. The threat failed, for Russia had been stockpiling cash for decades, and had forged close trade ties with China to meet its consumer needs. A more critical card was left to play. Russia's wealth is derived largely from the sale of fossil fuels, which it leveraged quickly by cutting off oil supplies to the US and its allies, should they retaliate against Russia's invasion of Ukraine.

Russia is also the single largest fertilizer producer and exporter in the world, so threatened to curtail those exports to any country that would impair Russia's free will, to the detriment of key food producing nations of the world—the US, Brazil, and others (Colussi et al., 2022). In response, the US Department of Agriculture provided US $250 million in incentives to increase domestic production of fertilizer. However, the cost of fertilizer production is closely tied to the price of fossil fuels, which Russia largely controls.

The economic volatility whipped up by Russia, a single player in global market capitalism, is nothing new. Global market capitalism requires corporations and industries be loosely connected via production processes and supply chains spanning multiple countries. Volatility is not the only byproduct of this tenuous dependency. Global market capitalism has stoked the production and distribution of cheap goods around the world, matched by a level of global consumption exceeding any previous epoch. In the process, wealth has become concentrated into fewer and fewer hands.

To be clear, the concentration of wealth is not a problem in and of itself. Anyone is free to amass as much wealth as they desire. Who am I to say how much is too much? There are thresholds, however. For instance, when concentrations of capital are so great that the control of media, banking, and other institutions falls into the hands of fewer and fewer people, whose innate desire is to maintain the very system that gave rise to their wealth. Or when high concentrations of wealth result in a diminished productive capacity, lower productivity growth rates, and unemployment across entire regions (i.e., the China Shock). Then it is a problem.

Beyond the Global Market Economy

We exist in the realm of global market liberalization across governments of all persuasions. This includes communist-leaning countries like China, which increasingly gain their global power via sale of goods to communist-fearing consumers in America. Meanwhile, citizens across the globe become more discontent with each passing decade as we endure repeated periods of economic instability, chronic poverty, flat real wages, social unrest, and other social and environmental impacts at the hand of global market capitalism (Greenspan, 2007; Pew Research Center, 2008; Spash, 2017; Stiglitz, 2002).

After a mere fifty years of unrelenting growth, is the world now bracing for globalization's demise? If so, what does this mean for earth's leading capitalist nations, let alone those trading partners with which they form an economic whole?

Though the US dollar remains the leading currency across the world, many capitalists fear the control over global capital has become dispersed over a growing number of countries (e.g., China, Taiwan, Malaysia, etc.). While others posit the globe is simply working through another transition of global economic power. Exactly who will emerge as the leader, or how long they might dominate the global economic stage, is unclear.

Or will global capital continue its dispersal across more nations and regions, rather than being concentrated in the hands of the few? Some economists do believe global market capitalism naturally causes capital, and hence wealth, to become more equally distributed across developing nations as they become more productive and profitable. The most profitable countries receive a greater share of global investment, leading to a *convergence* of wealth and capital between rich and poor nations.

The concept of convergence, while tempting, has been marked with serious flaws by economists such as Piketty (2014). First, while it may result in a more equal dispersal of capital, convergence does not equate to an increase in per capita income in developing countries. Even if foreign investment does succeed in increasing the productivity of a developing country, a significant portion of the resulting wealth will be owed to the foreign entities who invested in those gains.

Second, the historical accounts show that external investment (i.e., capital moving between developed and developing countries) is not the key factor driving the convergence of rich and poor nations. Rather, Piketty's research suggests that domestic investment and other factors are more important to stimulating domestic growth. We must further question convergence, should it require a greater homogenization of culture and industry across the world, which may only increase the susceptibility of developing countries to greater cycles of economic collapse.

Reflecting on the cycles of capital accumulation and decline over the history of capitalism, Arrighi noted a self-defeating mechanism. The expansion of the global market economy has always increased the value of capital. However, the growth in global trade and production that drives such expansions ultimately drives down the rate of profits for producers, and thereby diminishes the value of capital itself (Arrighi, 2010). This trend is also observed by Piketty (2014), based on his analysis of the rise and fall of national incomes and capital accumulation in Europe and the US over the course of centuries.

In essence, as investment is increasingly directed toward the production of global commodities, the market for those commodities becomes oversaturated, driving down their profitable trade. Cooperation between trading centers can continue only if the global system of traders can avoid plowing profits into the further production of global commodities. As Arrighi observed, humanity has yet to witness such restraint.

The Elusive Structure of a Self-Regulating (Sustainable) Economy

After seven centuries of evolution, the global market economy's core structure remains elusive. On the surface, an economy is little more than the geographic area in which the production, distribution, and consumption of goods and services occurs in the most efficient manner possible. To date, capitalism has proven the best means of attaining that efficiency. Just as self-regulating ecosystems thrive on the free interaction of species, capitalist economies thrive on the unregulated interactions (i.e., natural feedback loops) between sectors, industries, and businesses, and between all levels of production and consumption. In a poorly structured economic system, however, these interactions may not yield the efficiencies that capitalism promises.

Our Economy is Just Another Complex Self-Regulating System

Self-regulating systems abound on earth, from simple cells to the complexity of the entire biosphere. For all living things, self-regulation means external instructions are not required in order to maintain vital functions, such as breathing or eating. So involuntary are the most vital functions of our organs, they are often taken for granted. Yet innumerable chemical signals such as hormones, nerve impulses, and other conveyors of information are constantly at work to ensure our body's proper functioning.

By extension, we easily grasp the relationships between key body parts, such as the lungs, heart, and digestive system, and the influence external forces have on our body. When it's too cold, we shiver. When it's too hot, we sweat. When we get dehydrated, we drink. Even if someone could control such vital functions, would we want them to?

Ascending the ladder of complex self-regulating systems, such as a forest, the roots of trees form underground networks with other life forms (e.g., fungi), which facilitate communication between the trees (Simard, 2018). Through these interactions the forest can respond quickly to external threats, such as insect outbreaks or drought. But there are no external instructions *per se*. There are only cues from the environment, such as a drought, or a hoard of sap-sucking insects, requiring that the forest make adequate adjustments in order to survive.

Thousands of species of plants, fungi, insects, bacteria, and other lifeforms exist in an ecosystem (i.e., billions of individuals), comprising innumerable interactions between species and their environment. It is no wonder we struggle to see the key structural parts—the foundational components—of a system that is more complex than ourselves, let alone understand the invisible bonds between ourselves and the greater ecosystems with which we interact.

Many economies encompass multiple ecosystems, making those economies equally complex. Even at the local level, the complexity of an economy is far greater than a mere collection of roads, buildings, warehouses, gravel mines, farms, smokestacks, bustling consumers, hundreds of trading partners, forests, and more. They are so complex that as we walk the aisles of a supermarket, or navigate a city of skyscrapers and onramps, our ability to witness key components is cloudy at best.

Instructions are unnecessary to inform consumer or producer behaviors in such a complex system. And to be clear, the fact that an economy is self-regulating does not mean that government actions should not occur, such as monetary policy, investment in education, healthcare, watershed restoration, or the military. The collective behavior of consumers, businesses, and governments defines life within every self-regulating economy, just as the forest thrives upon the collective interactions of fungi, plants, herbivores, and predators.

It is the architecture and management of an economy's core components (i.e., diversity, energy, and trade), though, that determines the efficacy of government regulations, private investment, the programs of non-profit organizations, and other actions within an economy. Mismanaging these foundational components can lead to broad scale systemic failures. For instance, subsidies and global trade policies have led to a vast depletion of soil fertility, which represents a decreased productive capacity of US farmlands. Global trade policies may also be tied to the demise of economic diversity across the Midwest, a seven-state region which has endured high rates of unemployment, low wages, rampant suicide and drug addiction, etc. Such problems can further obscure an economy's core components.

The Social, Environmental, and Industrial Context of our Economies

To discover an economy's core structure, we must peel back the external layers of the system—its context. In his groundbreaking book, *The Theory of Economic Development*, Joseph Schumpeter distinguished between those forces that are external to an economy (e.g., war, bad harvests, pandemics, climatic cycles, supply chain disruptions, etc.) and those that comprise the economic system itself. Critical to this discussion, Schumpeter observed that external forces are those that cannot be eradicated by changing the structure of an economy. But those forces can be moderated, or exacerbated, in response to a particular economic structure. Like economists before him, Schumpeter did not provide a clear picture of the core structure of an economic system, nor its foundational components. Nonetheless, Schumpeter's revolutionary ideas advanced the search.

A summary of the external forces acting on an economy are provided in Figure 2, some of which are referred to as factors (e.g., geology, climate, latitude) throughout this book. In an unregulated manner, external factors and factors continually interact with an economy's foundational components (i.e., its core structure), forming feedback loops with those components. Those feedback loops are essential to bringing the system back into balance when necessary. Feedback loops can also represent what many economists explain as *volatility*, such as a dramatic decline in flour prices following an especially abundant harvest of wheat, or spikes in petroleum prices in response to global political shifts.

In extreme cases, conditions such as agricultural degradation have stimulated feedback loops as drastic as social upheaval (i.e., the Dustbowl of America, the Potato Famine of Ireland), and even the collapse of entire civilizations (i.e., the Maya). Those failures stemmed in large part from a lack of understanding of the environmental context of the economic system. The US Soil Conservation Service was itself a result of the Dustbowl, and labored for decades afterward to restore degraded farmlands. A national system of native plant production centers was established, which today provides the very seeds necessary to restore impacts of mining, forest fires, floods, etc.

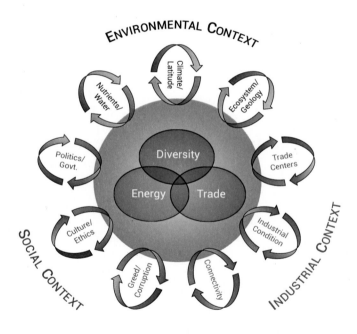

Figure 2. *The structure of an economy consists of its foundational components—diversity, energy, and trade—and the external factors interacting with them. A few common external factors are represented in the chasing arrows, which form feedback loops with the foundational components.*

Even the most routine interactions, such as supply and demand behaviors, can have far reaching impacts across industries and sectors. The increased price of petroleum puts upward pressure on the price of ethanol. In turn, more corn is directed to the tanks of automobiles, which can increase the cost of food. Increased fuel consumption contributes to global climate change, which is threatening agricultural productivity in many parts of the globe. Meanwhile water used in fracking for oil reduces the availability of water for farmers or other industrial needs, which can further increase the cost of domestically produced food. In turn, the demand for imported food is likely to rise.

The presence of feedback loops (i.e., interactions) does not invalidate an economy's foundational components. Diversity, energy, and trade are still operating, yet are in constant flux as external forces rise and fall. Similarly, principles and theories such as supply-demand theory cannot compromise the structure of an economy. They are merely a reflection of basic human behaviors within the system, and together with other external factors comprise the context of an economy—the outer layers we must pull back to reveal the inner structure of the system.

An economy's context defines the distinctive form of its communities. The interwoven picture of weather, highways, skyscrapers, warehouses, forests, meadows, government buildings, cultural values, farms, etc. is what we experience on the surface. For convenience, that context is partitioned into three parts: social, environmental, and industrial.

The *social context* includes cultural values, behavioral norms, religious preferences, and attitudes toward diversity traits such as race, gender, or sexual orientation. Additionally, the social context includes perceptions of wealth and poverty, preferred forms of governance, aversions or attractions to technology, population density, educational variables, productivity expectations, and other demographic values. In an economy where wealth and industrial productivity are not highly valued (e.g., Papua New Guinea), the precise structure of diversity, energy, and trade will look different than in those economies that place a higher value on productivity and wealth (e.g., the US, Japan, or Germany).

The *environmental context* can wield an even greater influence on the form of an economy than its social context. This includes soil fertility, precipitation, latitude (i.e., a driver of temperature), elevation, the quality of natural resources (e.g., have the forests all been cleared and the ore and groundwater stripped), and biological diversity. Just as one's social context varies, their environmental context varies considerably from region to region across the globe, and can greatly influence the productive capacity of their economy.

Similarly, the environmental context of an ecosystem dictates its distinctive productive capacity. Colombia's lowland tropical jungle is one example, which exhibits a high degree of diversity and net primary production, supported by abundant rainfall and intense solar radiation. Every species in the jungle, coupled with the jungle's environmental context, comprise a unique set of conditions on earth. Should one attempt to relocate a Colombian tropical jungle to the Sonoran Desert of Mexico, the water-demanding plants will certainly perish, together with the animals that depend upon them.

Similarly, a nation's distinctive socio-economic factors—productive capacity, technology, legal structure, etc.—cannot be transplanted to another nation and still function as they did in their original context. Such blind transfers may trigger social and/or environmental forces to react in unpredictable ways, potentially destabilizing the social or economic balance of a country, or at least jeopardizing its productive capacity. For instance, the USSR failed miserably in trying to implement American-style capitalism (Stiglitz, 2002), due in part to Russia's unique social-industrial context. In contrast, China has succeeded to assimilate free market ideologies while respecting its unique social and industrial context.

The *industrial context* of an economy includes factors that are neither environmental nor purely social in context. This includes the quantity of trading centers such as cities and industries, as well as the connectivity of those centers (e.g., the quality and density of highways, railways, waterways). An economy's industrial context is further defined by the quality and quantity of infrastructure such as farms, factories, banks, and other businesses within its centers of trade. Technological and communications infrastructure, such as high-speed internet or cellular networks, are also part of an economy's industrial context.

An economy's industrial context is a reflection not only of the region's environmental and social context, but its economic history. As such, the industrial context of an economy is constantly interacting with its social and environmental contexts in unpredictable ways as the entire system evolves. These factors are referred to as an economy's social-environmental-industrial context (SEI) in the remaining chapters.

The moment an economy's SEI context is viewed opportunistically, rather than as a constraint, ingenuity may more effectively generate solutions to social, economic, and environmental challenges. For example, in tropical regions with abundant water, communities are pioneering micro-hydroelectric systems for power generation that do not require erecting dams across entire rivers. In the windiest areas of the American West and Midwest, such as Wyoming, Colorado, and Illinois, wind is harnessed to power homes and businesses. In the Netherlands, methane and other biofuels power their economy. Even in the urban confines of San Francisco, food waste is diverted from scarce landfills to compost centers, and used to enrich soils for local food production.

As we ponder our economy within its context, important questions can be put into proper perspective. If the productivity of our economy was scaled to its SEI context—rather than attempting to circumvent that context—would greater or lesser economic stability result? Would such an economy be better insulated against future volatility from around the globe? If so, would that economy be more (or less) capable of sustaining economic, social, and environmental values?

Humanity is Not the Center of the Universe,
and Humans are Not the Center of the Economy

As humans, it is difficult to believe that we are not a foundational component of our economy. We created the economy after all, and our behaviors and decisions form unavoidable feedback loops within the system.

It is also true that animals and plants comprise the living matter of ecosystems. And as with humans in an economy, the behaviors of all species within an ecosystem occur within a constantly changing environmental context. Under drought conditions, many plants will close their stomata—the components of leaves that regulate gas exchange—to conserve water. Many species of tropical trees will increase their toxicity to animals when a member of the population is under attack by an herbivore. Innumerable species of plants across earth are known to release chemical compounds that make the environment around them less favorable to other plant species.

Countless self-regulating actions are constantly at work in a forest, and species are no doubt key parts of all living systems. However, plants and animals do not comprise the foundational components of a complex self-regulating system, for the system is far more complex than any of them. Should a species of ant become extinct, the ecosystem continues to thrive. And should drought strike, plants do not perish. If the system is structured well, the plant community merely shifts in response to a drying climate, with more drought tolerant species filling the voids left by drought intolerant plants.

Similarly, basic human instincts such as greed, love, hunger, and basic survival mechanisms form feedback loops within an economy. These behaviors translate to production and consumption behaviors, specific rates and types of innovation, legal structures, high or low savings rates, etc. But such factors do not constitute the structure of an economy, for an economy is more complex than any plant, animal, community, business, or industry. A single person in demand of an automobile, or even a small population of consumers, is insufficient to support the rise of an automobile industry in an economy.

The consumer base must have ample income to afford the automobile; the demand must be consistent enough to provide confidence to the entrepreneur to develop an automobile plant; ample supplies of raw materials and energy must be available; a road system must be in place; etc. The complexity of an economy, and hence the structure that defines it, is far greater than any one species, community, or industry.

Unknowingly, the structure of an economy's *foundational components*— those parts responsible for producing the greatest shifts with the least effort— can influence the behavior of the people and businesses with which they form a unified whole. The more invalid an economy's structure, the more magnified are the external forces acting on the economy, and hence on its people and businesses. In response to those forces, more resources (i.e., capital) must be allocated to combat graft, corruption, social unrest, environmental degradation, etc. That same capital is then unavailable to build or maintain an economy's productive capacity and desired levels of productivity.

The opposite is also true. From a more valid economic structure flows a more efficient distribution of resources. That is, when the foundational components of an economy are operating well, the influence of external forces on the system's productive capacity and productivity is moderated. The foundational components are in balance with their SEI context. And from such a condition, fewer decisions and inputs are required to meet the needs of an economy's primary beneficiaries: humans. More capital may instead be directed toward restoring or maintaining the economy's productive capacity, or to sustain other social, environmental, or economic benefits.

Extreme Cases of Human Behavior

The Sicilian mafia is an extreme example of a universal external force: greed. The research of Dimico et al. (2017) shed light on a wide range of economic and political variables during the birth of the mafia, concluding that "the mafia arose as a response to an exogenous shock in the demand for oranges and lemons." To keep the story brief, citrus fruits had become a common cure for scurvy in the mid-1800s. Sicily, graced with the ideal environmental context, became a global leader in citrus production. But it was the spike in the value of citrus in the late 1800s—largely due to increased demand in New York—that created sudden and great profits. Those profits were greatest in Sicily.

Important questions remain. Was the lemon market to blame for the sudden rise of the mafia? Or was it the weak rule of law following the fall of Feudalism in Italy? Or was it the increase in small, unprotected farm parcels?

Setting fresh eyes on 19th century economic data from Sicily, Dimico and his team discovered an interesting relationship. Mafia activity was *not* strongest where the weakest protection efforts existed on private property, nor where the greatest number of small farms existed. Further, a weak rule of law and high levels of poverty were present in countless other provinces throughout Italy at the time, where the mafia did not exist. Where organized crime emerged was very specific. It was in those towns where the greatest profitability of oranges and lemons existed.

Digging deeper, we may discover an intractable relationship between trade, diversity, and an economy's external forces. Sicily's 19th century wealth had been built on strong foreign markets at the expense of economic diversity. But the moment Florida began growing citrus in the late 1880s, coupled with a severe drought in Sicily, Sicily's agricultural industry began suffering serious decline (Acemoglu et al., 2020). It was in the aftermath of Sicily's agricultural decline that waves of Sicilian immigrants fled to New York, giving rise to the Mob.

Economic volatility and corruption are merely external forces, which may be magnified when an economy's foundational components are out of balance with its SEI context. With this construct, I interviewed Brandon S. Lewis (personal communication, May 2020), who develops environmental education projects in Mexico, the most corrupt country in the G-20 and in the Organisation for Economic Co-operation and Development (Rodriquez, 2018). Brandon and I questioned if a greater diversity of smaller businesses would more effectively distribute a nation's concentration of wealth, such as to diminish the incentive for corruption in countries such as Mexico. Though we fell short of a sound conclusion, Brandon and I did agree on one thing. Battling corruption or graft will not solve the problem, for external forces such as corruption and greed have no bearing on an economy's structure. They serve only as a testament to its validity.

TWO

The Global Market Economy:
Failing to deliver in a
Rapidly changing world

While there is no shortage of capitalists who champion the benefits of the current global market system, a growing number of economists (e.g., Alan Greenspan, Giovanni Arrighi, Milton Friedman, Joseph Stiglitz, John M. Keynes, Herman Daly, etc.) warn of the social and environmental impacts left in its wake. Many of these economists also berate government efforts such as tax-based social and environmental programs, interest rate adjustments, bailouts, global trade deals, or subsidized agribusiness. Such actions, I agree, fail to address the structural economic issues responsible for creating the problems they aim to fix.

Economists are not the only skeptics. After nearly a century of struggling policies and actions, an expanding mass of US citizens are questioning if the global market economy has made any meaningful progress. That same doubt continues to grow throughout other nations such as Germany, England, and France.

Putting Economic Progress Under the Microscope

Clearly, ample technological progress has been made over the past fifty years in the US and other developed nations. But if there has been any social, economic, or environmental progress made by the US economy over the past fifty years, it's questionable if said progress can be sustained. Perhaps more importantly, if the benefits of technological or economic progress are not equally shared among all citizens of a nation, does it matter? More fundamentally, should economic pundits and politicians claim progress toward key economic goals, are those goals correct?

Economic Productivity and Economic Goals: Bridges to Nowhere

The course of the US economy has been charted to achieve several cherished goals: freedom, stability, full employment, growth, and equity. By definition, then, when the US economy is performing well, these goals should be met. America's economic performance, as with many developed countries, is measured by *Gross Domestic Product* (GDP), the total value of goods and services generated in one year.

Without question, America's GDP has been outperforming itself repeatedly over the past century, making it the top performing economy on earth. Under such conditions, then, Americans should be freer. There should be more equity among all Americans. Such a fiery economy should leave us all with a deep sense of stability. Our anxiety levels should be lower. Every able-bodied adult should be gainfully employed.

Despite a century of unprecedented GDP growth, it is questionable if the US economy has met its most cherished goals, let alone fulfilled basic human expectations. For instance, while the US unemployment rate has been fairly low over the past sixty years, it has bounced between 3.5% and 10.5% (Figure 3), spiking to about 15% in 2020. Given America's labor force of 160 million people, a 15% unemployment rate translates to about twenty-four million jobless.

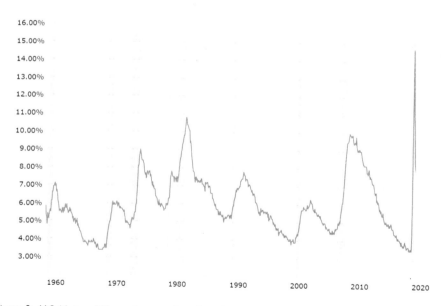

Figure 3. U.S. National Unemployment Rate from 1960-2019. Vertical gray bars indicate recessions. Source: Macrotrends. https://www.macrotrends.net/1316/us-national-unemployment-rate.

Just as important as having a job is the quality of that job, and how stable that job is. During America's most recent economic downturns, about one hundred million workers were employed in the service industry (Desilver, 2019). Not only were these employees highly vulnerable during the downturn, but they were among the lowest paid people in America. This scenario underscores the weak purchasing power of laborers, and the unintended consequences of America's transition to a service economy. Volatile unemployment and flat real wages are a few bruises resulting not simply from a flawed economic structure, but the fact that America's economic goals are invalid.

To begin, *stability* and *growth* are not goals. When one kneels down to the forest floor to examine the growth of a sapling, and ponders its role in the greater ecosystem, or when we experience the death of a loved one, or the birth of a child, the full picture of life comes into focus. Growth—a premise of every living system—is merely one phase within the dynamic cycle of life. It is irrational for any economy to pursue growth as a goal. Just as the purpose of life is not merely to avoid death.

Further yet, growth and stability cannot be decoupled in self-regulating systems. For instance, while destabilizing forces such as wildfires cause the death of some species, such as trees, they stimulate the growth of others, such as wildflowers and grasses that have laid dormant for decades under the dark forest canopy. Growth, stability, and instability are merely processes, not endpoints.

This leaves us with full employment, equity, and freedom remaining to be tackled by an economy's productive prowess. However, they too are unworthy goals. There are ample societies throughout history who have amassed tremendous labor forces that were fully employed—but not free. The slaves of British colonies during the Industrial Revolution are one example. Even those slaves who built Jefferson's Monticello were no doubt fully employed. But they were equally poor. Ironically, Thomas Jefferson himself, the architect and owner of Monticello, was fully employed, though he died deeply in debt. Yet he walked the earth a free man.

Freedom is a problematic goal for a more fundamental reason. One individual's freedom to pursue, for instance, a profit, often infringes upon another's freedom to hunt, fish, access clean water, breathe clean air, seek solitude in the wilderness—the list is long. In light of this quandary, it is preposterous to expect a capitalist system charged with maximizing profits for the individual, to concurrently provide freedom for all. Even within the SEI context of America's fifty states, under the umbrella of a strong federal government and rule of law, the freedoms of its people are constantly challenged.

Now expand the SEI context of America's economy to its 120-plus trading partners around the globe, many of whom lack the protective laws of the US. Across this interconnected global market economy, America cannot deliver freedom, equity, or stable employment. To believe anything more is nothing less than irrational exuberance. Undeniably, freedom and equity are essential to social justice in America and its trading partners. But they are inadequate as economic goals.

A Single Economic Goal: Fulfillment

Commingling the conditions of freedom, equity, and full employment, a worthwhile goal may emerge: fulfillment. To begin to understand how personal fulfillment is related to economic structure and function, imagine a scenario whereby the great diversity of people that exists in your community work in a single industry or business. For a moment, let's not be preoccupied with their happiness. Rather, ponder their fulfillment—the deep satisfaction awakened when one's abilities and talents are being fully engaged for the betterment of themselves, their families, the community in which they live, and by extension, their country.

If we are honest with ourselves, we cannot imagine a scenario whereby a single industry or business ensures the fulfillment of everyone in any community. Yet history is full of examples where entire communities are dominated by industry groups such as automobile manufacturing, logging, agriculture, meatpacking, service, higher education, or corn. The structure of the global market economy demands homogenization. Even when basic needs such as income and food are met by a *single-industry economy*, history has repeatedly revealed that homogenized communities are more susceptible to external economic forces than are communities with a more diverse economy. The notorious American Rust Belt, the potato famine, and the repetitive boom-bust cycles in mining and oil are notable cases.

In single-industry economies such as monoculture farm communities of the Midwest, those who can flee, do. Or, when the inevitable downturn arrives, unemployed residents have no choice but move to a stronger job market, whether or not those jobs are fulfilling. There has been a mass exodus of young, bright minds from the heartland of the US since the 1950s, fracturing communities to the point that once thriving towns are now dead. In Oakdale, NE, the high school—at one time the pride of the community—is boarded up, and warning signs are posted outside of crumbling churches.

Many of those souls that are left behind turn to drugs or suicide. America suffered similar drug epidemics in the wake of the auto industry collapse. Sadly, drug overdoses in America's rural communities exceed those of its urban counterparts according to the Center for Disease Control and Prevention (2017). If there is a link between fulfillment and economic performance, it may be concluded that drug overdose, homelessness, rising mental health and physical health issues, and other factors epitomizing one's lack of fulfillment have coincided not with the lowest performing economic era of the US, but the apex of its productive might.

I do not take issue with aspirations such as full employment, security, happiness, growth, or freedom. However, they are not worthy economic *goals*. If they were, the global market economy that the US champions has failed to deliver. Perhaps the global market economy has succeeded to provide a higher quality of life.

Quality vs. Quantity

As a measure of fulfillment is currently unavailable, we can call on measures such as quality of life, which also have their challenges. The World Health Organization defines *quality of life* (QOL) as "an individual's perception of their position in life in the context of the culture and value systems in which they live and in relation to their goals." That is, measuring one's quality of life is as difficult as measuring how much you really love your significant other.

A nation's GDP is not a proxy for the quality of life of its citizenry. Case in point, America's GDP in 2021 was about US $23 trillion (Bureau of Economic Analysis, 2022), making it the richest nation on earth. What may be news to some Americans is that the US is not among the top ten countries in terms of quality of life. Indices such as The Numbeo Quality of Life Index (Numbeo, 2020) show that Denmark, Switzerland, and Finland top the list of high-quality living. The Numbeo Index draws upon several indices such as purchasing power (higher is better), pollution (lower is better), housing price to income ratio (lower is better), cost of living (lower is better), safety (higher is better), health care (higher is better), traffic commute time (lower is better), and climate (higher is better).

The Numbeo index is a good starting point. But to gain a more complete understanding of fulfillment, the QOL index should be expanded to include measures of homelessness, mental health, job diversity, and access to clean water, clean air, and open spaces—to name a few. Finally, a crude indicator of a desirable economy may be net migration into the economy. That is, are more people moving into the economy than out, or is there a net migration out of the economy to seek fulfillment elsewhere? While it may seem that the US has a high immigration rate, due to the number of people entering its borders for seasonal employment, its net immigration rate has actually been declining since 1998 (Macrotrends, 2021).

High Standard of Living, Unhappy Life?

In reality, far too much variation in cultural values and economic expectations exists across the globe for there to be a universal measure for quality of life or standard of living. But considering the great weight economists and politicians place on America's *standard of living*, we owe it to ourselves to examine this measure. Encyclopedia Britannica defines standard of living simply as a measure of the aspirations of an individual or a population for goods and services (Britannica, 2018a).

Standard of living roughly equals the sum of all goods and services consumed by an individual or group. It is our material comfort, and includes services that improve our sense of well-being, even though they are not under our direct control: the quality of bus or train service, roads, the energy grid, etc. One's sense of well-being (i.e., their comfort) can also include breathable air, clean water, fertile landscapes, and access to parks and natural spaces.

While it is intuitive that a higher standard of living is good, there's a catch. Social scientists note that one's standard of living is strongly influenced not just by their own consumption patterns or income, but also that of their peers. In other words, our standard of living is relative.

Consider the life of Darwin, a young man who recently moved to Quito from the rural jungle of Ecuador. While Darwin's standard of living, relative to that of the family he left behind, may grow along with his new wages, so will his perception of inequity. Pondering life from his one-bedroom apartment (if he's lucky) in southern Quito, the lavish lifestyles of the Bellavista neighborhood to the north leaves Darwin feeling inadequate.

Furthermore, with access to a plethora of television and a continual bombardment of other social media, Darwin can now compare his windfall—life above the poverty line—to that of the average American, European, or wealthy Argentinian. Consequently, Darwin's standard of living has but one fate over time: to decrease, regardless of his higher income. And yet, there is a more fundamental challenge to Darwin's rising income.

Over the course of three years, I was privileged to work with Engineers without Borders and the local residents of Malingua Pamba, an Ecuadorian village in the high misty peaks of the Andes. This is one of many rural Ecuadorian communities where rampant erosion undermines water supplies and food production, from which children are streaming to urban centers such as Quito or Latacunga, to seek a greater life.

When someone such as Darwin *arrives*, he is met by a few predictable fates. First, he may not earn enough for even the shoddiest of apartments, and winds up roaming the poorest of neighborhoods, where trash and urine often fill the streets. Abundant food and medicine abound in the high rises and plazas surrounding them, but Darwin cannot afford such luxuries. Tens of thousands of people suffer a similar fate amidst Ecuador's wealthier cities.

An alternative fate for Darwin is that he experiences a financial windfall and moves into a low-end apartment. His family cheers for him, until another financial reality strikes. As Darwin's new community increases its collective consumption, his ability to reach a higher standard of living slowly erodes. Darwin is now faced with ever-increasing costs of food, medical services, and other living expenses (e.g., housing, infrastructure, taxation, etc.), which rise in tandem with a higher standard of living.

Eventually, Darwin may come to discover that even in the wealthiest cities of America and Europe he will trip into potholes, breath polluted air, experience high crime rates, find inadequate medical services, encounter poverty—to name a few. In these wealthy cities an ever-increasing mass of citizens struggle to keep pace with the ever-rising cost of living. Should the poorest citizens of the world somehow claw their way to a higher standard of living, their ability to maintain that standard is becoming increasingly difficult.

Systemic Threats to our Quality of Life and Standard of Living

There is at least one elite economist—Alan Greenspan—who has no qualms warning of the threats to the stability of earth's most productive nation, and hence America's ability to maintain the quality of life and standard of living so many citizens expect. Greenspan served as the Chair of the US Federal Reserve under four presidents between 1987-2006, a perspective gained no other way than having the most important economic job for the world's wealthiest nation. Greenspan highlights several fundamental threats to the stability of America and other developed democratic countries: the ever-increasing wealth disparity, rising income gaps, and high stress and anxiety among market participants (Greenspan, 2007).

At the same time, Greenspan and other economists credit the global market economy for lifting the poor out of poverty and raising the standard of living for billions of people across the globe. If the global market economy is responsible for accomplishing such a feat for some, is it doing so at the expense of others? The answer depends on the country in question, and is likely to change the longer we measure the social and environmental impacts of the global market economy. In the meantime, the claims that the global market economy is lifting billions of people out of poverty, and providing food security for the world, should be questioned.

Misperceptions of Poverty and Food Security

Earth harbors over five thousand diverse cultures, making a universal definition of poverty impossible. Regardless, in 2015 The World Bank defined poverty at a global scale as earning less than US $1.90/day—the absolute poverty line. With such a low bar, it is no wonder global market capitalists are quick to praise the global market economy for lifting billions of people out of poverty.

Global leaders such as Pope Francis are not fooled by poverty measures that focus solely on earnings. In his Encyclical Letter, *Fratelli Tutti*, Pope Francis noted that poverty is actually increasing globally, rather than declining (Francis, 2020). He points out that the global free market economy has been succeeding to reduce poverty only because we've been defining poverty incorrectly.

Quite eloquently, Pope Francis observed, "There is no poverty worse than that which takes away work and the dignity of work." Besides the matter of work, poverty is a reflection of a country's ability to feed its citizens, which Greenspan and others also attribute to unfettered global trade and an ever-rising global GDP. While per capita GDP globally has been increasing steadily since 1960, reaching about US $11,000 per person in 2020, averages at such a scale tend to be more deceptive than constructive. For instance, the average temperature in Death Valley is 77o Fahrenheit. Drawn by such facts, many people would flock to Death Valley, were it not for the fact that for about five months of the year they would be coping with temperatures above 100 degrees.

Similarly, due to the fact that most of the world's GDP is concentrated into so few hands, the average annual income of most people on earth is far below US $11,000. For the poorest people of the world, it is less than US $700 per year.

Food production has also ballooned since 1960 thanks to the Green Revolution. Another hallmark of global economic progress, this agricultural revolution was a defining moment along the greater evolutionary path of technology. The Green Revolution saw a huge leap forward in the success of hybrid crops, and surgical applications of pesticides, herbicides, and fossil fuel-infused fertilizers to stimulate those crops. Essential to our understanding of economic progress and food security, however, the Green Revolution stimulated a vast increase not in the quality or diversity of food, but in the yield per acre of *monocultures*: farm fields dominated by a single species.

Economists and politicians rushed to praise the Green Revolution as proof of the benefits of globalization. On the surface, the praise sounds plausible, until we take a closer look at the impacts. Through decades of research, doctor Pingali of Cornell University provided a deep evaluation of the economic, environmental, and social impacts of the Green Revolution (Pingali, 2012). This includes the decreasing food security for hundreds of millions of people across the earth.

The Food and Agriculture Organization (FAO), mandated to eradicate hunger around the world, defines food insecurity as insufficient access to safe and nutritious food, to the extent that normal growth and development cannot be attained. Together with the World Health Organization and others, the FAO summarized a wealth of global data in their 2019 report, *The State of Food Security and Nutrition in the World*. Among dozens of important findings, this report revealed that the number of people experiencing moderate to severe levels of food insecurity has reached 26% of the world population—close to two *billion* people. To put that number into perspective, earth's human population prior to the Green Revolution was about two billion people.

If the prodigious increase in food supply following eighty years of dramatic global market expansion has failed to meet the most basic needs of two billion people, it is imperative we ask if poverty can be resolved simply by growing more food, increasing rates of global trade, and achieving a higher global GDP. And considering tremendous advances in roads, shipping, rail systems, refrigeration, etc., adequate food *distribution* is rarely the problem.

While we call into question the ability of the global market economy to resolve poverty and food insecurity, we must mind some these related concerns. Global supplies of cheap fossil fuels and clean water, both essential to modern agriculture, are expected to decrease by the year 2050, alongside an additional two and a half billion mouths to feed. The real challenge to food security (and hence poverty) stems not from an inadequate global GDP, but from a modern agricultural system that cannot be maintained without cheap energy and ample water supplies. Basic supply-demand economics dictate the cost of energy and water must rise as supply decreases and demand increases. Therefore, the cost of food must increase. Based on past trends, the result is likely to be a global food supply in the form of more empty calories.

Global food security is often reported by pop culture news in terms of the *quantity of energy* provided by food, such as the calories found in sugars and fats. But high-calorie foods do not necessarily meet the basic nutritional needs of the human body, while they are directly related to cardiovascular disease and type 2 diabetes. The dietary essentials for a healthy life—fiber, protein, and vitamins—are notably swept aside by the obsession many capitalists have with a high yield agricultural system.

The narrow focus on calories and crop yield further ignores growing concerns over adequate sources of clean water and soil fertility. Access to clean water is expected to become more challenging as watersheds across the world become degraded by various economic activities, and as many of the Green Revolution's leading crops—corn, rice, almonds, etc.—directly contribute to the lowering of aquifers. At the same time, high yield farming methods decrease the amount of organic matter in the soil, which reduces a farmland's ability to capture and hold water. The most recent estimates are that about 35% of America's Corn Belt—about 33 million acres of land—has completely lost its organic rich soil horizon, its topsoil (Thaler et al., 2021). This translates to about US $3 billion in lost revenue across the Corn Belt annually. The cost of restoring that fertility, as calculated earlier, is about US $1.1 trillion.

A perfect storm is brewing. Ever-decreasing soil fertility will be met with rising energy and water costs, or at the very least high market volatility of these inputs. Atop this financial struggle, significant shifts in precipitation and temperature patterns are unfolding in many of the world's most important food growing regions, including the US Corn Belt.

The US Department of Agriculture (USDA) analyzed the Corn Belt's changing climate, revealing that temperatures have risen in all seasons, growing seasons have lengthened, precipitation patterns have shifted, and extreme precipitation events have become more frequent (USDA, 2021). While some of these changes can be beneficial to some producers, the changes also mean increased losses of soil organic matter, reductions in the size and quality of grains, and greater financial uncertainty (Schilling, 2020). To be highlighted in Part II, US farm policy has created a less diverse agricultural system, which is more vulnerable to external forces.

Despite the rhetoric, neither global market capitalism nor the Green Revolution have provided a greater degree of security for humans. Instead, they have created a situation whereby food and energy security grow more tenuous with each passing harvest. In the interim, the standard of living of the global consumer will likely continue to deflate, alongside their happiness.

Consumption, Happiness, and Affluence

The US is full of consumers who, in blind faith, believe the global market economy will pull people out of poverty and eliminate hunger. So, we swipe and consume, enjoy a brief endorphin rush, and feel proud we are doing the right thing—for the sake of the poor! The biological rationale is quite basic. Consumer psychologists such as Darren Bridger have revealed how shopping provides an emotional high that keeps us seeking out pleasure and reward. (Dizik, 2016).

We have all felt it. The simple act of buying something provides a sensation at the same level as eating or doing drugs. Strong feelings of guilt can follow a purchase, according to consumer psychologist Kit Yarrow (Yarrow, 2014). Like doing drugs, the buying experience leaves consumers with the need to get high again. The mere act of shopping a sale, and then the very point of purchase, causes dopamine to be released in the brain, arousing our most carnal sensation—pleasure.

Of course, shopping does not actually raise one's quality of life, let alone their happiness, which is one reason happiness is not a key economic indicator for most capitalist nations. Emotions like happiness are fleeting, influenced by factors largely unrelated to an economy's performance. Blaming the economy for one's lack of happiness is akin to criticizing the plow for the failure of a crop.

That said, happiness among Americans has been relatively flat since the 1970's, coinciding with flat real wages and a ballooning GDP. The flatness of happiness has been tracked by the General Social Survey, an ongoing project of the University of Chicago (Smith et al., 2015). According to the survey, genetics accounts for about half of an individual's *happiness portfolio*. Another 40% of the happiness portfolio is made up of short-term events such as promotions, graduating, getting married, and other life events.

Corroborating the General Social Survey results, economist Arthur Brooks summarized decades of research into "A Formula for Happiness." Brooks's work identifies the portion of our happiness that is not attributed to genetics or major life events. He breaks the remainder of our happiness portfolio into four key elements that we do have control over (Brooks, 2013):

- *Faith — Our framework for making sense of life, suffering, and death*

- *Family — A home life with mutual affection, where the well-being of others is as important to you as is your own happiness*

- *Friends — At least two*
- *Work —The number of other people who benefit from the work you do*

Interestingly, *material abundance* is not among the list of what makes humans happy. Once any of us rises above the abject poverty line, even large windfalls of income such as inheritance fail to elicit a lasting smile. Travelers to those places on earth where GDP is low can vouch for this. Some of the happiest people I've ever met lived in a dirt-floored hut, their interior walls decorated with drying ears of corn from the rural hillsides of Guatemala, and they were as untethered as is humanly possible from the global market economy. Life there, Brooks would agree, is embellished not with material abundance but with faith, family, friends, and work.

Can Global Market Capitalism Resolve the Problems it has Created?

Many readers are aware of the social and environmental externalities cast upon the people and ecosystems of exporting countries when we consume imported products. These externalities include watershed degradation, water pollution, air pollution, soil degradation, species extinction, impacts to the health and wellness of humans, etc. Even economists such as Milton Friedman (1982) and Greenspan (2007) grasp the economic impacts of externalities produced by an economy's material consumption, costs that are easily missed in our collective consumer blind spot. And the longer the supply chain, the larger the blind spot.

Long Supply Chains: Self-inflicted damage in a global market economy

We stand at the leading edge of the 21st century, sensing with anxiety the failures of the global market economy to resolve a host of basic and expected disruptions (e.g., civil injustice and unrest, trade wars, weather and climate uncertainties, global political uncertainties, an attack on the nation's capital). All the while, the voice of many leading economists and capitalists is aggregated firmly against any limits to growth. That voice is echoed by citizens spanning both sides of the political divide, who have blind faith that technological progress will outpace our burgeoning human population and their voracious appetites for cheap imported products. That is, until a novel virus spreads from plane to plane and town to town across our tightly interconnected economic web.

Yet COVID-19 did not cause the subsequent global economic calamity, just as heavy snow cannot be blamed for crushing a rotten roof. The pandemic simply shed light on the tenuous connections between countries, producers, and consumers across the globe. Humanity witnessed how easily an economy can undermine its productive capacity and resilience via dependence on global markets. The shallowness of America's productive might, and that of countless others, was highlighted the moment global supply chains began to snap.

A *supply chain* is simply the journey a product takes across oceans, through multiple corporate hands, along train tracks or highways, and over several political boundaries to reach the final consumer. In an economy dependent on the global marketplace, this journey includes the supply of essential products such as medical supplies, food, and toilet paper.

Alcoa Corp, a global leader in the aluminum industry, and utterly dependent on bauxite exports from China, reported supply chain bottlenecks just days after the coronavirus outbreak in Wuhan. Agilent Technologies Inc, a global supplier of laboratory supplies, reported losses of up to US $50 million in the first quarter of 2020 due to the shutdown of China's economy. The first dominoes had fallen. Apple Inc, Walt Disney, Coca-Cola Company, and other transnational companies reported instant financial losses stemming from a single outbreak in one trading partner, even before the virus appeared on US shores.

Soon after, the lack of semiconductors reaching US ports became a critical bottleneck in automobile manufacturing. Entire plants shut down due to this one missing part, resulting in the lay-off of laborers with nothing to make. This trickled down to retailers, who laid off sales staff with nothing to sell. The pandemic cast a similar light on the fact that China and other Asian countries are leading producers of solar panels and related components for the US and others. When it comes to productive capacity, the US must own up to one embarrassing fact: the productive capacity of the US is weak.

Once the gravity of the pandemic became clear, the Federal Reserve dropped the federal funds rate to a quarter of one percent, a historic low. This translated to a prime rate of about 3.25%, the rate at which banks lend money. Such an expansionary monetary policy is aimed at one purpose—recovery. But the federal funds rate was already hovering at historic lows, leaving America's chief economic recovery tool—lower interest rates to stimulate consumption—ineffective. In the process, America's national debt ballooned to historic heights.

While a rising tide lifts all boats, in the interwoven sea of global market capitalism a lowering tide causes them all to sink. Citizens across the globe witnessed such declining economic tides during the pandemic, as long supply

chains between producers and consumers magnified disruptions at the furthest ends. This phenomenon is so common it has been dubbed the *bullwhip
effect*. In a very long whip (i.e., supply chain), small shifts in consumer demand
produce an increasing magnitude of interruptions as those shifts trickle upstream to distributors, wholesalers, and then manufacturers on the opposite
end. Tremendous inefficiencies can be produced along the way.

Even within the US, the length of supply chains can be mindboggling.
Hawaii ships nearly all its cattle to the mainland for processing, and then
imports their steaks and burgers. That's a 4,000-mile roundtrip journey. The
preferred shipping method is 747 cargo planes (Bechtel, 2014), which cannot
achieve liftoff or stay aloft without tremendous fossil fuel inputs.

Besides the obvious energy consumed in transportation, long supply chains
generate financial inefficiencies, byproducts of natural human responses to uncertainty and risk. As supply chains lengthen, uncertainty and risk increase. To
buffer against those risks, producers often accumulate *safety stock* at each node
of production and distribution. Safety stock (i.e., ordering more than what
consumers are demanding) not only increases the cost of production and distribution, but demands greater energy throughout the production-consumption
cycle. In many cases, long supply chains require producers and distributors to
amass a greater amount of perishable (e.g., bananas) or other short-lived stock
(e.g., fashion items), despite the fact they are likely to become unsalable before
reaching the hands of consumers.

The US cannot escape the insecurities guaranteed by a system that fills its
collective pantry with food originating an average of 1,000 miles away, or that
stuffs our medicine cabinets with raw ingredients manufactured over 7,000
miles away. These are the self-inflicted wounds of a global market economy,
and are not limited to the US, nor to food and medicine.

Unavoidable Externalities of a Global Market Economy

The longer the supply chain between producer and consumer, the easier it is
to underestimate (or plainly ignore) the unintended impacts at the furthest
ends. Hence long supply chains tend to exacerbate the social and environmental
impacts of our consumption. What we do not see we do not believe. And that
which we do not believe does not change.

The concept of *externalities* stems from the economic efficiency studies
of Italian economist Vilfredo Pareto (1848-1923) in the waning days of the
Industrial Revolution. An externality results when a product cannot be produced, delivered, or disposed of without making at least one other individual

or their environment worse off. A classic example is the economic, social, and environmental costs of water pollution caused by innumerable manufacturing processes.

Externalities are nothing new. The high productivity of the Industrial Revolution was largely fulfilled by child labor, excessive work hours, unhealthy working conditions, and significant air pollution throughout Great Britain (Braudel, 1984; Marx, 2015; Smith, 2019).

Regardless of Karl Marx's conclusions regarding communism, he provided keen insights into the externalities—unavoidable byproducts—of global market capitalism. This included boom-bust cycles, destructive competition, labor injustices, and other issues that would come to pass following his publishing of *Das Kapital* (Marx, 2015). According to Marx's work, children labored 16-hour days, seven days per week, for months on end during the Industrial Revolution. A managing partner of a Manchester factory reported, "For all these, children and adults alike, the average work for the last 18 months has been at the very least 7 days, 5 hours, or 78 ½ hours a week. For the six weeks ending May 2nd this year (1862), the average was higher–8 days or 84 hours a week." (Marx, 2015, page 170).

Two and a half centuries later, Britain and other developed countries have minimized the worst local social and environmental impacts of their domestic production. This has not proven Marx wrong, but rather that social and environmental externalities flourish across thousands of export-based communities around the globe—suppliers of sheltered first world consumers.

The centuries-long trend of dispensing externalities across the earth is unresolvable by global market capitalism. This is due in part to the fact that, to remain competitive amidst a globe of greatly disparate SEI contexts, transnational corporations must continually relocate their operations to countries where labor costs are as low as possible. Or they relocate factories to countries willing to accept degradation of their land, water, and air, regardless of the health impacts to their people, so that global consumers may enjoy the lowest possible price tags on the shelf.

Unresolved Environmental Externalities

Externalities flourish even in the wealthiest countries on earth. The toxic earth left by smelting operations at Anaconda Copper Mine in the late 1800s is still impacting the lives of ranchers and residents of rural Montana. Among the lingering externalities are acid drainage and metal toxicity that render waters undrinkable by downstream residents. As many US taxpayers now know, these externalities are too large even for earth's biggest economy to undo. Well over US $100,000,000 has been spent since the 1980s to clean up the Anaconda waste site, and the work continues as of this writing. If the world's leading capitalist nation cannot afford such clean-up efforts, nor protect farmers and ranchers from a single mining company, can any developing country be expected to protect their citizenry against the litany of externalities wrought by the global market economy?

Externalities arise also from paper manufacturing in, for instance, Washington State or Wisconsin, where dioxides and other pollutants are dumped into rivers, lakes, and oceans. The farther away consumers are from paper manufacturing facilities, the fewer pollution impacts they witness. Another famous externality is the stormwater runoff from North Carolina's nine million hogs, or from Iowa's 23 million. The pollution created by these hog farms is so fetid it made national headlines several times in 2018 to 2019.

These examples are not an assault on mining companies, paper users, or pork products. They are a spotlight on an economic system that systematically dumps externalities on unsuspecting communities across the globe. As long as the lakes and streams outside of our office windows and neighborhoods remain clean, we remain blissfully ignorant of the environmental externalities caused by America's export-based paper and pork manufacturers, or the social conditions of China's export-based industries.

Unresolved Social Externalities

A country's economic health is closely tied to the health of its citizens, which remains woefully unmet for a growing number of Americans. The United States—the number one global importer, with the world's highest GDP—has some of the greatest rates of mental health issues in the world (McPhillips, 2018), while its physical health grade is below average (World Population Review, 2021). America's health problems strike not only those at the lower end of the economic spectrum, but the demand for mental health services is expected to outgrow the number of counselors and other mental health providers in coming years (HRSA, 2020). Even if the gap in mental health providers is filled, it is questionable, considering the lingering flat real wages in the US, if future wage earners will be able to afford the services. Many cannot afford them now.

While pondering this scenario, consider that America's past half century of unprecedented growth has been accompanied by ever-increasing rates of homelessness. Searching for answers, the National Coalition for the Homeless (2009) has amassed one of the most comprehensive datasets in US history. As many might guess, the research indicates that homelessness results primarily from decreased job opportunities and increased housing costs, both of which have risen in America under its global market economic model.

Other factors influencing homelessness include mental health, drug and alcohol abuse, and weak social ties (Council of Economic Advisors, 2019). There has been a slight decline in the homelessness rate over the past decade, but changes to the federal definition of homelessness are largely responsible. The longer-term trend has been an increase in homelessness (National Academies of Sciences, Engineering, and Medicine, 2018). Worse yet, America's children—the future leaders of the richest country on earth—have suffered increasing rates of depression, drug abuse, and teen suicide in concert with the greatest period of economic growth in US history (Twenge et. al., 2019). Much of this stems from rising stress and anxiety levels, which impact health regardless of one's age.

Brief moments of stress are an expected part of life for every living creature. However, the stress stoked by regular disturbances within an ecosystem (e.g., high winds, severe frosts, drought, etc.) hone rather than dull the resilience of species within the system. In contrast, the economic structure of the US and other developed countries tends to produce chronic and severe stressors: a litany of social and environmental externalities that degrade personal health and wellbeing, or the destructive forces trickling down from the global market economy to lay waste to local business communities. Underscoring this point, Greenspan points to Silicon Valley corporations, the poster children of induced obsolescence of technology, who are forced to reinvent large segments of their business every few years to compete in the global marketplace. In turn, staff become obsolete, so are forced to reinvent themselves at a faster and faster pace.

Other impacts include the intense division of labor in industries such as textiles and steel fabrication. The degree of labor specialization required of globally-oriented factories creates "big-economy" problems for employees and employers, such as *Repetitive Strain Injury* (RSI): the collective pain, strain, and damage to muscles, connective tissue, and joints—physical stress. RSI has cost US businesses upwards of US $20 billion in lost productivity and direct costs annually (Microsoft Corp, 2013).

Even before Henry Ford's advanced degrees of specialization, factory managers in Italy associated repetitive strain injuries with mundane tasks—maladies that result from pulling the same lever, pushing the same button, or repositioning the same fender too many times over the course of too many days. Hours of drudgery, until you or the factory dies.

As America's vast shift toward a service economy unfolded, one might have expected RSI to be a ghost of industrial past. Instead, RSI was reincarnated into ailments such as tennis elbow, trigger finger, and carpal tunnel syndrome. As the ever-quickening pace of modern technology has penetrated further into the social fabric of America, "iPod finger," "Blackberry thumb," and "PlayStation thumb" have also materialized. Mounting stress doesn't end there. Mind-numbing environments on the factory floor and in the cubicle produce psychosocial disorders the medical profession is still struggling to understand.

At least three natural options exist. Work through the pain, risking further injury. Slow down, in an attempt to reduce the pain or stress. Or go to the hospital and stop working completely. Either way, productivity suffers.

Still Failing to Deliver

In response to an abundance of externalities, hundreds of non-governmental organizations (NGOs), corporate programs, and government actions have been launched globally over the past seventy years. In the US, this includes our Clean Water and Clean Air Acts, Endangered Species Act, zero waste initiatives, zero energy districts, the transition town networks, the rise of homeless shelters, fair trade and organic food certifications, etc. Besides federal and private efforts, hundreds of states and cities have developed aggressive recycling, carbon-reduction programs, minimum wage laws, equal rights acts, and much more.

As important as these actions are, they are merely compensating for a poorly structured economic system. Our best intentions cannot keep pace with ever-expanding global market forces. For instance, after sixty years of toil organic sales are only five percent of overall food sales in the US (Organic Trade Association, 2020). Rioting in the streets of America, deadly attacks on the US capital, and mass emigration from multiple developing countries indicate social injustice and unrest are largely unresolved, if not billowing under the current global market system. In the US alone, decades of political challenges to environmental laws pose ongoing risks to air, water, and wildlife, while the unrelenting trend of global mergers and acquisitions threaten corporate policies aimed at social and environmental justice.

Even at the height of America's economic and technological might, basic needs such as healthcare, nutrition, and housing remain unmet by a growing number of citizens. The wealth gap continues to expand, while higher education grows further and further out of reach. Globally, fair trade purchases were a mere US $9 billion in 2017, less than one percent of the world's GDP (Freund, 2018).

With regard to environmental protection, great advances in recycling technology and government-led campaigns have flourished across the US over the past fifty years, to reduce dependency on landfills and impacts of raw materials extraction. Yet America still sends over 50% of its waste to landfills. Similarly, despite government subsidies and tremendous technical achievements in agriculture, the fertility of US farmlands continues to erode. Globally, habitat destruction remains a leading cause of species extinction.

In 2020, legislation was passed in the US to waive pollution responsibilities for the oil and gas industry, which employs about 150,000 people—a fraction of one percent of the American workforce (Bureau of Labor Statistics, 2020). About sixty additional environmental rules and regulations were rolled back at the federal level by the end of 2021. Should any future administration succeed to restore those rules and regulations, the fate of federal environmental protections over the next decade of growing political tension is highly questionable.

Where government action fails to address social or environmental degradation, corporations have increasingly stepped up to the plate. A recent example is the Blue Dot Network, an initiative formed by the US, Japan, and Australia to assess and certify infrastructure projects around the globe. The US Overseas Private Investment Corporation announced the initiative at the Indo-Pacific Business Forum in Bangkok in 2019, stating that the development of critical infrastructure, when it is led by private industry in a socially and environmentally responsible manner, will lead to widespread economic empowerment.

Such corporate-led efforts are noble, but certainly not novel. And like the hundreds of social and environmental initiatives that have preceded them, they are constantly threatened by unrelenting global economic forces, the bottom-line mentality of individuals in corporate offices, unpredictable political forces, and the actions of special interest groups. Also at risk are the laborers of export-based nations, unshielded against the transnational corporations' constant search for the lowest social and environmental costs of production. A high-level manager of a global corporation (I cannot cite him here, out of professional respect) told me with some consternation that when the bottom line is in question, the environment doesn't matter. Most Americans know that, at least intuitively.

Until the fundamental structure of the global market economy changes, any social and environmental benefits we have coaxed from it will remain at risk of ever-shifting political extremism, the next disruption in global energy supplies, changes in global labor valuations, trade wars, destructive competition, or the next pandemic. In the meantime, the ill structure of the US economy requires every citizen run faster to capture the American dream, while the rate of technological change only quickens.

The Ever-Quickening Pace of Technological and Economic Change

During the earliest epochs of capitalism, the development and adaptation of technological advancements required decades or even centuries to ripple through society. A famous example of the natural delay between an invention and the useful application of that invention comes from the textile industry. So influential was this one industry to global economics, it was described at length by Paul Hawken in *Natural Capitalism* (Hawken et al., 1999), as well as by Adam Smith, Alfred Marshall, Fernand Braudel, and others.

The art of weaving goes back centuries before the Industrial Revolution. But it was in the late 1700s that technological advancements such as the Spinning Jenny and coal-powered looms allowed Great Britain's textile production to expand 120-fold. The resulting economic gains were so great that British-made garments were cheaper than imports from India, whose labor costs were far lower. The wealth of many British citizens increased, allowing some consumers to buy larger homes and cram more expensive trinkets inside of them. Change wrought by the textile industry has been credited with stimulating dozens of other economic advancements in the 1700s and 1800s.

Instrumental economic changes unfolded, included the perfection of steel lathes, the refinement of long-distance transportation, easier access to credit, the efficient utilization of coal in production, and improved agricultural methods. There were short-term gains for many, no doubt, alongside great economic and social instability. Dozens of uprisings and revolts erupted across Europe. The American Revolution made its mark on Britain and its textile industry, as did the uprisings in dozens of other colonies across the globe. By the late 1800s, wages in England fell and a great depression struck Europe (Marshall, 2011; Braudel, 1984). Yet the global textile industry lurched forward.

Today, the global textile industry is so cost-effective that, according to a survey of 18,000 American households, half of the clothes we purchase don't leave the closet but once a year (van Elven, 2018). More curious, a behavioral phenomenon exists where shoppers buy clothes that are never worn at all (Yarrow, 2014).

Alvin Toffler's *Future Shock* outlined the ever-quickening advance of technology throughout history (Toffler, 1970). Prior to the first Agricultural

Revolution, new technologies required hundreds or thousands of years before being broadly adopted. By comparison, the twenty-first century consumer witnesses the invention and adaptation of new technologies within days or weeks.

Regarding transportation, an essential means to a growing global market economy, Toffler documented a near exponential evolution in the speed of travel (Figure 4). The pace of change nearly replicates the growth of bacterial communities in a petri dish injected with sugar. From such growth patterns, a crash always results. The quickening pace of global finance has also fueled the engines of globalization, with the rate of trade in currencies and commodities limited only by the speed of digital processors.

The same year that Toffler released *Future Shock*, Intel founder Gordon Moore predicted the growth rate of transistors on integrated circuit chips. His prediction, coined *Moore's Law*, was that circuit chip capacity would double every two years. Moore was spot on. In 2021, humanity witnessed the computing speed generated by over 10 *billion* transistors per microprocessor. In 1971, a mere 10,000 transistors existed in a processor. Such change is possible because technological evolution has not occurred linearly, but exponentially. As such, the rate of change 365 days from now will be greater than it is today—computers become faster and more efficient with each passing year.

It is hard to know when a threshold has been crossed, as the evolution of technology and innovation can unveil itself so sluggishly that changes in economic and social momentum are difficult to witness. That is, until one day you wake up and bemoan the amount of time wasted shuffling through your drawers and closets to find something you might wear. Or search for lost keys. Or, due to the boundless distractions of social media, you cannot sleep at all.

Absent a global economic implosion, might the pace of technological change outstrip the rate of human evolution needed to keep up with the resulting societal changes? Perhaps prophetically, Alvin Toffler believed our accelerated rate of technological change would leave people disconnected and suffering from shattering stress and disorientation. Even Keynes's 1930 article, "Economic Possibilities for our Grandchildren", published 40 years prior to *Future Shock*, warned of the fast pace of technological change preceding the Great Depression. As Keynes lamented, "the very rapidity of these changes is hurting us and bringing difficult problems to solve." And to think, Toffler's and Keynes's concerns arose before the pervasive influence of computers, Blackberries, smartphones, the internet, artificial intelligence, social media, joy marketing, the firehosing of falsehood, and fake news.

Blind faith is required to believe technological progress is our salvation from the social and environmental problems caused by the current economic model. Such faith manifests itself in statements such as, "improved communication will compensate for inefficiencies in ever-lengthening supply chains," or "modern technology allows us to enter into negotiations, make purchases, or forge trade deals with the necessary knowledge to make economically and ecologically sustainable decisions." And perhaps, "improved technology will reduce the social and environmental externalities across the globe." Or, "increased mechanization will reduce the need for labor, freeing us up to…"

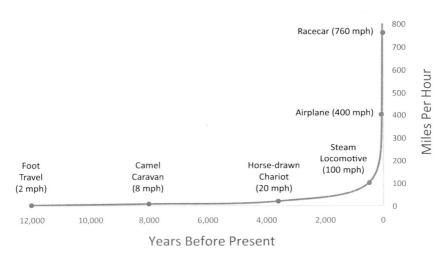

Figure 4. Change in speed of travel over time. Data from Toffler (1970).

In contrast to such statements, recall that at the height of our current over-information age COVID-19 caused a rush of irrational consumer behavior, leaving entire city blocks devoid of toilet paper. As I can personally attest, medical needs went unmet and pasta shelves were barren. Unemployment reached record highs. Supply chain disruptions led to food processing challenges and interruptions in the manufacture of cars. Based on the evidence, it is easier to believe technological change is inept against the world's most critical social and environmental challenges, as long as our economic foundations remain in shambles. Technology, too, is external to the foundational components of every economy. It is merely a tool, whose improper use is a danger to the patient.

More likely, the ever-increasing web of global market dependents (i.e., trading partners who exchange their self-reliance for dependence on others), coupled with the ever-quickening pace of technological change, may simply magnify the intensity of external forces upon our economies. Consumers and nations will respond in unimaginable ways to increasingly unpredictable global market forces. The result may likely be greater economic volatility and chaos.

There is an alternate path. The structure of our economies can mirror that of complex self-regulating ecosystems.

THREE

THE ARCHETYPE OF A
SELF-REGULATING
(SUSTAINABLE) ECONOMY

As we seek stable employment, a high productive capacity, resilient economies, etc., we owe it to ourselves to examine the system most capable of
producing these results for the greatest number of individuals. Systems that
have survived millions of years of earth's most disruptive events, while actually
increasing their resilience and resistance to those events over time.

These systems, of course, are ecosystems. Like our economies, ecosystems
are highly complex self-regulating systems. They are comprised of innumerable subsystems at the same time that they are nested within the greater biome.
Unlike ecosystems, however, our current economic model struggles to attain
high levels of resilience and resistance to disturbance, sustain a high productive
capacity, and yield other beneficial traits that ecosystems naturally produce. To
comprehend how self-regulating ecosystems and economies are structured, and
how they function, we must first understand systems thinking.

Systems Thinking as Applied to
Ecosystems and Economies

Systems thinking is the branch of science that examines the structure and interactions of key components within living and non-living systems. It provides a
foundation of knowledge to better understand our ecosystems and economies.
As one of science's newest branches, systems thinking has evolved considerably in recent decades. The first comprehensive book on the subject, *Systems
Thinking*, was written by Australian scientist Frederick Emery in 1969, and
spans social, physical, and biological systems. Nearly five decades later, Capra

and Luisi (2014) produced a book on systems thinking that is difficult to rival: *The Systems View of Life: A Unifying Vision.*

In *The Systems View of Life*, Capra and Luisi describe how systems are nested one within another, and grow more complex with each higher level of organization. The cell, for instance, is comprised of many lower order systems: the cell wall, mitochondria, nucleus, etc. Millions of interconnected cells constitute a system such as the human heart, which is part of the larger and more complex circulatory system. When a network of organ systems become arranged uniquely, a new species such as *Homo sapiens* will emerge.

Whether our focus is physical, social, or biological systems, the smaller units of organization within each system (e.g., cells, organs, species, wires, factories) are often referred to as parts, components, or subsystems. In living systems such as the human body, none of the components (e.g., heart or lungs) can survive without the body that houses it, and *vice versa*. While each subsystem exists as an identifiable unit, it must also interact with surrounding systems for survival. For instance, the particular form of a seahorse results from a unique arrangement of several body parts, which provide ample advantages in its environment—the ability to change skin color to match its background, a covering of spiny plates for protection, and a uniquely-shaped had that creates a nearly undetectable movement during ambush, giving them a much higher predatory kill rate than sharks.

Humans, or any other species, cannot persist without constantly interacting with the greater systems they inhabit. And those systems, such as the ecosystems upon which our economy depends, are in a continual state of flux. This reality demands every species live by one carnal rule: evolve or die. In turn, multiple species interact with one another in competitive and collaborative ways to form entire communities, which are also self-regulating.

Ascending the ladder of complexity, several communities coalesce into larger ecosystems, such as a ponderosa pine forest. As an identifiable unit, every forest is shaped by local environmental factors such as soils, climate, latitude, elevation, and others. The ponderosa pine forest exists alongside other ecosystems to form ecoregions such as the Southern Rockies, stretching from Santa Fe, New Mexico to Casper, Wyoming. The Southern Rockies ecoregion is nested within a larger biome, the Temperate Coniferous Forests of North America. Ultimately, all biomes are nested within the biosphere, which houses every living thing on earth.

Just as ecosystems exist at multiple scales, the economy exists at local, regional, national, and global scales. However, we must question whether the global market economy can thrive when the national and regional economies comprising it are operating poorly. For perspective, can any higher order eco-system, such as an ecoregion or an entire biome, persist if the subsystems comprising them are functioning poorly? Can a patch of America's tallgrass prairie thrive when the individual plant communities comprising it are malfunctioning? Can your body function optimally if your heart or lungs are ailing? The answer is a resounding *no*.

However, when the lower-order systems (e.g., individuals, communities, regional economies, etc.) within a greater system are functioning well, a synergistic byproduct arises. When those lower order systems are thriving, the higher-order system achieves a level of resilience and resistance that exceeds the sum of its parts. High levels of resistance and resilience are critical to the long-term survival of any system that is under constant threat of disturbance.

The Quest for a Self-Regulating Economy, and its Benefits

The desire for our economies to operate in a self-regulating manner dates back to 18th century views on free markets, and arguments against government interference with natural market forces (Smith, 2019). As important as Adam Smith's understanding of a self-regulating economy was, ecological research over the past two centuries has revealed key insights into how self-regulating systems are actually structured. For instance, abundant research on biological diversity, evolution, energy transfer rules, and nutrient cycling in ecosystems now exists. However, economists and ecologists have yet to identify diversity, energy, and trade as foundational components of self-regulating economies and ecosystems, nor clarified the role these components play in the efficient acquisition and distribution of resources.

In a well-structured economy, the fewest possible government interventions are necessary to maintain its productive capacity. Many would agree that this same structure must also ensure a broad range of social, economic, and environmental benefits are met. Throughout this book, the term *highly functional* is used to describe an economy that attains a desirable level of productivity from the fewest resource inputs, and with the least government intervention, without jeopardizing the social and environmental assets upon which it relies. Productivity, in this regard, is not measured by GDP but by *net domestic production* (NDP). NDP is the productivity of an economy after accounting for depreciation and maintenance, and will be described more fully below.

A highly functional economy must also sustain desired *economic benefits*, such as stable employment, profitability, satisfactory jobs, wages that are adequate to cover living expenses, and other basic human needs and expectations that vary from region to region. A highly functional economy must be able to maintain its productive capacity and produce economic benefits in the face of expected regional, national, and global turbulence. That is, an economy must attain high levels of resistance and resilience to disturbance. The restoration of such an economy is the focus of Part III of this book. In the interim, we will explore the *emergent properties* of an economy.

Emergent Properties and Feedback Loops in Ecosystems and Economies

The *emergent properties* of a system are those that are not present any of its parts, but *emerge* in response to interactions among the parts. In turn, the whole is different than the sum of its parts. The emergent properties of your body, for instance, are such that multiple organ systems continually interact to maintain a stable environment, a homeostasis. Bodies that cannot maintain *homeostasis* perish.

Your body's homeostasis is maintained through a great number of *feedback loops*, involuntary responses to external stimuli. High levels of carbon dioxide in your blood triggers faster breathing, which more quickly removes carbon dioxide from the body. Similarly, should your body reach too high a temperature, your brain signals your skin to start sweating, and your body cools. Such reactions are examples of negative feedback loops. Despite their name, *negative feedback loops* are not necessarily bad. They are simply a means to bring a system back into balance. They are essential to maintaining a relatively stable state in an economy or ecosystem, or to make corrections when the system deviates from its course (Katz & Kahn, 1969).

Positive feedback loops, on the other hand, are those that produce an amplifying effect. Milk production in nursing mothers is an example of a positive feedback loop that is essential to the survival of the species. As the baby suckles from its mother's breast, her body releases a chemical signal that stimulates more milk production.

The Benefits of Maintaining a Dynamic Equilibrium, and the Costs of Disequilibrium

Humans thrive when they maintain their body temperature, oxygen levels, blood pH, etc. within acceptable limits, regardless the environmental conditions of the moment. We are adaptable to normal fluctuations in temperature, seasonal food sources, etc. Should we waltz into an environment where stressors are more constant and/or severe, however, more resources must be allocated toward maintaining our homeostasis rather than our growth and reproduction.

Today, an increasing concentration of metals and chemicals in our air, water, and food are directly impairing the fertility of the human race. Toxins are causing decreased sperm counts in men, while women are suffering progressively poor ovulation, impaired implantation, and loss of fetal viability (Pizzorno, 2018). While an increasing number of individuals chooses to avoid parenthood altogether, perhaps due to rising population pressures and the resulting social stressors. In total, the birth rate has declined by 50% in the past sixty years according to Pizzorno.

Should environmental stressors continue long enough, or become severe enough, the body's ability to maintain homeostasis eventually suffers. That is, the capacity to self-regulate becomes impaired. To the extreme, death will result.

But as individuals form populations, and populations form a species, and hundreds of species interact within communities, the increased complexity of the system exhibits features that are not present in the individual. The more complex a system is, the longer it can persist. For example, an entire population of humans (i.e., the Rapa Nui people of Easter Island) does not perish when the homeostasis of any individual fails. Nor did the human race go extinct when the Rapa Nui population vanished.

An entire community of species attains far higher levels of resilience and resistance than the species within. As a community survives each passing threat, such as a drought or wildfire, its ability to survive future threats is fortified. In this way, eons of disturbance and recovery have molded ecosystems into a *dynamic equilibrium*: a relatively stable condition under which resources are most efficiently distributed to species within; where processes are balanced at a landscape level. Predator and prey populations may rise and fall over time, but system-wide diversity—on average—remains fairly stable (Loranger et al., 2016). Ecosystems in a state of dynamic equilibrium certainly experience fires, droughts, etc., but those disturbances are essential to maintaining landscape level diversity, which correlates to high biological diversity (Huston, 1994).

In our economies, basic human responses to our ever-fluctuating SEI context help maintain its dynamic equilibrium. When the price of corn rises, we may consume more palm or canola oil. When crude oil becomes too expensive, we tend to drive less or purchase more corn-based ethanol. When interest rates fall too low, bond values increase. When interest rates climb too high, consumer spending decreases. And when there is a glut of capital, together with low interest rates, a risk of deflation emerges.

The concept of a dynamic equilibrium is contentious even among ecologists, or is at least challenging to understand in a system that evolved alongside constant environmental change. For perspective, consider the opposite condition, *disequilibrium*: a condition whereby, in the face of regular and expected disturbances, the system cannot maintain an efficient distribution of resources, high net primary productivity, diversity, or other necessary conditions for the survival of species and individuals within. Degraded ecosystems exhibit disequilibrium when, for instance, a shift in plant and animal populations results in an increase in wildfire frequency. This is the case in rangeland habitats of the Colorado Plateau, where the introduction of cattle grazing, together with the introduction of cheatgrass, an annual weed that dominates millions of acres, has resulted in a decrease in biological diversity and low net primary production. Wildfires now burn every three to five years, rather than once every five to ten decades.

Poorly functioning economies can also experience disequilibrium, and struggle to maintain productivity and efficient resource distribution during recessions, depressions, supply chain disruptions, or other disturbances. Such economies can also exhibit lower diversity, as well as high degrees of volatility. Volatility can arise in the form of unpredictable supply chain disruptions, rampant market shifts, threats of high inflation or deflation, etc.

Highly volatile economies are less capable of distributing goods and services efficiently to citizens, maintaining high employment, supporting a high quality of life, or ensuring that a community's most important social and environmental values are met. Stress and anxiety among individuals, businesses, industries, and trading partners rise accordingly, stimulating volatility further. Unpredictable feedback loops form, in an attempt to stabilize the system. The examples are numerous: panic buying during the COVID-19 pandemic that left grocery store shelves bare, panic selling of stocks that stoke market crashes, the oil glut that resulted from decreased global trade in 2020-2021, etc.

Countless feedback loops interweave an economy with the greater environment in which it is nested, so that economic volatility may also erupt from a variety of environmental forces. When massive flooding or drought strikes the Midwest, the corn industry is jeopardized. A warming and drying climate in the Rocky Mountains causes larger and more severe wildfires, which threaten water supplies and downstream infrastructure, and destroy personal property. This brand of feedback loop can incite additional economic stressors, such as disruptions to supply chains, health risks, increased costs of water, rising costs of food production, or social unrest.

In response to volatility, more capital must be allocated to maintenance. The examples are abundant: military activities, police, jails, watershed restoration, physical and mental health expenses, environmental clean-up costs to maintain air and water quality, job training and retraining programs, etc. Every dollar spent on maintenance is then unavailable to invest in restoring the productive capacity and resilience of an economy, or to support important social and environmental values.

Is the Global Market Economy on a Path to a Steady State, or the Opposite State?

The concept of dynamic equilibrium is similar to a *steady state economy*, described by Herman Daly (1991) as one that seeks an equilibrium between productivity and population growth, and is capable of thriving amidst mild economic fluctuations. Through their efficient use of energy, labor, and other resources, steady state economies can maintain higher levels of production and consumption than economies in a state of disequilibrium, or instability.

Words such as *stability* and *security* are difficult to avoid in the context of economics. *Security*, used here, relates to a nation's ability to sustain its productive capacity while delivering basic goods and services to its citizens, regardless of volatility in the global market economy. From that capacity stems more stable employment, secure food supplies, sufficient medical supplies, military might, and other essential goods and services, regardless of the economic conditions of other nations. *Stability* is used here to portray a relative condition, as no self-regulating system is perfectly stable at all times. For perspective, major global economic depressions and recessions, boom and bust cycles, and similar events are signs of a relatively *unstable* economic system.

A steady state economy, it can be argued, has not been the trend throughout the history of global market capitalism. A more peculiar trend has befallen the capitalist system over the course of its evolution. As capital is increasingly re-invested in global trade, and into greater scales of production that global trade requires, the *economic space* required to keep financial returns high tends to deteriorate (Arrighi, 2010). One's *economic space* refers not only to the geographic area of their economy, but the number of trading partners and the degree of trade among those partners, financial systems, business diversity, and other socio-economic conditions of that space. It is a self-defined area in which goods, services, people, and capital move freely.

As capitalism has become increasingly global, another peculiar trend has emerged. Documented by Arrighi, Fernand Braudel, Alfred Marshall, and others, the duration of each new capitalist model has been shortening as the global market economy has evolved as a system (Table 1). This curious condition—a system's persistence decreases as it evolves—has not, in my experience, been witnessed in ecosystems.

Table 1. Epochs of capitalism. Data from Arrighi (2010) and Braudel (1984), with duration reflecting time between signal crises. Signal crises occur in periods of comparatively stable governance.

Epoch of Capitalism	Dominant State	Approximate Time Period (AD)	Duration from signal to signal crisis (years)
Mercantile	City-states of Northern Italy (Genoa)	1340 - 1560	220
Mercantile	Dutch	1560 - 1740	180
Classical	Great Britian	1740 - 1870	130
Classical	United States	1870 - 1930	60
Keynesian	United States	1940-1970	30
Global Market	?	1970 - ?	?

Global market capitalism rests on two crutches, both of which raise doubt as to whether or not the system can persist, let alone achieve a steady state. First is the significant degree of government actions (e.g., subsidies, tax breaks, trade restrictions and promotions, bailouts, manipulation of prime interest rates, etc.) required to prop up productivity and employment, manage instability, and maintain other economic values in the US, and in other countries wed to global market capitalism. Second is the significant reliance upon imported resources (e.g., energy, labor, materials, investment, etc.) to support domestic needs. Together, these conditions have jeopardized the productive capacity and resilience not only of the US economy, but of those economies the US is bound to via trade.

The global market economy is functioning more like a bicycle, with an over-reliance on external resources and external "instructions" in order to move forward. Though an unstable bicycle, tasked with navigating an increasingly volatile world.

The ever-expanding mass of wealth concentrated into fewer hands stimulates such instability and volatility (Greenspan, 2007; Stiglitz, 2015b). The social justice riots in the summer of 2020, followed by the attack on America's capital on January 6, 2021, were simply a few steps down a path of social upheaval that has been brewing alongside America's ascension to global capitalist superpower. Until the structural faults of the system are corrected, volatility will most likely intensify. Alternatively, the rules of self-regulating ecosystems may provide a guide to restoring our economies to a more stable—less volatile—state.

Ecosystems as Models for Sustainable (Self-Regulating) Economies

An ecosystem is little more than an assemblage of living organisms interacting freely with one another to extract the greatest quantity of resources possible from the environment they occupy. An ecosystem's environment includes variables such as oxygen levels, the amount and type of precipitation in a given year, the angle of sunlight striking the landscape, the type of soil, number of frost-free days, and other nonliving factors. An ecosystem's living and nonliving components are interconnected through energy flows and material transfers between all species, both above and below the ground, and between the thin crust of life on earth and the atmosphere above.

Coined by Arthur Tansley in 1935, the word *ecosystem* has its roots in *oikos* (home), which it shares with another word from ancient Greek: *economy*. Literally, economy means "household management", and describes the means by which a society manages its material resources. But the more important relationship between ecosystems and economies is far deeper than their shared Greek root, and exists beyond a mere analogy.

Some readers may shun the notion that knowledge of ecosystems can inform the structure and functioning of something as complex as an economy. Their first response may be that analogies between the two systems are imperfect, making any conclusions false. And if economies and ecosystems were merely *analogous* to one other, I would agree. Likening an economy to a bicycle is one such false analogy. The chain of a bicycle, one might conclude, symbolizes the distribution of energy to the wheels. The handlebars might represent policies that steer the economy. Abundant analogies exist, all of which break down when we begin asking basic questions. What happens when the chain breaks, or the tires go flat, or when the cyclist jumps off?

The analogy fails because fundamentally a bicycle is not a self-regulating system. It is a simple, closed system, lacking any redundancy in functions, or the ability to maintain its form and functions over time without external inputs. When one component fails, such as a broken hub or flat tire, the bike simply stops. Without external resources and instructions, a bike cannot maintain itself.

Despite the Greek roots, a house is also an inappropriate analogy for our economy. Even though a home is built from dozens of sturdy components, it cannot repair itself when those components degrade due to external stressors. Because houses and bicycles are not self-regulating, they have but one fate—to deteriorate over time at the hand of storms, fires, freeze-thaw cycles, rust, and so on.

As in ecosystems, the persistence, resilience, and efficiency of an economy result from the interaction of several self-regulating components—multiple businesses and industries, communities and cities, and a great variety of ecosystems with which any economy forms an integral whole. And like ecosystems, economies are nested one within another.

The actual structure of ecosystems and economies are equal. They are *homologous* to one another, rather than mere analogies. Ecosystems and economies are not only complex self-regulating systems, but they have become interdependent, with the human species serving as the vital connection between both. When we treat them as interconnected and homologous, the principles and rules of one are readily applied to the structure and functions of the other.

Still, when comparing the structure and functioning of economies with that of ecosystems, something appears amiss. Shouldn't our economy be capable of sustaining its productive capacity without the continual input of resources from far beyond its borders? Why does the current US economy require the constant manipulation of policies and laws to prop up production, maintain social and environmental assets, and reduce the risk of depressions? More importantly, shouldn't our economy be increasing (not decreasing) its resilience and resistance to disturbances as it evolves?

The Roots of Resilience and Resistance

Over the enduring course of evolution, earth's ecosystems have developed levels of diversity and complexity that allow them to thrive in the face of constant disturbance. That is, self-regulating ecosystems have a high degree of *resistance* to disturbance. They can withstand the expected (i.e., normal) range of disturbance events without becoming significantly degraded. And following a "normal" disturbance—drought, insect outbreaks, heavy winter snows, floods—the system's ability to maintain its productive capacity remains high, and its ability to transfer resources throughout the system remains secure. In fact, net primary productivity and diversity often increase following disturbance in a highly functioning ecosystem. This is a sign of *resilience*: the degree to which a system can continue producing and distributing biomass (i.e., resources, capital, etc.) during and following a disturbance.

The concepts of resistance and resilience are exemplified by the fences erected throughout Rocky Mountain National Park to protect meadows from overgrazing by elk. Elk have reached abnormally high populations in response to the loss of the wolf, a keystone predator. The wolf would otherwise keep elk constantly on the move, so they would not overgraze any specific valley, forest, or alpine meadow.

Today, with the elk lazing in the meadows like cattle, the vegetation upon which the whole system relies has been dramatically altered. The willows that once stabilized soils and sustained beavers have become denuded. In turn, the beaver dams that once dissipated floods, maintained high water tables, and sustained lush vegetation in the valley have disappeared. Formerly lush meadows have become drier and less productive.

In response, park managers have erected elk-proof fences over the years to help restore willow communities and lush meadows throughout the glacial valleys. But like bicycles, fences are simple closed systems with minimal *resistance* to the most basic disturbances such as elk, floods, fires, wind, frost, rust, and the like. When any of these forces undermine the strength of the fence, external resources are required to repair it, lest the elk rush back in.

Fences are not solutions to restoring complex self-regulating systems. Park managers know this, and so for decades have championed the reintroduction of a key component: wolves. In 2020, Coloradans narrowly passed a proposition to bring gray wolves back to Colorado. Yet ample uphill battles exist before wolves reappear in the state, including concerns that wolves will wreak undue economic damage to cattle operations. That said, the presence of wolves in parks such as Yellowstone have been economic boons to the region.

Given the interdependency of economies and ecosystems, economic solutions likely exist to the ecological degradation in Rocky Mountain National Park. Whether or not political divides will keep such solutions from succeeding is yet to be seen. In the meantime, the park has no option but to invest in closed systems such as fences and other resource-intensive means of protecting the productivity and health of the park. Protections which will eventually fail, for they are not self-regulating.

In contrast, ponder the tens of thousands of years of ecosystem evolution, shaped by countless disturbances, constantly chiseling away at the system's structure and functions, and that of the species within, while enhancing its ability to efficiently produce and distribute resources to the greatest number of individuals possible. Barring some cataclysmic disruption, such as a collision with a mile-wide asteroid or continent-wide volcanic eruptions, the resilience and productive capacity of the system only increases over time.

The Role of Disturbance and Succession in Maintaining the Productivity of Ecosystems and Economies

It may appear counterintuitive, but ecosystems garner their resilience, resistance, and productive capacity not in spite of but *due to* their experience with disturbance. Through eons of evolution, ecosystems have developed traits that allow them to persist in the face of a wide range of disturbances (e.g., fires, floods, severe drought, deep freezes, etc.), just as our bodies have developed traits that confer persistence in the face of cuts, colds, viruses, droughts, broken bones, and other disturbances.

Economies and ecosystems are in a constant state of recovery from some past disturbance. From the right perspective, disturbances can be viewed simply as a means of testing the system's resilience, resistance, and general health. A healthy body has little trouble healing from a cut or a broken bone. The healthier the system, the better it can withstand disturbance while maintaining its productive capacity.

A Gross Error in Calculating Economic Productivity

Before proceeding further, a critical distinction must be made in how economic productivity is measured. Gross domestic product (GDP) is a standard measure of an economy's performance, and is tied to boundless historical data. As such, GDP is referred to throughout this book as necessary. However, *net* domestic product is a far more realistic measure of an economy's ability to sustain its productivity, efficiently distribute resources, and maintain other values in the face of continual internal and external threats.

Traditional measures of net domestic product begin with GDP, then account for the depreciation of capital assets (e.g., the natural deterioration of homes, factories, warehouses, office buildings, roads, machinery, etc.). In essence, NDP accounts for the maintenance needs associated with economic production. Should the equipment and infrastructure of a business or industry go unmaintained, their ability to continue producing goods and services will decline. NDP is equivalent to the Net Primary Productivity of ecosystems, which accounts for energy consumed to sustain metabolism, and various maintenance requirements of the entire system.

In the US and other economies, NDP ignores many maintenance and depreciation costs associated with production. To begin, degradation of natural resources caused by various economic activities is rarely accounted for in the same year in which the related economic activities occurred. As a result, NDP (and certainly not GDP) does not fully account for the degradation of the system resulting from those economic activities. The tens of billions of dollars spent to clean up the Chesapeake Bay from past economic activities (e.g., degraded water quality, habitat loss, impacts to fisheries, etc.) was not accounted for in the years that degrading economic activities contributed to the productivity of the US economy. GDP and NDP were therefore artificially inflated in those years.

Similarly, soil fertility losses caused by modern agriculture were not accounted for in the decades when high farm productivity contributed to gross domestic product. Restoring even a portion of America's degraded soils, using traditional methods, would require about thirteen billion cubic yards of compost to be added to 65 million acres of land. Half of that land has lost all its topsoil, and the other half has moderate to high topsoil loss. Assuming a cost of US $85 per acre for materials, shipping, labor, and tilling operations, the cost of restoring fertility to this one region of American is about US $1.1 trillion. This does not include the cost of restoring fertility to degraded farmlands in California's Central Valley or Scott Valley, or anywhere outside the Corn Belt.

Traditional measures of GDP and NDP also fail to account for the mental and physical health costs associated with hyper-productive economic activity. GDP is therefore a gross overestimate of economic performance. If only we could drive our cars like our economies, without worrying about replacing the tires or changing the oil.

To better account for the cost of maintenance, a more accurate definition of NDP is needed. To be in alignment with complex self-regulating systems, I propose this definition of *net domestic product*: an economy's productivity after accounting for the depreciation of capital assets, social assets, and ecological assets. When using NDP throughout the remainder of this book, it represents this more comprehensive definition, rather than the inflated value that is typically reported.

Measuring the health of an economy in terms of NDP, rather than gross domestic product, has far-reaching implications. For starters, economies that accurately account for maintenance costs such as watershed restoration, public health, restoring soil fertility, and water quality, have an economic incentive to minimize maintenance costs throughout the production-consumption cycle. Economic activities that minimize maintenance costs, without reducing production levels, can result in higher NDP.

The examples are endless, so I will mention just one. Selective logging can be employed to improve water quality (and quantity) in many regions, lower the risk of severe wildfire, reduce firefighting costs, contribute to carbon neutrality, and reduce the costs of restoring watersheds after a fire. The timber is used to build and heat homes in the region, instead of being consumed by wildfire. Ample clean water can be maintained at a lower cost. In some forest systems, new trees do not need to be replanted after selective logging. Road maintenance costs can be lowered, and so forth.

Succession and Net Primary Productivity in Ecosystems and Economies

It is not intuitive, but the net primary productivity of an ecosystem—equivalent to the NDP of an economy—is typically highest in the early to middle years following a significant disturbance (Gough et al., 2016; Kira & Shedei, 1967; Odum, 1969; Tang et al., 2014). Following a wildfire or some other disturbance, the recovering forest is dominated by quick-growing species, each capable of high rates of productivity. As the years go by, diversity increases, biomass accumulates, and an increasing quantity of resources is directed toward system maintenance. Eventually, an equilibrium is reached between community-wide production and maintenance.

Absent another significant disturbance, the forest becomes dominated by towering trees, which demand yet more maintenance, and are less productive. This is the late-successional stage of an ecosystem, sometimes referred to as a "climax" community, which has not received significant disturbance in a relatively long time.

Succession is the process of plant community changes over time, and is as important to our understanding of productive economies as it is to productive ecosystems. A late-successional community—an old growth forest, a tallgrass prairie that has not been grazed or burned for many decades, etc.—rarely exhibits the highest net or gross primary productivity, compared to early- or middle-successional communities. Nor is it the most diverse system.

Studying America's temperate deciduous forests, Gough et. al. (2016) found that the middle successional stages achieved the highest levels of productivity (Figure 5). In these middle stages, the actual structure of the forest is being shaped by a higher frequency of small-scale disturbances, such as blowdowns of individual trees. The result is a more complex and diverse forest. An increase in diversity imparts the system with a greater capacity to efficiently capture and distribute resources—what economists refer to as *allocative efficiency*.

Uninterrupted successional processes are essential to the productivity and diversity of most terrestrial ecosystems, not just forests. Work in North American grasslands by Tilman et al. (1997) revealed that prairie communities with higher degrees of structural diversity—plants with varying canopy heights within the same patch of land—and greater species diversity exhibited the greatest production. Tilman's work also showed that prairies with greater diversity captured more energy and increased the total amount of plant-available nitrogen for the community. In the diverse prairies, species such as legumes convert nitrogen from the atmosphere, making it available to grasses and other plants.

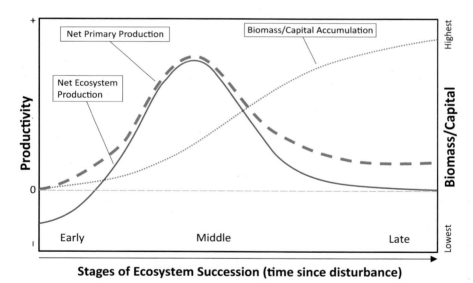

Figure. 5. Predictions of aboveground net primary production (NPP), net ecosystem production (NEP), and biomass over the course of ecological succession (after Gough et al., 2016; and Odum, 1969). NEP is the difference between the gross primary production of vegetation, and total ecosystem respiration, and represents the total amount of organic carbon present (Lovett et al., 2006). After a wildfire, or under intense agriculture, NEP can be negative due to carbon losses to the atmosphere.

In contrast, the global market economy tends to achieve its highest levels of productivity (as measured by GDP) immediately prior to significant disturbances, such as depressions and recessions. Recall the roaring 1920s that preceded the Great Depression, the booming US economy prior to the 2007 Great Recession, and the record-breaking GDP and market performance prior to the COVID-19 crash. Long before that, a booming European economy in the mid nineteenth century was ended abruptly by a global depression of the 1870s to 1890s, what some have labeled the Long Depression. Much earlier, the booming Florentine textile trade ended with a cataclysmic crash in 1338, impoverishing tens of thousands of laborers throughout Florence for four decades (Arrighi, 2010).

As in ecosystems, essential feedback loops exist between disturbance and productivity in our economies. In an economy, disturbances such as recessions and industry shake-ups (e.g., disruptive technologies) can provide opportunities for new business entrants. Those new entrants tend to grow more quickly than larger and older businesses following a downturn, making new entrants essential to the future productivity of the economy, and to maintaining stable economic growth (Eliasson, 1991; Eliasson et al., 1995; Haltiwanger et al., 2010; Schumpeter, 1934).

Unfortunately, the economic opportunities that disturbance can provide are often suffocated in countries such as the US, via government interventions like subsidies and bailouts of large industries. Such interventions place downward pressure on the number and competitiveness of new entrants, as well as existing small businesses, who can take advantage of a downturn more quickly. Interferences occur throughout all successional stages of the US economy. For instance, *subsidies*—direct or indirect financial support of specific industries—have been used to stimulate the production of a given product or service regardless of the presence of any meaningful disturbance.

More damaging, some of America's largest subsidies and bailouts go to its largest corporations; industrial behemoths whose corporate structure, client base, and ingenuity rarely meet the future needs of a rapidly evolving economy. To the degree such subsidies and bailouts diminish the complexity and diversity of an economy, they also jeopardize its productive capacity. In essence, such interventions push the successional stage of the economy farther to the right side of Figure 5. It is in this late-successional condition that economies throughout history have experienced decreased growth rates, and industries have witnessed declining profitability (Arrighi, 2010; Piketty, 2014).

Economic Evolution and Endogenous Growth Theory

As in ecosystems, evolution is the basic process by which economic diversity builds. Economic diversity is sparked the moment a structural or technological adaptation imparts the slightest advantage to any business, industry, or sector. While such adaptations are often viewed in terms of new gadgets, innovation has a far less glamorous side—the structural changes within businesses and industries necessary to bring new products to market. This includes new organizational structures, transportation networks, or novel means of production such as assembly lines, or advances in agile manufacturing, to be described more fully later.

At the same time, no structural or technical innovation occurs inside a bubble. Innovations coevolve with greater industry changes, and certainly in response to larger economic changes. The invention of the steam engine, for instance, had little influence on the global economy until coupled with an adequate energy source, coal. Coevolving with other technological advancements during the Industrial Revolution, industrial-scale steam engines gave rise to the possibility of coal-powered trains and ships, new niches for business to fill.

Similarly, Leonardo Da Vinci invented the automobile in 1495 as a four-wheeled, spring-powered model with rack-and-pinon steering (Corby, 2019). His invention needed to coevolve with new industrial processes such as assembly lines, and become coupled with systemic economic shifts (e.g., higher wages, cheap gasoline) before customers would accept cars as a practical means of transportation—four centuries later. Politicians and economists hotly debate exactly what is required to stimulate such innovations.

Innovation cannot be merely added to an economy; a reality that may explain why investment can have limited impacts on innovation. For example, though the US has been praised for high levels of technological progress, the return on investment into innovation has been diminishing for decades (Romer, 1994). Concurrently, economic diversity in the US has been declining at national, state, and regional levels, which may explain why the per capita GDP growth rate has dropped from about 8% per year in the 1970s to about 3% in the twenty-teens (Macrotrends, 2020b). The increases in productivity that innovation must deliver, in order for an economy to support further innovation, are declining.

One theory struggling to explain the role of innovation on productivity is *endogenous growth theory*, pioneered by Nobel Prize Economist Paul Romer in the late '80s (Romer, 1994). This theory maintains that economic growth is primarily the result of internal rather than external forces. Therefore, growth is stimulated by investment in a nation's human capital. Building that capital requires a nation develop new forms of technology, including more efficient and effective means of production.

Yet Romer, as recently as 2018 in an interview with Bloomberg, still champions investment in innovation to stimulate endogenous growth. In its current form, endogenous growth theory appears to violate the basic rules of complex self-regulating systems. Like many such theories, endogenous growth theory confuses external forces and internal components. Investment, when it originates outside an industry or economy, is an external force. Hence adding more investment to an economy does not necessarily stimulate productivity, diversity, or innovation for any meaningful length of time. In fact, *exogenous* investment (i.e., investment originating outside one's economic space) is more likely to degrade an economy's productive capacity, as has been the trend in the US and other developed nations.

For example, several Asian countries—South Korea, Japan, Taiwan, China—have achieved high levels of economic growth in the past half century due to internal investment in physical and human capital domestically, not from exogenous investment (Piketty, 2014). Piketty and other economists argue that raw population growth is the key ingredient in economic growth, for half of all past economic growth has been correlated with increasing population, which has ballooned in China and India.

But what explains the other half of the economic growth equation? Part II will tackle this question, while part III proposes a definition of growth that better aligns with the realities of a self-regulating economy. In the meantime, I posit that for endogenous growth theory to be valid, any economy's foundational components—diversity, energy, and trade—must function according to the principles of self-regulating ecosystems, which is the core discussion of Part II.

Self-Imposed Threats to Innovation

To better grasp how innovation might be stymied (or stimulated), imagine you had the power to remove innovation from an economy, or at least diminish it considerably. Here is how that might happen, at least at the level of industry. A novel innovation such as the electric-powered assembly line attracts investment from outside the industry and regional economy. Those business receiving the greatest investment grow quickest, attracting yet more external investment, stimulating greater levels of automation. Increased automation places downward pressure on business diversity and labor needs in the impacted industry. Short-term increases in profitability stimulate more investment, including foreign investment. The scale of production further increases, generating a vicious cycle of diminishing diversity and labor needs. Eventually, this process reduces not only the number of humans in the industry, but the number of businesses competing in the industry. Absent human ingenuity and business competition, innovation stagnates.

If the above scenario sounds far-fetched, recall that such a decline struck the American auto industry prior to its collapse in the late 1980s (Ingrassia & White, 1995). The same trend has befallen America's agricultural industry, as well as manufacturing at large, retail, and even high tech.

Ingenuity, a trait of individuals, lies at the core of innovation. Yet as we speak, artificial intelligence is delivering an increasing number of problem-solving services, once the work of humans. Speech recognition. Routing problems. Military strategy. Navigation on congested highways. Medical doctors are also employing AI outputs, which synthesize hundreds of medical journals to inform proper care for patients.

Simple tasks can be completed by AI, thus reducing the need for people to solve rudimentary problems. But absent human involvement, and absent moral judgement, AI is limited to routine cognitive tasks. While navigating down a steep winding road, what decision does an AI-driven car make when a boy on a bike appears suddenly in the double yellow line around a blind turn? Does it direct the car to swerve, and risk killing the family in the car, or does it strike the boy on the bike?

AI also lacks the ability to create. Would AI, if presented with the ingredients of rubber and steel, know to create the bicycle or the car? If so, for whom? That is, can AI anticipate human needs? Can it call a military bluff, and avoid hitting the nuclear launch button? Will advances in AI result in a more fulfilling life for workers, should it create another wave of job-replacing automation? And while aiding in decision making, will AI ultimately degrade our collective ingenuity, and therefore our rates of innovation?

Absent innovation, economic diversity has but one path over time—decline. As diversity declines, the threats of external forces are magnified. Yet, to combat such threats, greater diversity must be stimulated. But here is the rub. As observed by Emery (1969), continual additions of energy are a way to maintain the existing structure, not create a new structure.

Are There Limits to Economic Growth?

This book was published on the 50th anniversary of *Limits to Growth* by Meadows et al. (1972), who argued an economy cannot grow perpetually without depleting the very resource base required for its survival. With all due respect to Meadows and her team, I counter that growth in and of itself is not the issue. Growth is a natural property of all self-regulating systems. Economic growth simply needs to be redefined in the image of ecosystems. When focused on restoring an economy's foundational components, growth is essential to sustaining humanity and the planet we inhabit.

That said, growth can no longer be focused outward, on ever-increasing scales of production for a global or national market, demanding continual inputs of energy and resources from beyond our economic borders. This one shift requires a chain reaction of changes. The next three chapters explore the role of diversity, energy, and trade in restoring a nation's productive capacity, diversity, and net domestic production. This hinges on an economy's ability to efficiently transfer resources throughout the system, which requires it abide by one simple truth: Earth's resources are limited.

A challenge for any country, then, is to wield its ingenuity and resources to maintain its productive capacity without degrading its social and environmental resources. The moment this challenge is accepted, we may discover there are no limits to growth. We need only redefine *how* an economy must grow, such that our economic systems do not undermine earth's ecological systems. What forms of growth will sustain economic prosperity for the greatest number of people, while imparting great degrees of resilience and resistance to our communities? To thrive as a self-regulating system, at what scale must our economy be fully functional—local, regional, national, global? Before addressing such questions, we must understand how an economy's foundational components serve as a fulcrum of sorts, to produce the greatest shifts with the least effort.

PART II

The Foundations of a Self-Regulating (Sustainable) Economy

FOUR

DIVERSITY CONFERS RESILIENCE TO ECONOMIES AND ECOSYSTEMS

If there is one variable economies and ecosystems can depend on over time, it is uncertainty. A case in point is Colorado, with its alpine peaks and temperate forests giving way to great plains and rivers flowing out to the east. Today, a tremendous reservoir of fossil fuel lies below its short-grass prairie, where a vast inland sea once teemed with ancient tropical life. Ecologically and geologically speaking, Colorado has been the recent recipient of a makeover.

Some 300 million years ago, when fossil fuels around the globe were just forming, the area we know as Colorado was situated closer to the Yucatan Peninsula of Mexico. Ever since those pre-human days, life-exterminating events carved and molded Colorado's natural history while tectonic movements nudged it ever-northward. Severe disruptions were continually unleashed upon the globe. The Himalaya Mountains rose, causing a shift in the global airstream and earth's climate. A monstrous asteroid struck near present-day Yucatan, extinguishing the reign of dinosaurs and driving three out of every four plants to extinction. Oxygen levels dwindled, and the age of mammals was ushered in.

Primates climbed down from the safety of the trees as dense tropical forests dissolved into open savanna. Over time, humans ventured into North America, where they eliminated some of the continent's most influential herbivores, which had never before experienced the speed and accuracy of a spear or bow. For thousands of years, native tribes used fire to shape Colorado's prairies. Then modern humans began converting vast tracts of diverse prairie into monocultures, suppressing forest fires, extracting fossil fuels to power the extraction of other resources, piping water across the continental divide, and pumping it from deep aquifers, etc.

Yet in the face of these cataclysmic events, Colorado's ecosystems did not collapse. They stayed their course, maintaining optimal performance given the environmental context of the day, and sustaining as many "old" species as possible while evolutionary pressures gave rise to new ones. And with the addition of each new species, the diversity and complexity of the system allowed it to efficiently sequester ample energy and other resources. In turn, the productive capacity of the ecosystem remained secure over time.

The Benefits of Diversity

Biological diversity, at its most basic level, is the quantity and distribution of species in an area. *Economic diversity* is simply the quantity and distribution of businesses in an area. There would be little point to discussing diversity were it not for the benefits (i.e., advantages, it imparts to ecosystems and economies. One notable advantage, often overlooked, is that diverse ecosystems are capable of harnessing more energy from their environment than less diverse systems, thereby increasing the system's productivity (Cadotte, 2013; Odum, 1969; Odum & Odum, 2003).

Energy efficiency is just the beginning. Systems with high diversity tend to maintain a high net productivity in the face of drought, insect outbreaks, floods, and other disturbances. That is, they have high resistance to disturbance. Diverse systems are also more resilient following a disturbance (i.e., they are able to recover more quickly) than are low-diversity systems. They can maintain a dynamic equilibrium in the face of continual minor disturbances (Loranger, 2016). Do diverse economies produce advantages similar to those of ecosystems, or is just the wishful thinking of ecologists?

The Benefits of Economic Diversity

An in-depth analysis of US industrial data going back to the 1980s reveals that states with greater diversity are more economically stable and have higher rates of employment (Tran, 2011). Research by Paul Templet (1999) over the same period shows that high industrial diversity yields high economic productivity. We could stop here, and be satisfied. But diversity graces an economy with advantages beyond stability, higher employment rates, and higher productivity. Diverse economies have also been shown to provide higher wage growth (Felix, 2012). Alison Felix of the US Federal Reserve System drew that result from a seven-state region of the US, which also showed greater stability and employment in diverse economies.

In economies harboring a high diversity of manufacturing industries, for instance, the failure of one industry does not result in the collapse of the entire manufacturing sector. When America's monolithic auto industry suddenly collapsed across a seven-state region in the 1960s, few manufacturing businesses remained, and hundreds of thousands of people were left jobless, or at least underemployed. The losses in manufacturing trickled into the service industry.

Fundamentally, low-diversity economies are more susceptible to volatile business cycles, global and national trade shifts, energy shocks, etc. Excessive volatility causes growth to decline over time. As growth declines, out-of-work employees are less likely to find a new job in their local economy, leaving workers with two basic options: find employment elsewhere, or stay where their friends, family, and home are, and remain unemployed.

Most economists and politicians agree that stability and employment are essential to a healthy economy. However, many fear trade-offs between economic diversity and business profitability, or diversity and wages, or diversity and growth, so they wage policies that support large-scale export-based businesses, to bolster short-term productivity gains. It can take a few decades for the findings of diversity studies like those of Felix, Template, and Tran to impact the actions of politicians, economists, and business leaders. But the benefits of economic diversity are beginning to take root, and can have the greatest impact when implemented regionally, locally, and at even smaller scales.

Diversity also yields financial benefits for individual businesses. For instance, diverse farmlands are more profitable than monoculture farms (LaCanne and Lundgren, 2018). At Colorado's Ball Corporation, a diverse portfolio of aerospace and canning divisions has provided resilience and sustained profitability for decades, as the continual-shifting global marketplace demands one service over the other. My own business, a small ecological restoration firm in Colorado, has witnessed tremendous resilience and financial stability due to a diversity of services and clientele.

Oddly, diversity has yet to become a leading indicator of America's economic health. This is a remarkable failure in leadership considering that long before Charles Darwin outlined the role of diversity in productive ecosystems, Adam Smith extolled business diversity for its role in the productivity, and therefore the wealth, of nations.

While Adam Smith was writing *The Wealth of Nations*, the benefits of economic diversity were being etched into the foundations of American democracy. Alexander Hamilton wrote in *The Federalist Papers* that "Commercial enterprise will have much greater scope, from the diversity in the productions of different states. When the staple of one fails, from a bad harvest or unproductive crop, it can call to its aid the staple of another." (Carney, 2001) The understanding of diversity in complex systems has expanded significantly since the time of Smith and Hamilton, giving ecologists and economists a fuller toolbox with which to work.

Eight Types of Diversity in Economies and Ecosystems

Fundamentally, consumer wants and needs drive new business opportunities in an economy. Should those opportunities go unfilled, they represent—in both ecological and economic terms—a vacant niche, which business abhors. It is the job of the innovative business to determine how an empty niche is filled, and in doing so it creates more niches. Economic diversification, under this lens, can be viewed as a mere byproduct of an entrepreneur's craving for a vacant niche. When the system is structured and functioning well, that craving is satisfied.

Mimicking the biological diversity of ecosystems, eight or more types of diversity may flourish in our economies, when they are structured well. This includes business richness, business diversity, functional diversity, structural diversity, functional redundancy, regional diversity, entrepreneurial diversity, and cultural diversity. These are described below, as they relate to economies and ecosystems.

Richness and Diversity

The most basic measure of biological diversity is the number of species present in an area—what ecologists refer to as *species richness*. A valley harboring 300 plant species is far richer than one with three plants. But when the species are evaluated with respect to their relative "dominance" in the valley (i.e., how much biomass each species produces compared to the others), we get a picture of how evenly each species is distributed across the system. For instance, a meadow with a hundred species of plants is more *diverse* than a meadow with just ten, assuming each species contributes equally to the biomass (i.e., capital) of the system. This measure of diversity is quantified by Shannon's Diversity Index (Shannon & Weaver, 1949) and similar indices.

The greater the degree of diversity in a meadow—or forest, or desert, etc.— the greater the system's resistance and resilience to disturbance. When drought strikes a highly diverse meadow, ample drought-tolerant plants may thrive in the void left by the less efficient water users. When fire rages across the meadow, those species whose seeds require smoke and heat to germinate will expand their population. In years with excessive rain, plants that can best take advantage of ample water will likely out-compete most drought tolerant plants.

The diverse networks of freely-interacting species in ecosystems (i.e., they are unregulated) impart not simply resilience and resilience to the system, but greater productivity, compared to less diverse systems. For example, atop the smorgasbord of primary producers in the meadow, an even greater diversity of pollinators and other insects flourish, which contribute to ever-higher levels of production within that ecological space. Not only does insect diversity increase with plant diversity, but the actual quantity of insects—their total biomass—rises as the diversity of plant life increases (Borer et al., 2012; Hallman et al., 2021; Welti et al., 2017).

This abundance stimulates more diversity, ultimately weaving an invisible web of hundreds of grazing animals, seed-eating mice, nectar-loving insects, insect-eating birds, and bud-eating bugs, each with their own preferences for a specific group of plants. And in waltz the top predators, chasing herbivores across the landscape, keeping their numbers in check lest the grassy meadows be grazed to the ground. In a review of over forty studies across the globe, a team of researchers discovered that the total biomass of ecosystems was directly correlated to the diversity of the system (Cadotte, 2013; Cambardella et al., 2016; Cardinale et al., 2007).

To understand how diversity promotes resilience and resistance in our economies, consider two scenarios within America's automotive industry.

> *Scenario 1:* One hundred manufacturers exist, each of which garners 1% of the market share. That is, one large pie with 100 even slices.

> *Scenario 2:* Four manufacturers exist, but three of them comprise 80% of the market share of the industry.

The first scenario is highly diverse, more closely representing America's automotive industry not long after Henry Ford set up shop on Piquette Street in Detroit. Steadily thereafter, diversity began to dwindle, until the industry was dominated by four enormous manufacturers by the late 1970s (*Scenario 2*). Shortly afterward, the industry began collapsing beyond the rescue of government bailouts. The auto industry has since rebounded, and gained some additional diversity in the process.

Similarly, an agricultural industry with one hundred farms, each of them growing fifteen different crops, is more diverse than an industry dominated by one farm that produces a single crop. Should one out of one hundred farms fail, the industry remains strong and people are fed. Conversely, when the one-farm-one-crop industry fails, the result is obvious. And when demand for that one crop diminishes, the entire agriculture industry suffers commensurately. It lacks resistance to natural disturbances let alone to economic turmoil.

A Diversity of Functions

Ecologists classify every species according to the *functional group* it belongs to. At the coarsest level, species are grouped into one of three basic functions they provide in an ecosystem: producers (e.g., plants), consumers (e.g., herbivores), or decomposers (e.g., fungi). But given the grand complexity of ecosystems, far more than three functions are present. For instance, four species of birds that consume a variety of bugs in a forest occupy a very specific functional group: insect-eating birds. Other functional groups include insects that eat plants, rodents that eat insects, or foxes that eat rodents. Ecologists simply refer to these functions, the various levels of production and consumption in an ecosystem, as *trophic levels* (from Greek, *trophe* = food).

In reality, every species eventually becomes food for another, while also consuming some resource in the food chain below it. That is, ever species is both a consumer and a producer—two sides of the same coin. Plants are often considered an exception, as they are the primary producers of the entire ecosystem—the first trophic level. However, not even plants can produce fodder for herbivores without consuming (i.e., ingesting) water, carbon dioxide, or nitrogen.

Ecosystems containing a greater number of trophic levels (e.g., plants, insects, mice, snakes, eagles, decomposers) have high *functional diversity*. In such systems, the constant struggle for survival within every functional group (e.g., rodents) places continual pressure on species above (e.g., snakes) and below (e.g., plants). In a simple food chain—mouse eats grasshopper, and grasshopper eats grass—the number of interactions within and between trophic levels is very low. But as functional diversity grows, and food chains become intertwined into a complex web of interacting species, the number of interactions within and between trophic levels rises to extraordinary levels.

Important to our understanding of economic efficiency, ecosystems with high functional diversity are capable of producing more total biomass from the available resources—their net productivity is typically greater, compared with ecosystems with low functional diversity (Hodapp et al., 2019). One reason for this is that they have higher *resource-use efficiency*, compared to systems with low functional diversity. As discussed earlier, resource-use efficiency is also an essential means to increasing the net domestic production of our economies.

Functional groups and trophic levels also exist in economic systems. And every business in an economy, like any species in an ecosystem, is a producer of resources (or services) at the same time it is a consumer of resources. Farms operate equipment made of steel, which consume fuel. Nutrients and water are applied to the farm. The staff consume a great variety of food in the process of farming, etc. Tremendous resources are consumed so that a farm can produce food. Economists simply use different labels.

Table 2 provides an abridged list of functional groups in an economy, from industry groups to entire sectors. At the finest level, a group of similar businesses comprise a functional group, such as farming, food canning, distribution, wholesaling, retail, or composting. Just as ecosystems cannot thrive on a single functional group—just top predators, or just decomposers, or just insects—nor can an economy persist on a single economic function. A single-function economy (e.g., one in which only apples are sold, or only pie shops exist) has very low functional diversity.

The waste-to-resources function is so essential to maintaining the productive capacity and NDP of an economy that it is presented here as a new sector (Table 2). For perspective, in ecosystems without decomposers—fungi, bacteria, etc.—the wastes of animals and plants would simply pile up. Thankfully, an abundance of plant and animal species are constantly at work, transforming dead biomass into topsoil, bolstering the productive capacity of the entire ecosystem in the process.

To clarify, economists do not recognize a waste-to-resources sector in the US economy, and past economic policies (e.g., trade policy, energy policy, etc.) have not favored one. Lacking a robust waste-to-resources function, the wastes of an economy simply pile up in landfills, lakes, oceans, and the atmosphere—as pollution. The potential for the waste-to-resources sector to bolster an economy's resilience, wage growth, NDP, and economic diversity must be fully embraced.

In the image of ecosystems, a highly diverse economy naturally forms a complex web of interactions among businesses and industries. And there is a diversity multiplier when entire sectors harbor a great variety of industries within them, for every industry is capable of harboring multiple industry groups, each which can harbor a diversity of businesses. For instance, an agricultural industry harboring a diversity of industry groups (e.g., corn, wheat, dairy, composting, etc.) can support a greater diversity of businesses than one dominated by a single group (e.g., corn). Imagine, then, the multiplier effect of a regional economy housing all sectors: resource extraction, manufacturing, waste-to-resources, service, and knowledge.

Economic regions—or even entire Nations—have built their economy upon a single sector, such as manufacturing, or even a single industry, such as automobile manufacturing, and they have repeatedly failed, or at least fallen victim to a host of external forces. For comparison, try to imagine an ecosystem comprised of a simple chain of consumers (e.g., insects, rodents, and snakes) within the animal kingdom. Such a condition cannot persist. In order for animals to exist, a diverse plant kingdom must also exist. A thriving decomposer group must also be present, to provide fertile soil for plants, etc. Likewise, in the absence of several other sectors, the manufacturing sector cannot persist, or at a minimum such a low-diversity economy would not sustain important benefits to society for any meaningful length of time.

An economy managed for a great diversity of industry groups, industries, and sectors will naturally harbor greater functional diversity, richness, and other forms of diversity. From such diversity, a complex web of interactions forms between businesses across a multitude of industries and sectors. The web, if represented by a series of dashed lines connecting multiple industry groups, industries, and sectors in Table 2, would in reality create a three-dimensional image—a sphere of interactions that must thrive for a community or nation to sustain important social, environmental, and economic benefits.

A Redundancy of Functions

Bred for resilience, and constantly creating new niches, ecosystems take the idea of diversity even further, by means of *functional redundancy*. As ecologist Edward O. Wilson explains in *The Diversity of Life* (Wilson, 1992), ecosystems provide redundancies when a functional group such as "consumer of mice" is occupied not by a single species, such as a fox, but by several species capable of eating mice, such as snakes, owls, and hawks. Should one predator disappear, another is ready to fill the void.

On the receiving end, multiple species of rodents may thrive in a meadow, consuming a cornucopia of grains and insects. Should one species of rodent go extinct, the greater web of life remains intact, and predators continue feeding their offspring. But when a population of mice thrives, a portion of the grain they gather winds up sown into the soil, forgotten, left to naturally reseed the meadow.

Economies are similarly fortified when multiple businesses exist, for instance, to manufacture automobiles, install wind turbines, fell trees, or produce grass-finished beef. Redundancy provides not only resilience, but productive competition within each industry group. When multiple businesses exist in each group, greater functional redundancy exists in the industry. Higher up the economic ladder, when multiple industry groups (e.g., geothermal, solar, wind, methane, etc.) exist in a given industry (e.g., energy), greater functional redundancy exists. Should one fail, ample energy is delivered to manufacturing facilities, government buildings, and homes—assuming the economic space those buildings exist in has a diverse energy industry.

Table 2. Economy's functional groups, based on the North American Industry Classification System (NAICS) and other standard nomenclature. Note that NAICS breaks down groups into major and minor groups, as well as divisions, and does not recognize a waste-to-resources sector.

Sectors	Example Industries	Example Industry Groups
Resource Extraction	Mining	iron ore, bauxite, gravel, etc.
	Energy	oil & gas, wind, photo voltaic, coal, nuclear, etc.
	Logging	hardwood & softwood, wood biomass, small diameter, etc.
	Agriculture	pasture, corn, soy, cattle, sheep, vegetables, fruit, etc.
	Fishing	deep sea products, shellfish, fish farming, aquaponics, etc.
Manufacturing	Transportation	automobiles, tractor-trailers, trains, cargo ships, etc.
	Plastics	toys, bottles, car parts, tools, utensils, etc.
	Equipment	engines, motors, appliances, power tools, etc.
	Food	frozen foods, canned peas, meat products, etc.
	Textiles	shoes, high fashion, kids clothing, hats, linens, etc.
	Construction	residential, heavy industrial, light industrial, retail, etc.
Waste-to-Resources	Recycling (durables)	steel, aluminum, glass, plastics, etc.
	Recycling (organics)	residential & commercial compost, municipal biosolids, etc.
	Recycling (toxic waste)	biomimicry solutions, bioremediation, etc.
	Waste-to-Energy	biogass, biodiesel, wood biomass, etc.
	Energy Efficiency	heat pumps, smart grid systems, etc.
	Materials Efficiency	agriculture, manufacturing, logging, residential, etc.
Service	Financial	banking, brokerages, lending, accounting, etc.
	Retail	grocery stores, department stores, restaurants, etc.
	Entertainment	movies, theater, music, dance, comedy, etc.
	Insurance	medical, automotive, home, employee, etc.
	Medical	hospitals, physicians, mental health centers, etc.
Knowledge	Education	primary, secondary, trade schools, etc.
	Research & Development	applied research, product design, innovation, etc.
	Information Technology	computer networks, software, mobile phones, etc.
	Consulting	business, architecture, resource efficiency, etc.
	Health and Medical	pharmaceutical, physical therapy research, psychology, etc.

Millions of Californians experienced the downside of low functional redundancy in 2019, via their reliance on a single energy provider: Pacific Gas & Electric. The moment PG&E began to suffer financially, due to a series of wildfires it caused, millions of people were left at risk. Risk to Californians also stems from PG&Es reliance on natural gas pipelines from Texas, which cross the San Andreas and other unstable fault lines before reaching California's power stations. Forty thousand miles of pipelines cross high-risk earthquake zones before reaching households and businesses. California's energy industry is impoverished, as is the energy industry of nearly every other state, as it lacks ample diversity. California is a microcosm of America, which lacks adequate diversity to secure the livelihoods of its citizens in the face of a turbulent future, let alone provide short-term security.

Another example from "The Golden State" is Belcampo, once famous as an organic grass-finished fine meats company in northern California, which closed its doors suddenly in 2021. Fortunately, another grass-finished beef producer in the region, Five Marys Farms, was able to employ a few people who had suddenly lost their Belcampo job. But export-based Belcampo had grown so large that the food products industry within the local economic space, Siskiyou County, could not absorb the remaining employees. Dozens of highly trained and dedicated food industry workers were out of luck. Ample functional redundancy in that one industry did not exist.

California, nor the US at large, is not alone in its diversity woes. The trend throughout successive global capitalist regimes has been to eliminate functional redundancy across a multitude of industries in exchange for a few homogenized export-based businesses. A final example of declining functional redundancy comes from the consolidation of US flour mills and lumber mills into ever-larger scales of production, leaving a trail of factory skeletons strewn across the nation. In states like Nebraska and Kansas, this means lower economic richness, functional diversity, and functional redundancy. The result, of course, is a cheaper sheet of paper or bag of flour in the short term.

In the long term, decreasing levels of diversity coincide with increasing levels of destructive competition, as global manufacturers scramble to fill the same niches. An economy can limp along, as diversity dwindles alongside a growing global expansion. Eventually, though, a global market contraction will occur, leaving globally-oriented manufacturers struggling to keep "out of each other's way" in the domestic economic space in which their production facilities and staff exist.

For instance, when the global market for wheat declines, or when US wheat production is undermined by cheaper production elsewhere—the capacity of America's colossal export-based flour mills will be rendered "overbuilt" for domestic needs. For those who believe such a scenario cannot strike the US, note that these exact cycles have erupted across seven centuries of capitalist history in industries—and nations—whose growth strategy is built on the fickle global marketplace (Arrighi, 2010; Marshall, 2011; Smith, 2019).

In response, downward pressure is applied on domestic manufacturing wages as businesses are pressured to replace labor with technology, in a quixotic battle against an ever-shifting system of cheap production centers. Despite the wishful thinking of many economists, the trend of reduced diversity in favor of homogenous export-based corporations does not lead to decreased prices in the long term. Nor do trade pacts guarantee low prices for cooperating nations. Following the 2019 trade pact between the US, Mexico, and Canada (USMCA), lumber prices grew higher than any time in US history. The cost of paper and wheat were also at historic highs as of this writing, regardless of the size of mills or the power of trade pacts. What global trade pacts do ensure is a decline in economic diversity where it counts most, in the regional economic space—where you work, play, and try to raise a family.

Structural Diversity

Economic diversity is further stimulated when businesses of varying sizes exist in the same area—what ecologists refer to as structural diversity. The paragon of structural diversity is a tropical rainforest with multiple canopies of trees and shrubs, their roots intertwined and their canopies overlapping, all thriving within the same ecological space. The structural diversity of trees is higher there than in almost any other system, providing a multiplier for the number of other plant and animal species that exist there (Huston, 1994).

In contrast, a recently burned or logged tropical forest is dominated by a single canopy of fast-growing annual grasses and wildflowers, exhibiting very low structural diversity. Similarly, an industry group with only large or small businesses exhibits low structural diversity, as compared to one with businesses of all sizes.

During the Industrial Revolution, the manufacturing sectors of Europe and the US tended to be dominated by large monopolies, trusts, and cartels—the low end of the diversity spectrum. At the time, global free trade was a means for Great Britain and other European nations to protect consumers from such monopolistic enterprises, as well as to expand the empire. But the process of global expansion required a disproportionate number of large enterprises at the expense of a diverse network of small artisan producers.

The financial advantages of large global enterprise grew so unbalanced in the final decades of the industrial capitalism epoch that a litany of laws and regulations was required to dismantle monopolies, trusts, and similar threats to domestic economies. This included the Sherman Antitrust Act of 1890 and the Clayton Antitrust Act of 1914. But the root of the problem was not pulled. As the global market economy continued expanding, very large corporations continued applying competitive pressures on small businesses in domestic economies, and on each other at a global scale. Over time, wages and profitability in the affected industries trend downwards (Arrighi, 2010).

This being said, large businesses do play an important role in driving gross productivity. A manufacturer producing ten thousand toaster ovens a year has greater economies of scale (i.e., more units are produced relative to the plants fixed costs), so can sell each oven at a lower price than a business that produces only a thousand. When customers are faced with a choice between the two toaster ovens on the same retail shelf, typically the cheaper unit sells. Such pressure requires small companies to innovate in order to persist. Through innovation, small businesses stimulate industry-wide innovation necessary to produce a pipeline of future medium and large businesses. For the pipeline of structural diversity to flow, small businesses must be allowed to flourish.

Explained earlier, *disturbance* is an essential driver of diversity in complex self-regulating systems, so must be allowed to unleash itself from time to time in our economies. Subsidies and bailouts are two means of suppressing the benefits of disturbance in the US economy. Intentional efforts to minimize disturbance in ecosystems, such as the century of fire suppression efforts in western US forests, have resulted in hotter, larger, and more frequent wildfires. The more severe the fire, the more time is required for the forest to return to a dynamic equilibrium. America's intentional interference with wildfires has created forests that are not simply less resistant and resilient to disturbance, but less productive.

Regional Diversity

In 1987, a group of researchers led by Dean Urban illuminated the importance of diversity that exists across entire landscapes (Urban et al., 1987). A single ecosystem can occupy spaces ranging from one hundred square miles to several thousand square miles. Landscapes are composed of smaller habitat patches, each shaped by subtle differences in soils, precipitation, aspect, and other environmental factors to create a unique configuration of structural, functional, and other forms of diversity. Building upon this complexity, a wide range of disturbances such as fires, floods, and insect outbreaks are continually shaping the landscape, creating more patches of habitat within the same space.

A diversity of habitat patches is a multiplier of species diversity in a landscape. For example, the meadows created by wildfire harbor hundreds of plant species that do not exist in the adjacent unburned forest. Rocky Mountain elk require access to patches of forest and meadow to fulfill various forage, mating, and other needs, so they are benefited by wildfire. The same holds true for woodpeckers, martens, and of course humans. A regional economy, when harboring a patchwork of cities, farm communities, and various industrial centers, has high regional diversity.

Diversity, Innovation, and the Entrepreneurial Venture

Diversity and evolution form a self-reinforcing cycle in ecosystems and economies. At the most basic level, the more businesses there are collaborating and competing in an industry (richness), the greater the degree of innovation in that industry. In turn, innovation stimulates new businesses and industries (e.g., electric grids, alternative energy, computer technology, electric vehicles, etc.), which apply evolutionary pressure across entire sectors to create an endless course of economic evolution. As the entire economic space evolves, every business within is pressured to innovate, and the cycle keeps revolving.

Innovation, though, does not materialize evenly in any sector, industry, or industry group. To help understand why, the *Innovator's Dilemma* provides a detailed account of several large corporations that were handily defeated by "disruptive technology" and changing consumer demands that are ever-present in our economies (Christensen, 1997). As Clayton Christensen points out, behemoth corporations such as IBM certainly could finance the changes necessary to maintain strong growth in the face of destructive competition in the early '90s. But due to their rigid client relationships and business structure, IBM and other corporate titans could not actually enact the necessary changes; even if the necessary financial means were secured. In essence, the institutional gravity amassed by businesses who structure themselves to fulfill the needs of global markets—homogenized to meet the needs of mass production—creates an intractable dilemma.

Christensen provided the example of rampant evolution in digital disk storage in the final decades of the twentieth century, which IBM and other tech giants struggled to adapt to. IBMs corporate infrastructure precluded them from evolving, such as to meet changing consumer needs. Access to capital investment was certainly not a factor. However, global investors were best rewarded by stimulating the success of smaller businesses, nimbler than IBM and their cohorts. IBM survives today, but only as a miniature of its former might, just as the once-mighty dinosaur is represented today by the lowly lizard. If the world's most technologically advanced industries cannot evolve quickly enough to remain competitive, is it any wonder the world's largest manufacturing industries succumb so quickly to destructive global competition?

If homogenization is a threat to diversity, and diversity is an essential means to growth, resilience, net production, etc., then we should examine the drivers of homogenization? This search may be guided by our understanding of the entrepreneurial venture, the wellspring of economic diversity. In the thicket of the Great Depression, Joseph Schumpeter described five means of profit for the entrepreneurial venture (Schumpeter, 1934), all of which are important to the productive capacity of an economy:

- The development of a new product, and the successful delivery of that product to consumers who need or want it (e.g., smart phones, Minecraft, chia pets).

- The replacement of an old product with an equivalent substitute (e.g., cotton for wool).

- The development of novel trade routes, including new distribution channels.

- The successful application of new production means (not necessarily the invention of them), such that the unit cost of each product is reduced.

- The development of successful financing mechanisms for an existing business or industry (i.e., loans, trusts, stock exchanges, etc.).

As a small-business owner, and from countless collaborations with dozens of other entrepreneurs, I can firmly attest to Schumpeter's diverse means of profitability. I can further attest to something so many business owners fear: that none of the profits derived from these means of diversification are permanent. In response, our business has done what many businesses do: increase the diversity of services and products. A diversity of revenue streams yields stable profit margins, in the aggregate, and reliable profits are a basic condition for growth and maintenance.

The destructive competition among global trading centers (i.e., globally-geared manufacturing centers sprinkled across the nations of the world) provides a constant threat to economic diversity in those centers, and in turn threatens profitability, wage growth, stability, and other benefits that diversity yields. In light of this, how does any economy respond?

In the context of Schumpeter's means to a profitable venture, consider these two basic scenarios: (*a*) attain a more efficient means of production to meet the needs of domestic markets, or (*b*) stimulate scales of mass production to meet the needs of global markets. The key difference between scenario a and scenario *b* is that a greater tendency toward destructive competition exists in scenario *b*. *Destructive competition* arises in at least two forms. The first form includes short-term cost advantages that a manufacturer gains when besting a competitor in fulfilling the needs of a new niche somewhere on earth. As economists (and laborers) have witnessed over the centuries, those gains dissolve as the costs of labor and land rise in the economies where factories are located.

The examples are endless. As the cost of labor in America, Germany, and Italy increased in the 1970s and '80s, the production of textiles, clothing, and footwear (TCF) shifted to Southeast Asia and Latin America, where labor and land costs were lower (International Labour Organization, 1996). Though real wages have risen tremendously in SE Asia in recent decades, the data is deceiving. A third of the region's workers remained below the international poverty threshold, even following a decade of tremendous economic growth (International Labor Organization, 2014). Even in the US, ever-rising GDP growth has been accompanied by flat—and even decreasing—real wages in manufacturing and agriculture sectors in multi-state regions.

In the affected global production centers, a second form of destructive competition arises. Industrial centers in Southeast Asia, Mexico, China, and even the US are pressured to accept a litany of social and environmental externalities (e.g., declines in soil fertility, caustic levels of air and water pollution, poor working conditions, etc.) that degrade their net domestic product. Those countries with the lowest social and environmental standards are better able keep the costs of production low, applying a level of destructive competition that is unmatched by countries with higher standards. This vicious downward spiral will continue as long as the structure of the global market economy favors such trends.

In scenario *a*, scales of production are tailored to the domestic economy, where basic consumer expectations demand that businesses attain higher efficiencies of production, without necessarily attaining higher scales of production. This requires technological innovation be adopted across multiple sectors and industries (e.g., energy efficiency, materials-use efficiency, etc.), as well as innovation in organizational structures and processes (e.g., agile manufacturing, industrial clustering, cooperative business models, etc.). In short, scenario *a* provides upward pressure on business diversification and materials-use efficiency within a domestic economy, while scenario *b* relieves that pressure.

Given the centuries-long trend toward business homogenization, there exists a tremendous opportunity to diversify the number of businesses, industry groups, industries, and sectors within most economic regions across America and the globe. And those strategies that expand diversity within one's economic space provide boundless niches for the entrepreneur to fulfill. However, there is a more fundamental aspect of diversity that may constrain entrepreneurs, industry groups, and even entire industries.

Cultural Diversity: The roots of innovation

Humans form an inseparable bond between ecosystems and economies, which may explain why, when we conjure up diversity, the most immediate images entering our minds are people of various cultures. One's culture is comprised of dozens of traits, such as ethnicity, art, language, cuisine, dress, religious beliefs, and others that are shaped by the SEI context in which we live.

Earth has witnessed not only a wave of biological extinctions, but cultural extinctions in the wake of the rising global market economy. Take, for instance, the San Francisco Bay Area, where over fifty unique tribes once thrived. These tribes lived an unimaginably rich life in the Bay Area (Margolin, 1978; Solnit, 2010), with an abundance of diverse foods and cultures across a relatively small landscape. In some cases, one tribe's language was difficult to understand by neighboring tribes just twenty miles away, such as with California's indigenous Ohlone and Yahi (Kroeber, 1961; Margolin, 1978).

Today, San Francisco's indigenous cultures have been supplanted by dozens of other cultures from around the world. And while globalization has introduced new cultures to some cities, the net decline in culture diversity across the earth has been substantial. Intuitively, it appears that cultural diversity declines with mass production and consumption at a global scale. But can we go so far as to claim globalization is responsible for this wave of cultural extinction? That question may never be fully answered.

What is certain is that humans must obey the same carnal rule of any other species: In order to survive an unknown future, we must preserve the knowledge of our past. This requires we preserve the cultural diversity that gave rise to that knowledge. Should we fail to protect the fountain of knowledge itself—human diversity—our capacity for ingenuity will likely follow suit.

But quite beautifully, economic diversity is interwoven with cultural diversity. Cultural diversity lends to business diversity, which in turn provides for the diverse cultural needs of a community. The surest path to restoring the productive capacity of America is not through homogenizing its economy and citizenry, but through a strategy of diversification. To underscore this point, two American cases of industrial homogenization are provided below.

Economic Impoverishment in America

Under the banner of global market capitalism, the globe has witnessed the creation of several new industries and industry groups that did not exist even fifty years ago. This includes dozens of new groups in the information technology industry, the rise of the automotive industry, entirely new entertainment groups, alternative energy groups, etc. Yet when we step back to witness the decreases in diversity across multiple industries over the same period (e.g., logging, agriculture, transportation, food, textiles, etc.), it is difficult to conclude our economies have grown in diversity. Or, has economic diversity actually declined over the past century in leading global capitalist countries such as the US, and in those trading partners who have built ever-larger scales of production to meet the needs of US consumers?

The Collapse of Diversity in America's Automobile Industry

Shortly after Henry Ford mastered industrial automation, Detroit became the epicenter of America's automotive industry, and home to 500,000 people in the early decades of the twentieth century. The explosion in automobile manufacturing lured people from as far away as Italy and Poland. By 1950, the brief climax of Detroit's economic boom, their population reached two million (Sugrue, 2004). It had grown into one of the wealthiest cities in America. As was the case in other industrial cities such as Chicago, cultural diversity in Detroit was high. And with good-paying jobs being the norm, peace among the diverse working class was also high. Some say Detroit was the largest middle-class city in America, with square green lawns, white picket fences, cars in every garage, etc.

It was an artificial prosperity. A single industry group formed Detroit's economic backbone, leaving zero room for disruptions. Within a decade, destructive competition began tearing at the US auto industry from Europe and Asia. The Korean war stoked a sudden spike in US steel consumption, drawing raw materials and labor from Detroit to other industrial centers (Clark, 2019). Almost immediately following Detroit's zenith, the economic giant began to crumble.

Entire factories, and their suppliers, began seeking cheaper labor from southern states and Mexico. The economic destruction ripped through the Rust Belt, a multi-state region spanning from New York to the Midwest.

Massive unemployment gave way to rising poverty. A wave of riots ravaged Detroit throughout the '60s. The punishment did not stop there.

By the 1970s, the struggling auto industry witnessed the rise of a new global power: The Organization of the Petroleum Exporting Countries (OPEC). OPEC wield its power to manipulate global oil supplies, causing a sharp rise in American gas prices. All the while, competition from Italian, Japanese, and German auto makers continued to rail against flailing US automakers.

US automakers fought back by stepping up efficiencies in automation. Like Henry Ford, these auto executives were certain that automation would reduce labor needs, thus increasing profitability. Only, automation did not save the day. By the turn of the century, the once bustling city was described by many as a ghost town, or as the murder capital of the US. Abandoned lots comprised over half of residential real estate, while factories were left to decay (Figure 6). This is the endgame of destructive competition.

Figure 6. Detroit in 2020. The Russell Industrial Center, built in 1924 to supply Ford Motor Company with body parts. Across the street sits the empty Doverspike Machine Tools facility, once an essential supplier to the auto industry.

Industrial Impoverishment

Cambridge Dictionary defines *impoverishment* as the act of making someone very poor. History, if we choose to listen, teaches that low economic diversity is a path toward impoverishment. Americans have witnessed this trend not only in poverty-stricken and rioting communities, but in the decreased health and wellness of a growing number of people across the economic spectrum. For the first time in modern history, 2019 marked the year that Americans could look ahead, only to expect a shorter life than that of previous generations (Woolf & Schoomaker, 2019). The shorter life expectancy is primarily attributed to alcohol and drugs, organ failures, and suicide.

The drug and suicide crisis struck the Rust Belt especially hard, a shadow that has finally caught up with the slow and steady march of global market capitalism. The social and economic implications are obvious. Another indicator of economic decline is that the next generation of Americans is expected to be less wealthy than their parents (Pemberton, 2020).

Impoverishment in America's Heartland

While America's auto industry was imploding, thousands of less riotous collapses unfolded across the heartland, the breadbasket of the world. Only, destructive competition from around the globe was not the sole culprit. In towns like Oakdale, Nebraska, economic life has become governed by a single crop, corn. But this was not always the case.

Oakdale is one of dozens of small towns dotting the Elkhorn Valley of Antelope County, in northeast Nebraska. As pioneers settled the valley in the 1870s, a great diversity of products sprang from its fertile soils. According to the rich historical accounts in *Antelope County History* (Leach, 1909), Oakdale produced an abundance of oats, wheat, corn, potatoes, pumpkins, and a great diversity of squash and root crops. "Potatoes were so plentiful as to be of little value," wrote A.J. Leach. Moreover, the entirety of Antelope County was rich in oak and cottonwood timber, cattle, wild game, and more. From this abundance, Oakdale grew into a bustling community surrounded by hundreds of family farms. It was not long before Oakdale became the town seat, enriched not only by dozens of farm products, but a great diversity of urban businesses, including barber shops, banks, mercantilists, grocery stores, doctors' offices, manufacturers, etc.

Following a diversity-prosperity peak in the 1920s, Oakdale entered a slow and steady economic decline. Where dozens of farm families once flourished in the rolling hills and valleys around Oakdale, a century later that same space is now dominated by a single agricultural corporation (R. Ahrens, personal communication, June 2020). All remaining families are tied in some way to the success of corn alone. Even soil-enriching soybeans, a crop rotation occurring less frequently in recent decades, owes its existence in part to the demand for corn.

Oakdale's summer concerts in the park are no longer. Trees—not children—were growing up through the playground equipment when I visited Oakdale in 2011. Junkyards, rather than serving an economic function, were being reclaimed by forests. When I visited Oakdale in 2020, "no entry" signs were posted on schools and churches (Figure 7). Entire neighborhoods were abandoned or blighted. Such a tragedy is due not to any lack of fortitude, intelligence, or dedication of Nebraskans. Rather, something sinister has been at work: state and federal economic policy, including farm subsidies. Those policies, and the benefits of their eradication, will be explored later.

Hundreds of small Midwestern towns have suffered Oakdale's fate alongside the rise of subsidized agribusiness. In the process, a homogenous agricultural bubble has grown, nourished by abundant (cheap) fossil fuels and farming methods that require little labor. At the same time, the soil fertility America's future ultimately depends on is becoming more impoverished with each passing plow. All to the detriment of America's productive capacity and NDP, and by extension to the impoverishment of its citizens.

Figure 7. Oakdale NE, June 2020.
Top left: local church.
Bottom right: local high school,
once the pride of Oakdale.

Agricultural diversity in the US plummeted by five million farms between 1935 and 1974 (USDA, 2020a), with thousands more farms going extinct by 2020. Nebraska rancher and former state senator Al Davis summarized the trend in an interview with Time Magazine (Semuels, 2019), saying "Farm and ranch families are facing a great extinction." Echoing the sentiment of hundreds of American farmers, Davis voiced a stark reality, that "If we lose that rural lifestyle, we have really lost a big part of what made this country great." To expand on Davis's point, the health and diversity of a nation's agricultural communities form the foundation of its productive capacity. Adam Smith made this same observation in *The Wealth of Nations*, nearly a century before Nebraskans began tilling the earth.

Declines in agricultural diversity have negatively impacted the socio-economic status of people around the world since the Second (British) Agricultural Revolution. The most famous instance is the potato famine of the mid 1800s—the Great Hunger of Ireland—that afflicted those who relied upon a single crop for sustenance. The famine also struck England, Scotland, France, and Belgium, but was particularly devastating in Ireland, where nearly a million men, women, and children perished (Baker, 2017; Mokyr, 2020). The lucky ones were able to flee to America and other countries. In total, a quarter of Ireland's people vanished.

Ignoring key lessons from the potato famine, and the Dust Bowl of the 1930s, the US developed a highly homogenized corn industry, which was struck in the 1970s by the southern leaf blight. Ten percent of the harvest was lost in a single season. America has done well to develop rust-resistant strains of corn and diversify corn varieties since, but monocultures of corn still dominate ninety million acres of the US (Economic Research Service, 2020), an area nearly the size of California.

Homogenized farmlands have spiderwebbed throughout the US, including millions of acres of irrigated pastures and hayfields that appear bright green and productive. In reality, they too are decimating their soil fertility with each passing harvest. The impacts reach far beyond crop diseases and soil fertility losses. Honeybee populations, which provide free pollination for dozens of crops, have declined as meadows have been converted to monocultures, and as chemical-laden farming practices have risen.

Several other threats have begun testing America's high-energy and low-diversity agricultural industry. As global weather patterns shift, America's corn belt is expected to suffer significant increases in heat stress, flooding, and drought in coming years (Pryor et. al., 2014). Additionally, the revenue of commodity-based agribusinesses is intimately tied to the whims of foreign in-terests and a wide variety of social and economic disruptions across the globe.

If the above risks fail to spoil one's appetite for farming, the costs of es-sential inputs (e.g., fuel, fertilizer, equipment, and pesticides, etc.) swing ram-pantly from season to season, as they are at the mercy of the volatile global market economy. Of course, farms are also at constant risk of floods, droughts, insect outbreaks, rusts, etc. Considering the weight of all these risks, in the face of Greenspan's age of turbulence, belief that America's impoverished farming system can survive another generation is nothing short of irrational exuberance.

Alongside mounting instability and risk, profitability for commodity farmers has declined since the Green Revolution. This stems from ever-rising produc-tion costs and ever-declining income, according to US Agricultural Census data (Dreibus, 2019). Surviving such a reality requires corporate farmers develop even larger and more homogenized landscapes, reduce labor costs, and lobby politicians for more farm subsidies.

As the global market economy churns, the very foundations of America's productive capacity continue to fray. With every global market swing, Oakdale's neighboring towns take note. Ray Ahrens of the Antelope County Historical Society readily foresees the fate of neighboring towns like Neligh, based on past trends. "The youth are leaving, and the drive to succeed is just not there like it used to be," Ray shared with me one quiet summer day in 2020. When the ho-mogenized agribusiness bubble pops, it will affect not simply a few small cities but—akin to the auto industry—a multi-state region in the heart of America.

The Challenges of Quantifying Economic Diversity

In hindsight, it might appear obvious that diversity confers an economy with re-sistance and resilience to disturbance, while providing other benefits. However, just how to quantify diversity remains a challenge to budding economists as well as ecologists. Measures such as Shannon's Diversity Index have their im-perfections, the least of which is they are not tailored to economies, and do not account for the multiple aspects of diversity that exist. While diversity measures used by Felix and others do not account for natural demographic patterns (i.e., patches) within a region. Using such methods, rural economies, due to the nature of the agricultural industry, will have lower potential for diversity than an economy in a metropolitan region. Measures of economic diversity at large enough scales to include rural, industrial, and metropolitan regions will indicate higher levels of diversity—simply as a matter of scale.

Other shortfalls of economic diversity studies are the relatively short time periods they cover (e.g., one to three decades), and their heavy reliance on employment statistics—which vary naturally by industry—as a proxy for diversity. Studies that do measure regional diversity often compare results to a national benchmark, so that regional diversity is reported *relative* to national diversity. This begs the question, has the diversity of the American economy declined?

Economic Diversity Trends in America

Due to insufficient historical data, we may never know for certain if the great homogenization in manufacturing and agriculture resulted in a net decline in diversity across the entire US economy. Additional complications arise from the simple fact that the US population has grown, and per capita GDP has increased, alongside the rise of entirely new industries over the past century. That said, few Americans need scientific proof to tell them diversity has declined. They know first-hand there are no manufacturing or energy industry jobs in their local or regional economy. They know corn dominates their county. They have experienced the loss of auto industry jobs, or suffered through the vaporized wheat milling jobs, or felt left behind as the service and high-tech industries rose to primacy. Of course, not even America's service and tech jobs are safe from global market forces.

Some historical data does exist for a few industries, but for reasons stated above those data must be viewed with regards to shifting demographics such as population (i.e., on a per capita basis). For instance, Alfred Marshall (2011) reported that 238,000 manufacturers existed in America in 1900, when the US population was seventy-six million. In 2020, the US Census Bureau reported about 300,000 manufacturers in America, while the US population was three hundred and thirty-one million. By extension, the number of manufacturing businesses per person dropped by about 70% since 1900. If the number of per capita manufacturers had remained constant, about a million manufacturing businesses would have existed in 2020. This represents a per capita loss of about 700,000 manufacturing businesses over the past century.

This loss in diversity is amplified nationally by the fact that manufacturing provides significant value-added revenue, including the extraction of raw materials, demand for component parts, and the resulting consumption of other goods and services tied to manufacturing. The manufacturing sector's actual economic footprint is far larger than what appears on the surface, generating about seven indirect jobs for each direct job (Bivens, 2019). For perspective, the service industry creates about 1.1 indirect jobs for every person it employs.

Such data suggests what Adam Smith posited centuries ago—that manufacturing and agriculture are the foundation of a nation's productive capacity, and hence its wealth.

Even before America's century-long decline in manufacturing diversity, the Industrial Revolution laid waste to a great diversity of artisanal workshops across Europe (Braudel, 1984; Marx, 2015; Smith, 2019). But a new force—a confounding variable—may have compensated for these losses. As the global market economy has been expanding across the centuries, it has become dominated by the high tech and service industries, while the importance of agriculture and manufacturing, relative to GDP, have shrunk.

Can Services and High Tech Save the Day?

Alongside the tremendous growth in America's services and information technology industries, they too have become homogenized. Tech giants such as Google, Amazon, Microsoft, and Facebook consume smaller companies the moment they reveal ample profitability. The same global market pressures that cause homogenization in agriculture, manufacturing, and high tech are equally applied to the service sector (e.g., banking, retail, entertainment, etc.). For example, "Big box" stores—Target, Walmart, Home Depot, Bed Bath & Beyond, etc.—have displaced tens of thousands of businesses across the US, and thousands more across the globe.

Americans have witnessed the rise of monolithic retailers like McDonalds, Burger King, Taco Bell, In-and-out Burger—the list is long—since the 1950s. With 37,000 restaurants controlled by McDonalds alone, the impact one corporation can have on restaurant diversity is substantial, and reaches beyond the restaurant door. There is a multiplier effect that homogenization in retail produces throughout the supply chain. When the supplies, menu, and standards of operation are highly controlled by a single entity, such as McDonalds, the chances that a franchisee will grace your Big Mac with tomatoes, buns, or ground beef from a local small farm are slim.

A low-diversity economy is highly vulnerable to this century of global turbulence predicted by Greenspan. The COVID-19 impacts on retail and other service sector workers—among the lowest paid and most financially unstable workers in America—is but one recent example. Supply chain disruptions in manufacturing trickled even further down the chain. Lay-offs were unavoidable not only on the factory floor, but on the retail floor where Fords, Chevy's, and other cars are sold. While shopping for a John Deer tractor in 2021, I was warned it could take two years or longer to receive the desired product, for even this famous American product could not be assembled without parts from around the globe, which had stopped arriving. We might hop on our bicycles, but they too had nearly vanished from retail floors due to broken global supply chains. It would take years to retool the US manufacturing industry to rely on domestic suppliers.

No job is completely recession proof. However, a high-diversity economy provides more safeguards for jobs, higher economic stability, greater profitability, and stronger wage growth for workers. That said, no magic policy wand exists to diversify manufacturing industries, increase functional redundancy in agriculture, build greater structural diversity, or grow more diverse economic landscapes across America, Europe, Asia, and elsewhere. Diversity is not an external force that can simply be added to an economy.

Likewise, the US cannot wish away the high level of turbulence predicted by Greenspan (2007). The great recession, the 2019-2021 pandemic economy and race riots, the volatile energy markets of 2019-2022, the 2021 domestic attack on the US capital, and the Russia-Ukraine conflict are the most recent evidence of such turbulence. The US, or any other country, can no longer afford to ignore the role diversity plays in self-regulating economies or ecosystems, and expect to maintain the quality of life, freedoms, wealth, and countless benefits often taken for granted by its citizens. And while diversity cannot be simply added to an economy, it can be stimulated by another foundational component—energy. Quite beautifully, from the nature of feedback loops, diversity operates so as to liberate as much energy as possible from a complex self-regulating system, every second of every day.

FIVE

ENERGY'S INFLUENCE ON DIVERSITY

I am dumbfounded by the phenomenal display case of pastries and produce derived from a simple plot of land. Not to mention breakfasts, lunches, dinners, wine, beer, desserts—a boundless diversity of food and drink, from nothing but dirt, and the twenty thousand-plus species of edible plants rooted in the world beneath our feet. These plants owe their existence to a singular source of energy, sunlight, the electromagnetic radiation that is unavailable to an ecosystem until it is converted to biochemical energy by plants, algae, and other photosynthesizing life.

The unparalleled role that plants and algae play in transforming sunlight into useful energy is not limited to ecosystems. Even our economy's dominant form of useful energy—fossil fuel—owes its existence to earth's photosynthetic lifeforms. The way energy moves through ecosystems and economies, and the origins of that energy, has profound implications for the proper functioning of both systems.

The Nature of Energy in Complex Self-Regulating Systems

When pondering the importance of energy in our economy, it is natural to consider only the laws of thermodynamics, such as the fact that energy cannot be created nor destroyed. Or, we might consider only the quantity of energy being consumed. By extension, many policymakers, economists, and others fall into a logic trap: the belief that adding more energy to an economy is necessary to resolve socio-economic problems.

I have even heard environmentalists claim that an endless supply of cheap energy would forever solve the world's environmental problems. Not only would such an energy-intensive system violate the laws of thermodynamics, but it would likely speed an economy along a path of decline. An unavoidable chain reaction would ensue, for an economy's foundational components do not exist in isolation of one another. In an economy with a bottomless supply of cheap energy, diversity would likely dwindle, posing risks to resource-use efficiency, resilience, resistance, and equity, while yielding other unintended consequences.

The basic energy dynamics of economies and ecosystems were summarized well by Odum (1973) in "Energy, Ecology, and Economics." Leaning on decades of research by dozens of scientists, Odum illuminated how production efficiencies in self-regulating systems result from increases in diversity. The reason is quite simple. As the system gains a greater diversity of entities, its ability to capture energy increases (Odum & Odum, 2003). Other research on energy flow in economies can be found in the career works of Alfred Lotka (1922), Amory Lovins, and others. But there remains a critical gap in this work. Largely absent the discussion is the distinction of *where* a system's energy originates relative to where it is being consumed.

A Critical Distinction Between Exogenous and Endogenous Energy

When energy is referred to throughout this book, it is in terms of economically or ecologically usable forms such as carbohydrates, electricity, diesel fuel, coal, etc. Given energy's role as a foundational component of ecosystems and economies, the slightest change in the quantity applied can produce major shifts in the functioning of other components, and even alter the structure of the greater system. To an extreme, altering an economy's energy component can threaten its ability to maintain a relatively stable state and sustain its productive capacity.

A stark example is America's corn industry, whose productive capacity, as well as its resistance and resilience to disturbance, has deteriorated significantly the more dependent it has become on fossil fuels. To better understand energy's influence on this trend, we must first grasp the two basic origins of usable energy in complex self-regulating systems: exogenous and endogenous.

Exogenous energy is that which is not produced in the same time and place in which it is consumed. It originates outside the system. Fossil fuels are the most obvious example, having been created tens of millions of years ago, and typically imported to an economy from far beyond its border. Yet even electricity generated by wind turbines in Wyoming, and then transported to New York, is exogenous to New York's economy. Similarly, imported agricultural products (e.g., cattle, grains, fruits, vegetable oil, etc.) represent exogenous energy inputs to an economy, in the form of carbohydrates and other energy-infused products. To the extreme, Japan imports over 85% of its energy from other countries in the form of fossil fuels (International Energy Agency, 2021) and food, making it one of the leading exogenous energy economies of the world.

Endogenous energy is the energy produced and consumed by individuals and entities within the system's borders. The biochemical energy produced by the vegetation of ecosystems and agricultural systems is one example. When consumed within the same region in which it is produced, biochemical energy is endogenous. In the greater economy, when the wind, solar, or hydroelectric energy consumed is also produced within its borders, it is endogenous to the economy. A business or home is fully endogenous when its energy needs are met with renewable energy generated on site.

Energy can be neither created nor destroyed, and production of goods and services cannot occur without energy. This truism requires every economy be restructured so that it may sustain its productive capacity with endogenous energy alone. Ignoring this basic rule ultimately leaves us with few good survival options, such as burning down the house to roast the pig.

The terms exogenous and endogenous apply not only to energy, but to any resource utilized in economies and ecosystems. For instance, nitrogen is cycled between the atmosphere and the biosphere continuously. Yet, in its most abundant atmospheric form (N2), nitrogen is unavailable to plant life. It remains exogenous to a forest, meadow, or desert, until fungi and bacteria convert N2 into plant-available forms such as nitrate. Once nitrate or ammonium is assimilated by roots, nitrogen becomes an essential building block of amino acids, proteins, and cell walls, contributing to the productive capacity of the system.

Similar cycles exist with water, carbon, and other nutrients, all of which remain exogenous—external—to the ecosystem until they are assimilated by plants and animals. The impact of resource transfers on diversity is discussed in the next chapter. In the meantime, lodge this question in the back of your mind: Does biodiversity rise or fall with an increased application of nitrogen to an ecosystem?

Energy Acquisition and Distribution in Ecosystems

The moment that an ecosystem's primary producers, such as the grasses and wildflowers of a tallgrass prairie, transform sunlight into biochemical energy, it becomes endogenous to the system. Important to our understanding of the role energy plays in our economies, the vast majority of terrestrial ecosystems obtain nearly 100% of their usable energy from endogenous sources. That is, nearly every unit of biochemical energy that makes its way through the web of plants, animals, bacteria, and fungi is produced within the system.

The act of transferring energy and nutrients throughout a food web and to higher levels of consumers—mice, snakes, birds, deer, mountain lions—is tantamount to resource distribution in an economy. With each passing consumer and producer, energy leaves the system via metabolic processes, leaving just a fraction of usable energy reaching the top consumers. In this light, mice are merely distributors of energy from plants to foxes. Along the way, fallen leaves, feces, and uneaten carcasses are returned to the earth to build soil organic matter by the aid of fungi, bacteria, and worms. In essence, these decomposers consume the remnants of the ecosystem's biochemical energy, and enhance the system's productive capacity in the process.

As previously discussed, ecologists describe the distribution of energy and other resources through an ecosystem in terms of trophic levels: groups of organisms that comprise a specific level of production or consumption. *Primary producers* are the foundation of them all, while lions, bears, eagles, and crocodiles (top predators) represent the highest trophic level. Insect-eating animals comprise a trophic level between these two extremes.

Summarizing decades of research in *The Diversity of Life* (Wilson, 1992), E.O Wilson states that the maximum number of trophic levels that can occur in natural ecosystems is five. As an ecologist by profession, I have spent decades trying to find an exception to this rule. Thus far I have failed.

Grass, deer, lion. Nope

Grass, mouse, snake, eagle. Nope

Grass, beetle, sparrow, snake, eagle. Ah!

Once in a while a lion might eat an eagle, but it is a rare event, and both species exist in the same trophic level, as top predators. More realistic is that two top predators exist neck and neck in their competitive ability to hunt rabbits. Or they might fight over the same kill, without killing each other. Through their competitive struggle, the entire system becomes more efficient.

Ironically, that efficiency hinges upon the manner in which energy enters and cycles through the system. Little to no exogenous energy is applied to sustain any trophic level. The lion must obtain energy directly from its prey, which must obtain its energy only from that of grasses, wildflowers, and shrubbery within the system. No vegetation is hauled in from adjacent ecosystems.

The productivity of every plant community is beholden to the solar constant—the amount of solar radiation striking a given spot on earth in a year.

The transfer of energy between trophic levels is more efficient in communities with high diversity, which tends to peak in the middle stages of succession, along with a peak in net domestic productivity. In other words, mid-successional plant communities achieve degrees of efficiency Adam Smith was seeking in 18th century economies, as the key to building the wealth of nations. Only, at a time when exogenous energy—coal—was the primary means to propping up industrial efficiency, no concerns were voiced over the impact exogenous energy transfers would have on economic diversity, nor on the NDP or sustained wealth of nations.

Energy's Influence on Biological Diversity

It is difficult to comprehend how much energy is stored in nitrogen until tragedies such as the 2020 explosion in Beirut, powerful enough to cause a small earthquake. Ammonium nitrate, a common fertilizer, was the source of the explosion, killing over 250 people and leaving nearly 300,000 people homeless (Guglielmi, 2020).

Nitrogen has a less explosive side, one that underscores the intimate relationship between energy and diversity. From US grasslands to Brazilian rainforests, the evidence reveals that adding nitrogen to an ecosystem decreases its biological diversity (K. Dixon, personal communication, March 2018; Midolo et al., 2019; Soons et al., 2017). This critical finding is not the result of observations from a single meadow or forest, but from over 250 long-term studies across the earth. I was fortunate to gain first-hand knowledge of this nitrogen-diversity phenomenon in 1997, while studying plant community changes in Dr. Mark Paschke's short-grass prairie research plots in eastern Colorado. On plots where nitrogen—an energy metabolite—was added to the soil, the diversity of the plant community vastly diminished. Where nitrogen was removed, diversity increased.

Nitrogen also enters ecosystems via air pollution from distant economic regions, or as manufactured fertilizer applied to farms. Besides the negative impacts to biological diversity, there are economic repercussions. For ranchers in the Colorado Plateau, cheatgrass (*Bromus tectorum*, an annual weed with origins in Eurasia) has formed near monocultures across millions of acres of American ranchlands. Trivial as it may seem, cheatgrass has largely replaced a diversity of native perennial grasses, such as fescues, bluegrasses, and wheatgrasses, as well as hundreds of insect-pollinated plants. While historic overgrazing has hastened the cheatgrass conversion, excessive nitrogen inputs from the atmosphere and from fertilizers contribute to the weed's dominance.

Here's how the decline in diversity affects ranchers, hunters, and non-humans. Cheatgrass provides marginal forage for only a brief window in late winter and early spring, leaving little forage for cattle during the heat of summer. Beyond the needs of cattle, should cheatgrass contribute to increases in overall plant productivity, the resulting energy and resources are not necessarily transferred to higher consumers. For example, cheatgrass can produce significant quantities of seeds, compared to the native plant communities they replace, but this does not translate to more food for higher level consumers. Native mice do not find the same sustenance in cheatgrass seeds as they do native plant seeds, so can suffer population declines when cheatgrass becomes the dominant plant where they live.

Heavy cheatgrass invasions also cause Mule deer populations to decline, to the dismay of hunters, pumas, and wildlife viewers. Mule deer require a diverse diet of shrubbery, wildflowers, and grasses, all of which tend to decline under the pressure of cheatgrass. Insect diversity can also decline, which threatens not only the diversity of insect-pollinated wildflowers, but the diversity of birds and reptiles that forage on insects.

Insidiously, summer lightning strikes set ablaze the plethora of fine, dead, cheatgrass leaves. The total carbon of the system is decimated, leaving the net ecosystem production—the sum of all soil organic matter, aboveground biomass, animal biomass, etc.—lower than the NEP of the native ecosystem cheatgrass replaced. Cheatgrass-infested landscapes burn every two to five years, and those fires create the perfect conditions for yet more cheatgrass. For perspective, the historic fire frequency (i.e., the fire return interval) in the Colorado Plateau was once every hundred to five hundred years. Wildfires do more than vaporize competing vegetation and reset the successional clock. They often produce a nitrogen spike in the soil, which favors the establishment of yet more cheatgrass.

Vegetation forms the foundation of a diverse, resilient, and productive ecosystem. Small tweaks to that foundation can produce rippling effects throughout the entire system. Transferring exogenous energy into our economies can produce similar threats to economic diversity, net domestic productivity, efficiency, resistance, and resilience.

Our Upside Down and Backwards Economies

Considering the nature of energy in ecosystems, our economies are operating in reverse, or upside down if you will. Few goods or services in most modern economies exist without continual inputs of exogenous energy at every step of production and consumption. To extract iron from a mountain requires substantial exogenous energy to excavate, crush, and process rock into ore. Transporting the crushed ore to a smelter requires more energy. More exogenous energy is consumed to reach 2,800 degrees Fahrenheit, the heat required to melt ore into ingots. The ingots of steel (or gold, aluminum, etc.) must then be shipped to industrial centers where they are melted and molded into wires, wind turbines, combines, or tractors. Exogenous energy is applied at every step in this very long supply chain.

Despite the upside-down reality of the modern energy economy, the laws of thermodynamics have not changed. Energy cannot be created, only manipulated to do work. As is the case with water, its global circulation, and its distribution to economic activities are also driven by energy. Technology has not increased the amount of either of these resources over time, and it never will. Rather, the progression of technology has simply stretched our available resources to the very limits of what our economies can sustain, without continual inputs of exogenous energy. In the interim, the US economy has become less diverse, and more susceptible to disturbance.

Nearly every economy on earth operates completely opposite that of a complex self-regulating system. Rather than every level of production being sustained by endogenous energy, exogenous energy—fossil fuels, carbohydrates, electricity from a variety of sources, etc.—is applied from outside the system.

As native plant communities and agricultural systems are the primary producers of ecosystems and economies, a review of agriculture in America proves useful to better understand energy's role in maintaining the productive capacity of a self-regulating economy.

Energy as a Limiting Factor in Agriculture and Population Growth

The success of the first Agricultural Revolution made its mark on the human population about 12,000 years ago. The social transformation from hunter-gatherer tribes to agricultural communities required the design of new tools, the division of labor, rudimentary irrigation systems, etc. Yet the energy required to produce harvestable products and maintain the novel farming systems—the biochemical energy of animals and plants, and human labor—were produced within the system. It was an endogenous energy economy.

As the system grew more complex, humans pioneered plant breeding and the domestication of animals. About 6,000 BC, farmers began applying animal manure to crops to increase yields (Bogaard et al., 2013). New concepts of land ownership and governance materialized, and economies grew more complex. By 1,500 AD, the global population rose to 500 million. Atop this growth, a fundamental constraint was soon revealed, just before the second Agricultural Revolution.

Prior to the second Agricultural Revolution, most of the manure applied to farm fields originated in the same region where crops were produced (Bogaard et al., 2013). Manure was an endogenous energy source. That system worked until the early 19th century, when another 500 million humans appeared on earth. The increased demand for food made fertilizer, specifically nitrogen, humanity's most limiting resource. Yet the unrelenting march of industrial capitalism stoked an ever-increasing human population, causing a manure crisis.

Scientists of the Industrial Revolution knew nitrogen was essential to plant growth. They further knew that combining nitrogen with hydrogen would yield ammonium, a form of nitrogen easily added to farms, to stimulate plant growth. But economically, there was still no means of producing nitrogen-based fertilizers from the abundance of nitrogen existing in the atmosphere.

Crop yields would remain limited by the availability of manure. And as the supply of manure became overrun by demand, Europe's very future as a superpower fell into question. Nitrogen became a limiting factor even within America's deep and rich prairie soils, and the fertilizer crisis that enveloped the western world stoked a global race for natural nitrogen reserves.

In the thick of the crisis deep deposits of guano, the manure of ancient seabird colonies, were discovered to be rich in nitrogen and other essential plant nutrients. Guano quickly grew into the king of fertilizers, initiating a boom-bust cycle in the mid-1800s not unlike that of precious metals. Guano for European farms was sourced as far away as the Chincha Islands of Peru, where deposits ran 200 feet deep (Giaimo, 2015). Those deposits were scraped clean within decades, and earth's supply of guano was quickly outstripped by the demand for food. The population-agriculture-economic boom could not proceed until a more reliable source of exogenous nitrogen was discovered.

What the agricultural industry accomplished in the very next century went much further. Dozens of advancements occurred in agriculture between the 1830s and 1930s to support—or cause—a rapidly growing human population

(Braudel, 1984; Taiz, 2013). This included the Haber-Bosch process, which could create an abundant supply of nitrogen fertilizer from atmospheric nitrogen. This industrial process required the application of methane, coal, or other exogenous energy sources. Other technological breakthroughs included advancements in crop rotation; invention of the gas-powered tractor; mendelian genetics; irradiation; improved plant breeding; hybrid maize and wheat varieties; chemical pesticides (2, 4-D and DDT); the discovery of auxin as an essential plant growth hormone; the advent of gas-powered threshers and reapers, and much more (Taiz, 2013).

Global food production ballooned once again, and another billion humans arrived on earth, just as the Great Depression struck. Yet in just one more generation, a billion more were added. Reflecting on human population curves over time (Figure 8), is it possible that agricultural advancements did not respond to a quickly growing population, but rather stimulated such growth? Braudel (1984), in *Civilization and Capitalism*, raised such questions but stopped short of a definitive answer. Likewise, a thorough analysis by Gage and DeWitt (2009) failed to determine if the second Agricultural Revolution caused population growth, or if it simply accompanied such growth. But what of energy's role in food production, and hence population growth?

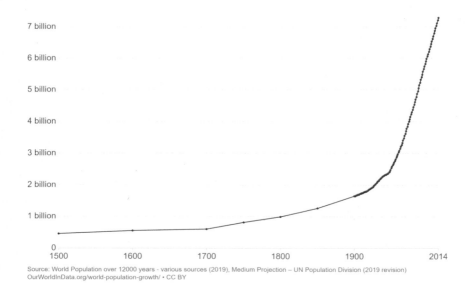

Source: World Population over 12000 years - various sources (2019), Medium Projection – UN Population Division (2019 revision)
OurWorldInData.org/world-population-growth/ • CC BY

Figure 8. World Population before and after the Industrial Revolution. Source: OurWorldInData.org. World Population over 12000 years (2019), Medium Projection – UN Population Division (2019 revision).

What we do know from the work of Braudel, Smith, Arrighi, and others is that the second Agricultural Revolution emerged at the same time fossil fuels— mostly coal—began making their mark on the global market economy. Scales of production vastly increased in manufacturing and agriculture. Levels of air pollution in England grew severe enough during the Industrial Revolution that the once-dominant white-bodied peppered moth (*Biston betularia* f. *typica*) was replaced by a much darker form (*Biston betularia* f. *carbonaria*), providing camouflage against coal-coated tree trunks that once shone white. At the same time, rapidly expanding monocultures of corn, wheat, potatoes, etc. devoured a plethora of diverse small farms.

Two catastrophic events unfolded throughout the century-long agricultural expansion—the potato famine of Europe, and the 1932 Dust Bowl in America—inflicted wide-spread social unrest and ecological degradation. But the question remains: is exogenous energy primarily responsible for the expanse of agriculture, and therefore population and economic growth? Is technology responsible? Or something else entirely?

To help answer these questions, note that the technology responsible for economic expansion during the Industrial Revolution—notably steam power—had been discovered centuries earlier. It was not until great quantities of denser energy forms (e.g., easily accessible coal seams throughout England) were discovered that the productive potential of the steam engine could finally be unleashed. As a result, the pace of technological change quickened.

Technological advancements that once required generations to develop and become adopted by society now required just years (Braudel, 1984; Toffler, 1970). This included the coal-powered steam engine, which allowed industry to manufacture machinery big enough and precisely enough to achieve mass production of industrial materials. With those materials, larger machinery could be produced, such as farm equipment. Thus, large-scale monoculture farming was limited by exogenous energy. This included the exogenous energy needed to produce synthetic industrial fertilizers, which would not impact global agricultural production until they could be manufactured cheaply.

Dozens of other technological discoveries were made that could transform the scale of high-yield agriculture. Yet, like the potential of the steam engine, those discoveries would have a minor impact on the scale and intensity of farming without adequate inputs of exogenous energy. That is, without ample energy the best technological breakthroughs collect dust on the shelf of great ideas.

Farming systems of the early twentieth-century required exogenous energy to transform ore into tractors and combines, pump water from aquifers, fuel equipment, etc. Those farming systems grew even larger during the Green Revolution of the 1950s-1960s, when industrial fertilizers that were being mass produced for explosives during WWII needed to find a new market. Fatefully, corn and wheat had been re-engineered to yield more grain under a regime of high nitrogen fertilizer and chemical herbicides (Pingali, 2012), both of which require great applications of exogenous energy. For perspective, even when accounting for the exorbitant fuel needs of modern farm equipment, over a third of the total energy consumed in modern agriculture is in the form of fertilizers and pesticides.

Today, monocultures of corn dominate landscapes from horizon to horizon across America's heartland (Figure 9). The last time such low levels of diversity existed in the Midwest was when great sheets of ice covered the land.

Figure 9. Monoculture of corn in Antelope County, Nebraska.

Behemoth monocultures require equal scales of capital. While visiting Oakdale in 2011, I had a chance to discuss the economic realities of modern agriculture with a few local farmers. Paraphrasing those farmers, to meet the financial demands of the modern "corn system" requires a farm of about 1,000 acres. For the operation to be profitable, the equipment, land, and other fixed capital would cost about US $3 million at the time. In the past decade, that cost has nearly doubled. In 2020, the cost of 1,000 acres of prime NE agricultural land alone was as much as US $8 million or more. The cost of fuel, labor, and fertilizer has also spiked. Likely, the amount of land required of a financially viable corn operation in eastern Nebraska is closer to 5,000 acres in 2022.

Agricultural corporations facing such realities cannot be concerned with the social, environmental, or economic needs of any one country, including the food security of its citizens. To survive, corporations must deliver food where it makes the most financial sense—exported to the highest value markets, whether or not people there are suffering food shortages. Additional exogenous energy is consumed transporting food to those distant markets. As fossil fuel prices continue their 70-plus year rise (EIA 2012), pressure is placed not only on transportation costs, or the cost of running farming equipment, but on the cost of fertilizer needed to stimulate yields. Even before the 2022 Russia-Ukraine conflict, some agriculture loan agents were beginning to press farm applicants to identify where their future fertilizer supplies will come from, and what the costs will be.

Under the weight of America's exogenous energy agricultural system, recall that the US has witnessed the loss of over five million farm businesses since 1935, with commensurate job losses (USDA, 2020a). In the process, economic volatility has ravaged multi-state regions of America as external forces tested the system's impoverished diversity. Volatility arrived not simply in the form of spikes and dips in commodity prices, but in major agricultural calamities over the past century. First was the 1920s agricultural depression, caused by overproduction. This was followed by the 1930s Dust Bowl, caused in large part by overproduction—drought was a secondary factor. In the 1980s, the US suffered another agricultural depression, stemming in part from another wave of overproduction stimulated by the Green Revolution. Such cycles are akin to a child that collapses after eating too much sugar.

In the wake of the 2019 trade wars and COVID-19 pandemic, corporate farmers dependent upon export markets suffered severe hardship due to another economic malady: long supply chains. In response to a multitude of interruptions in supply chains, farmers received billions in government bail-outs. A prime reason for such bailouts was to stabilize revenues, which had become destabilized by low diversity. In such a low-diversity landscape, the impacts trickle down to hundreds of small communities, some of which are among the poorest in the nation.

Does Exogenous Energy Destroy Industrial Diversity?

When an industry, or even an entire economy, maximizes productivity by applying more exogenous energy, history alone highlights the instability of the system. The low-diversity system is unarmed against disturbance, can suffer low wage growth, be susceptible to unemployment, etc. But is exogenous energy really the culprit? Or might some other external factor be responsible?

To help answer this question, we need to examine an era when electricity and petroleum were not influencing manufacturing or agricultural productivity, and when coal was just another useless rock in the ground. It was Alfred Marshall, author of *Industry and Trade*, who captured the era well, producing an in-depth glimpse into the relationships between energy, mining, financial capital, and mass production in the late 1800s and early 1900s (Marshall, 2011).

From Alfred Marshall's historical accounts, and as documented well by others (Arrighi, 2010; Braudel, 1984; Marx, 2015; Smith, 2019), it appears coal was a leading cause of unprecedented levels of mass production during the Industrial Revolution. Those nations and corporations with the cheapest (i.e., most abundant) source of energy gained an edge in the race for global domination. It just so happened that Britain had access to some of the most accessible—and therefore cheapest—coal seams in Europe.

Britain began mass-producing high-pressure boilers, a limiting factor to larger steam-powered generators, which were, in turn, essential in manufacturing sheet metal, I-beams, and other components of large-scale industrial systems (Braudel, 1984; Marshall, 2011). In a classic positive feedback loop, greater steam power was employed to more efficiently mine coal, which was used to generate more steam power. Enormous scales of production arose, giving rise to powerful corporate structures such as monopolies, trusts, and holding companies.

Quite possibly, Britain's domination over production and trade during the Industrial Revolution might never have materialized absent an abundant source of exogenous energy. For comparison, wood had powered British industry for centuries leading up to the Industrial Revolution, but with half the energy density of coal, wood's impact on productivity was limited. Just like manure in agriculture, wood became a serious limiting factor to industrial production in the waning days of the Industrial Revolution, so much so the poor could not heat their homes in the dead of winter—until coal was discovered. Productivity skyrocketed, but all too soon the coal-infused revolution would be eclipsed by another exogenous energy source.

A self-reinforcing cycle of industrial expansion and energy consumption had consumed European and American society. Industrialization produced ever-larger machinery and an increasing mass of consumer goods, which demanded more energy. Ground-breaking efficiencies in coal extraction in the final decades of the nineteenth century decreased energy costs on both sides of the Atlantic (Marshall, 2011). From this abundant energy, greater scales of production led to increased profitability.

Investment flowed toward profits, stimulating an expansion of the most productive systems. Alongside the growing network of global producers and consumers, demand for exogenous energy exploded. This included the vast quantity of fossil fuel needed to shuttle goods quickly across oceans and continents to a growing network of global trade centers. Those with the greatest sources of *coal* had dominion over the global trade network. That is, until vast reserves of petroleum—with twice the energy density of coal—were discovered in the US.

It was the close of the twentieth century, and the world was climbing out of the Long Depression. As the global market economy was recovering, it was America that bring cheap exogenous energy products such as fuel oil and crude oil to bear on global production and shipping. A monstrous increase in exogenous energy consumption (Figure 10) rocketed the young American economy into pole position.

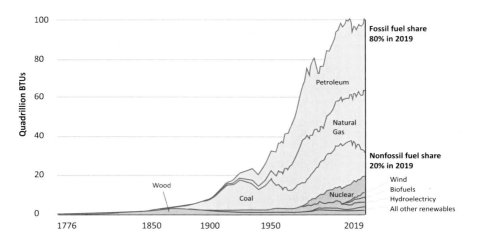

Figure 10. *Historic energy consumption in the US (1776 to 2019). Source: U.S. Energy Information Administration. July 01, 2020.*

Perhaps more important, an entirely new form of energy—electricity—began making its mark on productivity. Even before the roaring '20s had begun to boil over, industrial entrepreneurs began powering assembly lines with electric generators the likes of Thomas Edison's Pearl Street Power Station (Figure 11). Like the steam generators themselves, assembly lines were nothing new. Laborers had been collaborating for centuries to make agricultural tools, homes, buildings, equipment, ships—anything that could be more efficiently produced with the collective skills of many artisans than it could by the hands of just one. The introduction of electricity to factories simply allowed labor to be used more efficiently on assembly lines, which did not lend themselves well to cumbersome steam powered processes.

Through two world wars, two great depressions, rampant swings in economic theory, and political upheavals across the earth, the global market economy churned on. The forces of exogenous energy stimulated an explosion in automation, and ever-increasing scales of production. Transnational shipping grew cheaper, and a spiderweb of longer and more numerous supply chains became interwoven across an increasing density of global trade centers. Eventually, the electrified assembly lines that brought Ford Motor Company to prominence would come to bear on less charismatic industries.

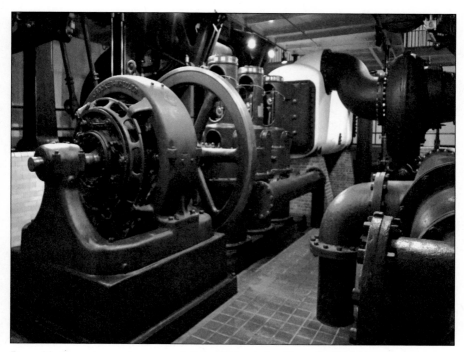

Figure 11. Steam powered generator built in 1912; used at Henry Ford's Highland Park Plant in the first quarter of the 20th century to power assembly lines. Preserved today at The Henry Ford Museum of American Innovation.

Energy, Diversity, and Jobs in American Bakeries

The unique nature of the baking industry meant that automation would take longer to make its mark on the diversity of bread makers and pastry producers in the world. And as with manufacturing at large, changes in the diversity of bakeries are difficult to quantify due to insufficient historical data (de Zwart et al., 2014). For instance, many New York "bakeries" in the late 1800s were home operations, many of which were not reported as legal business entities. Similar issues existed in the early days of the Industrial Revolution, whereby cottage industries and artisan workshops represented an incredible diversity of businesses, many of which were not officially documented. Further, much of the data collected in the 1800s was biased toward specific industries, or toward regions where significant economic activity occurred. Even as late as 1910, US census data was incomplete for many industries.

With the above caveats, New York census data at the turn of the twentieth century indicates there was at least one bakery business for every 1,010 residents (Phillips, 2001). While some reports show a higher number of bakeries per person, I use this lower value to be conservative, and extrapolated that ratio across the US. Using the estimate of one bakery per 1,010 residents, America's population in 2019, about 328 million people, would support about 327,000 bakeries. However, there are only about 8,800 bakeries in the US (Woodruff, 2019). Roughly, then, the US has witnessed a decrease of about 318,000 bakery businesses, relative to population.

As reported earlier, losses in business diversity—at an industrial or economic scale—should result in losses in jobs. On average, the New York baking industry at the turn of the 20th century supported one job for every 188 residents (Phillips, 2001). If we assume a similar job-resident ratio across the entire US baking industry, about 1.75 million bakery jobs would be supported by America's current population. Instead, America's baking industry employs about 800,000 workers. This represents an erosion of nearly a million jobs at the hand of a highly automated and consolidated industry.

This decline in diversity is not news. The US Bureau of Labor Statistics has documented a steady decline in manufacturing jobs for decades, including a loss of 2.7 million jobs since 1980 (Hernandez, 2018). Recall that each direct manufacturing job supports about seven jobs—indirectly—in other industries. A decreasing demand for direct and indirect jobs puts downward pressure on wages. And real wages in the US have remained relatively flat over the same period that manufacturing jobs have been declining.

In summary, abundant (cheap) energy throughout the 20th century spurred industrial automation, providing manufacturers with the profitability necessary to attract investors. From ample investment, automated industries attained monstrous scales of production and homogenization, with ever-dwindling business diversity and jobs as one byproduct.

Has America Experienced a Net Decline in Economic Diversity?

As America suffered through declines in manufacturing and agricultural diversity over the past century, a great number of new industries emerged. With those additions in mind, we should question whether *net* economic diversity (i.e., the difference between gains and losses across all industries) might have actually increased.

For instance, the automobile and airplane industry groups did not exist prior to the twentieth century. The novel inventions led to great increases in diversity in the manufacturing sector. By 1922, over one hundred automobile manufacturers existed in America (Scott, 2012). But the diversity bump was short-lived. A significant consolidation of automobile manufacturers occurred over the next 70 years as energy-infused automation erupted across the US, alongside other economic cycles. By 1990 just three auto giants dominated the American auto industry.

Alongside a steady technological evolution in the renewable energy industry, about fifteen new auto manufacturers have emerged in the US. This includes Tesla and other electric car companies. Not only can these cars run entirely on endogenous energy (i.e., solar and wind power generated in the same economy where the car is driven), but they consume far less energy per mile than vehicles powered by internal combustion.

Following the same pattern as the auto industry, three industrial giants—Grupo Bimbo, Flowers Foods, and Campbell Soup Company—dominated half of the bakery market share in the 2010s (Woodruff, 2019). Fortunately, start-up costs in baking are low, and the short shelf-life of its most profitable products requires that a bakery operate near its customer base (Doolittle et al., 2013). This may explain the resurgence in local bakeries throughout the US in recent decades, alongside an increased demand for locally grown and milled wheat, artisan meat producers, and locally-grown produce. Whenever I ask the owners of such businesses why they made the switch to local ingredients, two answers top the list: "It tastes better," or, "It just makes sense."

Thousands of new businesses, and entirely new industries, have emerged in America's knowledge sector (e.g., smart phones and computers, gaming and mobile app developers, consulting, etc.), many of which never existed at the turn of the twentieth century. Yet even in the tech sector, the drivers of business consolidation are constantly at work. Large corporations such as Facebook, Baidu, Google, and Intel are continually driven to consume smaller companies, chipping away at net diversity in the rapidly evolving information industry.

While these tech giants are known to pay higher wages, the number of jobs they support pales in comparison to those created by manufacturing. Manufacturing supported about 12.8 million jobs just prior to the pandemic, and comprised eleven percent of US GDP. While the entire information sector mustered about 2.8 million jobs, and comprised about five percent of US GDP. Relative to its contribution to GDP, manufacturing provides about twice as many jobs as the information industry. Additionally, tech giants can more easily "shelter" a larger share of their revenue overseas (Pemberton, 2020).

The question still stands—did exogenous energy cause business declines in manufacturing, agriculture, high tech, and retail in the US? Due to the lack of accurate and ample data going back far enough (i.e., a time before exogenous energy began to be applied to the US economy), an iron-clad answer may never emerge. But this much is known: An economic model that stimulates diversity in the manufacturing and resource sectors, while generating diversity in the service and knowledge sectors, will yield a net increase in overall economic diversity. We further know that transferring exogenous energy into a complex self-regulating ecosystem—and likely into an economy—places downward pressure on diversity. And a low-diversity system is less efficient at extracting resources, and its resilience and resistance to disturbance is lower than that of a more diverse system.

Arguments can be made that other factors place downward pressure on business diversity, such as greed, changing consumer demand, corruption, or competition. But like any external force, these human behaviors have no bearing on the foundational components of the system. Greed and corruption will always exist in society. How such behaviors influence business diversity is a matter of an economy's structure. An economy that ignores the influence of exogenous energy on its structure will ultimately jeopardize its own productive capacity, NDP, stability, etc.

Energy as a Limiting Factor to Economic Growth

Throughout humanity's experiment with global market capitalism, the relationship between food security, military might, and fossil fuel dependence has surfaced repeatedly. During America's 1970s oil crisis, I remember waiting hours in gas lines, crammed with my six siblings into a white station wagon. Of course, long waits and the increased cost of commuting are mere big economy problems. More importantly, what the 1970s oil crisis made abundantly clear is that the cost of food production can no longer be decoupled from the cost of fossil fuels. The cost of fertilizers, pesticides, building and operating farm equipment, transportation, etc. would rise or fall with energy prices.

As fossil fuel reserves continue to dwindle alongside a steadily increasing population, basic economic forces dictate that energy costs must rise. As energy costs rise, the cost of extracting and distributing energy must also rise, stoking a vicious positive feedback loop in energy costs. The mining and processing of oil shale in the Piceance Basin of Colorado, for instance, is an energy intensive operation. As the cost of energy consumed by bulldozers, loaders, and haul trucks rises, the cost extracting oil shale increases.

The same holds true in extracting uranium from salt water. Multiple renewable energy sources, such as wind and water, are available to extract uranium from seawater, but the extracted uranium must still be shipped to a nuclear plant and converted to electricity before reaching the end consumer. Not to mention the abundant technical challenges and associated costs this system must overcome in order to be economically viable (Slocum, 2017).

Similarly, hydrogen fuel cannot be produced without exogenous energy inputs. Certainly, renewable energy can be employed to separate hydrogen from water (US Department of Energy, 2020), but for every unit of energy produced, a near equal amount of energy is required to fuel electrolysis. The produced hydrogen fuel must then be shipped to the consumer, which requires more energy. Unless such solutions are able to yield more energy than they consume, they will not resolve any country's most basic economic needs.

In a world where finite energy reserves exist alongside increasing global energy demands, energy will likely become a limiting factor to food production, population, and manufacturing—and hence to raw economic growth (Piketty, 2014). Should the US desire to maintain its global leadership position, it must follow a radically different economic model. A model capable of producing essential goods and services not with more renewable energy, but by obeying the basic energy production and distribution rules of complex self-regulating systems. The US economy must be retooled to run on endogenous energy alone. Yet to achieve such a state, an economy must correctly leverage the third foundational component.

SIX

THE BALANCE OF TRADE

Trade has shaped communities since the time clans crawled from their caves to form tribes and territories. The evidence of ancient trade routes in America can be witnessed today in New Mexico's Chaco Canyon, Louisiana's Poverty Point, and elsewhere. The great majority of trade, though, was regional.

It wasn't until the twelfth century that a simple increase of money supply in Medieval Europe would forever tilt the balance of trade toward a global scale. Entirely new legal and financial mechanisms arose, providing merchants with much-needed confidence to trade goods across unknown social and geographical borders. Europe's population expanded accordingly, so much so that food supply could not keep pace. An increasing mass of food had to be imported, along with a growing number of luxury items, to meet the demands of an elite global consumer base. Still, most trade in Medieval Europe remained regional, as showcased by the series of elaborate fairs across England, Germany, and France (Spufford, 2002).

Bigger and bigger trade ships began blowing across the globe. But not just any trade route would work for the blossoming network of global market capitalists. Specifically, resources needed to be transferred from areas of cheap production to where consumers would pay the most. Those transfers offered the greatest potential for profit.

With trade routes now penetrating every continent on earth, many have begun to ask if the resulting concentrations of wealth and capital have grown tumorous. While pondering this, we must ask something more fundamental. When an economy becomes dependent on imported and exported resources (e.g., raw materials, water, labor, food, energy, etc.) to maintain high levels of productivity, can it persist as a self-regulating system, and derive the benefits thereof? Or is it being artificially supported? In humans, we call that life support. In an economy, we could call it dependency. It was such dependency, across a network of global trade centers, that was attributed to the collapse of society at the end of the Bronze Age (Cline, 2014).

Herein, trade within and between economies is evaluated according to the equivalent process in self-regulating ecosystems: the transfer of resources between two or more species, communities, or ecosystems. Through this evaluation, the natural cycles of trade (i.e., resource transfers) in ecosystems provides insights for questions society has struggled with since the earliest days of capitalism. For instance, at what scale—local, regional, national, global—should free trade flourish in order for an economy to provide the greatest and most enduring benefits to the greatest number of people?

The Structure of Trade in Ecosystems and Economies

We need not stretch our imagination to see how economies and ecosystems function equally with respect to resource transfers. In the process of trade, energy and materials are transferred from primary production levels (e.g., agriculture, mineral extraction, logging, etc.) to higher levels of production (e.g., apple sauce, cars, homes, etc.). Ultimately, materials are returned to the earth via landfills, burnt in incinerators, emitted as air and water pollution, or sent back into the production cycle as recycled material.

In an ecosystem, resource transfers (e.g., fat, micronutrients, carbon, protein, water, etc.) begin their journey of accumulation the moment plants convert sunlight into biochemical energy. Through a complex web of predator-prey interactions, the biomass of the ecosystem, similar to the capital of an economy, is transferred to higher and higher levels of consumers. However, the transfers cannot trickle up forever, for energy is lost in the form of heat waste at every point of consumption, in support of metabolism and respiration (Odum, 1957).

High-diversity ecosystems tend to consume less energy in acquiring and transferring resources throughout the system than do low-diversity ecosystems. One means to this efficiency is a diverse community of decomposers. In ecosystems, biomass doesn't stop accumulating at the highest trophic level—top predators. Leaves, uneaten fruit, carcasses, and other forms of biomass are eventually consumed by decomposers, whose actions improve soil fertility. In the process, the net productivity of the entire system is raised. As witnessed in most modern economies, the presence of an equally-thriving waste-to-resources sector is sorely lacking.

Another stark difference between resource transfers in ecosystems and economies is that nearly 100% of the biomass consumed within an ecosystem is produced within the system—it is endogenous to the system. In other words, until resources are captured by the plants and animals of an ecosystem, those resources remain exogenous to the system. For example, only a fraction of one percent of water on earth actually exists in the bodies of plants or animals. The rest remains uncaptured by the ecosystem. Likewise, only about two percent of the solar energy reaching earth is actually converted by plants into biochemical energy. The remainder is exogenous.

Similarly, resources entering from beyond an economy's border are exogenous to the system, while resources produced within the economy (e.g., paper, steel, food, car parts, etc.) are endogenous. When exogenous resources are transferred into self-regulating ecosystems, diversity declines, driving down the system's ability to capture and cycle endogenous resources. A challenge for every economy is to forge the proper balance between imported and domestic resources, such that its productive capacity and NDP can be sustained, without jeopardizing a nation's most important social, economic, and environmental values.

Three Forms of Trade

Early economists such as Adam Smith and Dudley North conceived of trade in three segments: the home trade, foreign trade, and the carrying trade. The *home trade* (i.e., the domestic economy) is that which is conducted between cities, regions, and states of a given country. *Foreign trade* (i.e., global trade) is the result of importing and exporting goods and services across country borders. Atop the trade pyramid rests the *carrying trade*, the highest and most nebulous echelon of global market capitalism.

The carrying trade embodies a system of financial transactions across a global network of national and transnational entities. To be consistent with early definitions of trade, yet considering the evolution of terminology over time, the carrying trade is described here in two parts. The first includes the physical and technological movement of products and services around the globe (i.e., via cargo ships, planes, information technology, etc.), without necessarily owning the cargo or being a legal entity in the countries of origin and destination.

The second part includes actions that facilitate global trade and the balance of power between countries. This includes direct investment in foreign markets, and the monetary actions of the International Monetary Fund, the World Bank, and the global system of national banks. It also includes the trade of currencies, which many refer to as the *carry trade*. The carry trade also includes "betting" on changing valuations of foreign currencies, investment in government bonds, asset-backed securities, etc. (Dohmen, 2014).

Less Obvious Resource Transfers and Their Economic Impacts

Clearly, the presence of financial resource transfers makes economies different from ecosystems. Economies utilize investment, subsidies, bailouts, loans, and credit to increase the transfer of other resources across economic borders. As such, financial resource transfers and exogenous energy transfers have similar influences on the production and transfer of physical resources.

The relationships between financial resource transfers, trade, and homogenization are not new. Adam Smith (2019) argued that Great Britain and other European countries discourage any encouragements, such as subsidies, that would interfere with the natural development of foreign and domestic trade. Smith also discouraged tariffs, which are one tool used to protect a nation's domestic economy from subsidized imports from other countries. To put Smith's stance on unregulated foreign trade into perspective, keep in mind two key factors. First, geographically, Great Britain is a relatively small nation, as are all countries comprising today's European Union (For perspective, the EU is about the size of the US). Trade between Spain and Italy is akin to trade between Colorado and Nebraska, or between northern and southern California.

Second, cheap exogenous energy and related industrial advancements had given rise to powerful monopolies and cartels (Marshall, 2011), which dominated European trade throughout the Industrial Revolution. Given the propensity for monopolies and cartels to drive up prices in their domestic economies, nations kept them in check by importing cheap products such as textiles from India, or steel from Germany. This would typically result in destructive competition, requiring the afflicted industries to develop even larger scales of production, to attain cheaper per unit costs.

Similar to the nature of energy in our economies, there is a positive feedback loop between financial resource transfers into an economy or industry, and the scale of production those entities can attain. The larger the mass of capital a company controls, such as the colossal capital of General Mills, the greater investments they receive. That is, a billion-dollar investment does not typically seek a million-dollar business. Rather, large investments stimulate ever-larger scales of production, and the capacity of a business to attract yet more capital increases—up to a point. The growth and homogenization of America's big three automakers coincided with an exorbitant level of capital accumulation, far exceeding that of the lean and more successful Japanese automakers (Ingrassia & White, 1995). The result was a collapse in the productive might of the US auto industry, which spiderwebbed throughout the greater economy.

Similarly, nations such as the US aggregate tax dollars from the entire country and transfers them into specific businesses via bailouts, subsidies, and loans. The result is often a homogenization of the affected industries, which places downward pressure on jobs and business diversity. In turn, the productive capacity of an industry or even an entire economy is diminished.

An abundance of unintended consequences can stem from subsidies and similar governmental resource transfers. For example, the cost of food in America increased following subsidies of the corn ethanol industry. As the demand for corn ethanol rises, the price of corn is driven upward. This price increase affects not only what consumers must pay for an ear of corn, but what they must pay for hundreds of other corn-based products.

Financial resource transfers that simulate industrial homogenization yield another consequence: over-reliance on global supply chains, which tend to be weaker and more volatile the longer they grow. In *The Wall Street Journal* article, "Wheat and Rice Prices Surge in Coronavirus Lockdown," Maltais and Wallace (2020) documented the global disruption in farm supplies as multiple countries restricted agricultural exports during the pandemic. In response, the price of the world's two most important staples, wheat and rice, rose sharply.

Maltais authored several other articles for *The Wall Street Journal* in 2020 to highlight supply chain weaknesses that the pandemic unveiled (not caused) within the corn ethanol market. From the global oil glut caused by a vast reduction in driving, the price of corn plummeted. This, in turn, placed downward pressure on the price of other farm commodities, meaning less revenue entered the farming industry. Maltais also documented the bailout of US pork producers, who were to euthanize hogs in the wake of large-scale processing plant closures (Bunge & Maltais, 2020). As many as 105,000 hogs a day had no factory floor to be processed on, and hence no product would reach the market. Global bicycle, tractor, and car manufacturing supply chains suffered similar disruptions, severing the pipeline of parts and products delivered to assembly plants, wholesalers, and retailers. In turn, demand for labor throughout the supply chain decreased.

Exogenous financial transfers, like energy transfers, tend to perpetuate the existing system—large scale industries whose ability to evolve is sluggish. Those industries often develop structural problems that can trickle up to the productive capacity of an entire nation. For instance, Sweden's MOSES economic model revealed that government subsidies in the early 1990s propped up the lowest performing industries (e.g., steel and shipyards), many of them utilizing obsolete equipment and production processes (Eliasson et al., 1995). In turn, Sweden lost its competitiveness within its SEI context, the European Union.

Finally, financial resource transfers tend to fortify barriers to new business entries into the market, and those new entrants are essential to restoring productivity following economic downturns. New entrants not only stimulate growth, but they tend to represent industries that are relevant to the economy of the future, not the past. America's subsidized agricultural industry, for instance, provides substantial obstacles to new farmers interested in rebuilding rather than degrading the productive capacity of US farmlands. Similarly, by bailing out producers who euthanize hogs, there is a disincentive to find a more innovative approach to the problem, an approach that would bring food to market while supporting a commensurate number of jobs throughout the supply chain.

When Trade Operates Counter to the Rules of Complex Self-Regulating Systems

In the early 1990s, US manufacturing jobs began vanishing as wave upon wave of cheap Chinese imports began streaming through American ports. The resulting social and economic suffrage across hard-hit manufacturing centers stemmed from President Carter's efforts to normalize trade with China in the late '70s. Reagan built on Carter's efforts with a strong US-China trade policy in the '80s. Doubling down on Carter's and Reagan's policies, Clinton enacted legislation at the turn of the century to further strengthen trade ties with China, with a single aim: growth.

Late twentieth century US policies that increased resource transfers across vastly different SEI contexts (e.g., China-US, Russia-US, Venezuela-US, Indonesia-US, Mexico-US, etc.) yielded predictable levels of destructive competition, laying waste to entire industrial regions of the US. The seven-state rust belt of the US is one such region, while the dramatic decline in paper mills all across the US is another. Economists of the '90s maintained blind faith that out-of-work laborers would get retrained, or find jobs in the billowing service sector. Or, perhaps, jobless factory workers would simply move to cities where new jobs were materializing, such as in Silicon Valley, where a high-tech boom was underway in the '90s.

Instead, a series of unfortunate economic events unfolded across America, summarized well by MIT economist David Autor and his colleagues (Autor et al., 2021). Dubbed the *China Shock*, the impacts Autor highlighted include rapid declines in wages, deflated housing prices, and lower tax revenues for impacted municipalities and states; and increases in unemployment, poverty,

drug and alcohol abuse, and mass filings for government aid in crippled manufacturing centers. The impacts lasted two decades beyond the initial shock. As
of 2018, China still supplied a quarter of US imports, with an additional ten
percent supplied by Southeast Asia.

Sound solutions to the China Shock still evade politicians and economists,
many of whom still fear a trade-off between economic diversity and growth.
Others argue that trade policies aimed at protecting domestic manufacturers
would actually hurt the US economy. Although, arguments against a strong
domestic economy are typically focus on impacts to a single industry or
product (e.g., auto parts, or import businesses), reflecting a deep ignorance of
the inter-relationships between trade, diversity, and energy.

Through some sort of collective economic amnesia, the reductionist arguments against a strong domestic economy—one free from the volatility and destructive competition of the global market economy—ignore the China Shock,
the rust belt, the monstrous assault on paper and lumber mills across America,
the millions of extinct farms, etc. They ignore the frail dependencies (i.e., lack
of resilience) the current global economic system creates among trade partners,
the repeated dismantling of communities and families, the degraded productive capacity and NDP of the US economy.

The reductionist arguments further ignore the litany of social and environmental externalities global market capitalism requires to survive. This has
been evidenced by yet another nation-wide cry for social justice, a relentless
rise in the cost of living, depressed employment and profitability in low-diversity states, an ever-increasing wealth gap, mounting mental and physical
health concerns, a rise in homelessness, and other socio-economic impacts. Of
course, Americans are not alone in suffering the consequences of an economy
functioning at the wrong scale, with trade operating counter to the rules of
complex self-regulating systems.

The list of external forces poised to threaten this unbalanced system is long:
the rampantly shifting price of oil, governmental and social unrest among
trading partners, subsidies to homogenized national and international businesses across the globe, threats of pollution and ecological degradation in
export countries, drought, flooding, wildfires, and more. To be clear, the past
seven hundred years of ever-expanding foreign and carrying trade have not al-
leviated such forces. If anything, it has stimulated those forces.

Acknowledging the impacts exogenous resource transfers have on both ecosystems and economies, it is unlikely any nation can resolve its social, environmental, and economic concerns by increasing its reliance on the foreign and
carrying trades. A more likely scenario is that a nation may diversify its way out

of such problems, and the benefits of such diversification are not restricted to the most developed countries.

The Organisation for Economic Co-operation and Development (OECD) and the World Trade Organization (WTO) view economic diversification as a means to managing volatility and providing a more stable path for equitable growth in developing countries (OECD/WTO, 2019). But not just any form of diversification. These transnational organizations admit that fostering business development (i.e., diversification) for export markets poses risks to economic stability for the exporting country, as global corporations must always seek those countries with the lowest costs of production. Corporations must remain profitable amidst a global network of destructive competition, or they will perish.

Eventually, export-based countries such as China, Taiwan, or Mexico experience a rise in the cost of labor, land, and other factors of production. In turn, their export-based industries become naturally less competitive, or they run the risk of tariffs, subsidies, or other tactics waged by importing countries in attempts to protect their domestic industries. Either way, production must shift to the lowest producer, so that the cheapest imports can continue their long trek into the hands of global consumers searching for the lowest price. In the process, the productive capacity of the importing country becomes flaccid as it grows overly reliant on the productive capacity of exporters. As for the abandoned export-based country, they are left with the socio-economic remnants of over-built (global-scale) industries, relative to their regional SEI context.

How Much "Stuff" Does America Import?

There's a gaping chasm between the nature of resource transfers in ecosystems, and resource transfers between the US economy and other economies. Even during the 2018 to 2020 trade wars with China and Europe, US imports broke records. With a collective value of about US $2.5 trillion in 2018, US imports included clothing, appliances, computers, cell phones, automobiles, toys, games, pharmaceuticals, sporting goods, food, equipment, parts, lumber—the *stuff* that fills our spaces and lives physically.

To fully understand the quantity of stuff the US imports requires some basic math. America's GDP, at the onset of the 2018 trade war with China, stood at US $20.5 trillion. However, most of this GDP was generated not by the sale of goods, but by service and knowledge industries such as education, finance, retail, consulting, insurance, entertainment, etc. Not accounting for such industries, America produced a total US $6.9 trillion in goods—about one third of its GDP (US Census Bureau, 2018). However, the US exported US $1.7 trillion worth of these goods. This left about US $5.2 trillion in *American-made goods* that US citizens and businesses consumed. Adding the value of imported goods (US $2.5 trillion), the value of all goods consumed in the US is about US $7.7 trillion.

In short, about one third of all US consumer goods are imported. This does not mean a third of all goods that Americans purchase originate in another country. The quantity of imported goods is actually higher, for much of what the US exports is of high value (e.g., high tech, oil, machinery, spacecraft, etc.), while most of its imports are cheap products (e.g., dolls, plastic parts, alternators, cookware, etc.). Accounting for this discrepancy, the quantity of imported goods is far greater. I estimate that closer to 60% of the *quantity* of consumer products in the US are imported. In most regional economies throughout the US, this number may be higher, while in dense urban areas the number approaches 100%. That is, nearly all of the products consumed are transferred there from another region or nation.

Forget for a moment how abnormal it is, relative to self-regulating ecosystems, for an economy to be reliant on ever-increasing resource imports, and ponder what such an imbalance means for the security and solvency of America. The total US trade deficit—the net balance between all imported and exported goods and services—has grown to the degree that for every US $1 received for exported goods and services, the US spends about US $1.25 on imports (prior to the trade wars).

Outlined well in a report by the Congressional Research Service (Jackson, 2019), America's lingering trade deficit is feasible largely because the US Dollar is the *de facto* global reserve currency. In other words, a stable US dollar provides economies around the globe with liquidity and a relatively safe place to store their assets. In essence, foreign entities are financing America's trade deficit.

America's trade deficit is further reinforced by the relatively high value of the dollar, which makes US exports less competitive than the majority of other countries. To solidify the discrepancy, manufacturing wages are higher in America than in China, Mexico, Vietnam and most developing countries. These conditions explain, at least in part, why the US does not tend to export toys and toaster ovens, but high-valued services such as intellectual property, computing, consulting, etc. One might ask, though, so what if we maintain a trade deficit?

The Impact of America's Foreign and Carrying Trades on its
Productive Labor and Productive Capacity

As declared by Adam Smith, it is the strength of a country's domestic trade—
not its foreign or carrying trade—that builds the foundation of its wealth.
That foundation, he argued, is sustained by a country's manufacturing and
resource extraction sectors, which comprise a nation's "productive labour." As
Smith observed, the service sector does not produce excess value, and therefore
wealth; it only consumes value. This holds true for the military, the knowledge
sector, and government services, all of which consume excess value (i.e., wealth)
generated elsewhere in the economy. Hence, the service and knowledge sectors
are categorized as unproductive labor.

To clarify, Smith was not condemning "unproductive" labor as invaluable to
society, but that such value cannot be realized without an abundance of productive labor elsewhere. Labor that is engaged in extraction, processing, transportation, and other productive parts of an economy must generate surplus
value (i.e., beyond the capital that is consumed in the production process) in
order for a nation to build its wealth. In the process, the productive capacity of
a country is built, enabling it to sustain high and stable employment and yield
other economic benefits.

As the US economy has become dominated by unproductive labor, its "productive" sectors and industries have dwindled significantly relative to its GDP.
While an increasing value of the products purchased in US retail outlets support
the productive labor of other countries, not the US. In 2020, US agricultural
production comprised less than 1% of America's GDP, while manufacturing
contributed a mere 11% (National Association of Manufacturers, 2020). In
the early decades of the twenty-first century, the remainder of America's GDP
has been derived from the following (Bureau of Economic Analysis, 2019):

- services, finances, and information (55%)

- trade, warehousing, and transportation (15%)

- federal, state, and local government services (12%)

- manufacturing (11%)

- mining, utilities, and construction (6%)

- agriculture (1%)

This represents a massive shift in the industrial context of the American
economy since the 1950s, when agriculture and manufacturing generated
about 50% of US GDP. In turn, the percentage of the US workforce employed

in manufacturing and agriculture has dropped significantly. Those losses produced commensurate impacts to labor demands in other industries (i.e., due to the high jobs multiplier manufacturing provides), placing downward pressure on real wages. Overall, the demand for jobs in US agriculture, manufacturing, and retail has been lower than the supply of workers.

In retail and other industries, this trend began to reverse in 2021 during the "great renegotiation." As if they were directed, laborers across the US began to realize that the only way to overcome their ever-increasing cost of living was to renegotiate with their employer. If that failed, they would negotiate with a different employer, desperate for employees. Those who could not find better wages elsewhere chose to remain unemployed, rather than remain in a stressful, unfulfilling, or otherwise undesirable low-paying job.

Furthermore, America has traditionally assessed lower taxes on services than it has on manufacturing, while revenues from industries such as consulting provide no tax revenue (Murray, 2020). Not until 2007 did the majority of US states begin to tax services at all. Taxes on internet sales still lagged behind their "brick and mortar" counterparts as recently as 2020. It's no wonder the streets of America's richest cities are littered with potholes, education is exorbitantly expensive, homeless shelters are grossly inadequate—the list is long.

While the general rise of America's service sector has partially compensated for declining labor demands elsewhere, this sector is known for some of the lowest paying jobs in the country. Furthermore, as the US economy has grown over-dependent on foreign trade, the viability of US service sector jobs no longer hinges on America's productive labor (i.e., manufacturing and extractive industries), but on the productive labor of other countries. A thriving US service sector is at the whim of global supply chains. Between 2020-2022, with tractor, automobile, bicycle, and other parts failing to arrive at US ports, US retailers had little to sell.

An ever-rising carrying trade delivers additional risk. As noted by Bert Dohmen (2014), a former contributor to *Forbes*, as the carry trade rises so does the value of the U.S. dollar, bond prices, and stocks. In return, commodity prices have a tendency to deflate. Dohmen and others are concerned that if and when the Bank of Japan (or other national banks) hikes its interest rates to combat rising inflation, the carry trade will unwind.

Like the proverbial frog in a kettle of water, slowly brought to a boil, a country's slow shift toward the carrying and foreign trades—and away from manufacturing and agriculture—feels comfortable during the early stages of building wealth. As a country's productivity heats up, excess value is created. The natural tendency for such excess is that it be invested in emerging foreign markets. In the process, those sectors responsible for the productive labor of a country are marginalized. In America, such a shift has not only suppressed real wages, but has engendered instability throughout entire industries, including agriculture, manufacturing, and retail.

This does not mean the US economy has failed to grow. Afterall, *per capita* GDP prior to the COVID-19 pandemic was the eleventh highest in the world. However, correlated with such growth has been a flat purchasing power for working class Americans—perhaps declining purchasing power, as inflation in 2022 reached at least 7.5%, a level not seen in forty years.

Equally destructive, an increased mass of wealth has become concentrated into fewer hands. As of 2020, the richest one percent of US citizens owned about thirty-one percent of all the wealth in America, or about US $34 trillion (Duffin, 2021). Some estimates are higher, that 72% of all wealth is in the hands of the top 1% of Americans, with the bottom half of Americans owning about 2% of total wealth (Piketty, 2014). Similar trends have unfolded across Europe.

To reiterate, the concentration of wealth into few hands is not a problem in and of itself, except for a few key facts. First, the foreign and carrying trades—not America's domestic economy—are largely responsible for this concentration of wealth. In other words, America's wealth is not dependent on the stability and productivity of America, but that of the global market. Recognizing this issue during the Industrial Revolution, Adam Smith declared that the foreign and carrying trades are a reflection, not the cause, of a country's wealth.

Economists today note a more tangible economic impact of a country's concentrated wealth. When the majority of a country's consumers experience a loss in wealth, they consume fewer goods and services (Greenspan, 2007; Keynes, 2017; Stiglitz, 2015a). With the income and assets of the millennial generation proving to be lower than that of the previous generation (Kurz et al., 2018; Pemberton, 2020), a drop in consumption, and hence production, is likely to result. In response, the economic might and stability of the US will decline. Should the wealth of America's top 1% be allocated across the US labor force, it would amount to about US $200,000 per worker. If those workers spent that money on the productive labor of America's domestic industries, the positive impacts to NDP would be significant.

The relationships between trade, wealth, and productivity go back centuries, when Adam Smith posited that a nation's increased reliance on the carrying and foreign trades jeopardizes their productive capacity. In effect, any excess value generated by a nation's agricultural, mining, manufacturing, or other productive industries, when used to conduct the foreign and carrying trades, becomes unavailable to building the productive capacity and NDP of the domestic economy. This trend is so pervasive today that Americans are investing in China and other foreign markets—wherever the greatest potential for profit exists—and they don't even know it (Schoenfeld, 2020).

To put a face to this unavoidable artifact of global market capitalism, I had the honor of interviewing Justin Brunson in 2020. As founder and head chef of Denver's River Bear American Meats, Justin strives to source their animal products within a 200-mile radius: a mission that would stimulate the productive capacity of America. But like many American entrepreneurs, Justin struggled through six sets of investors before acquiring the capital he needed to launch his business. Thankfully, Justin's biggest struggle today is meeting the insatiable demand for locally-produced artisan salami, bacon, sausage, and other delicacies (Figure 12). A less obvious challenge, not unique to Justin's business, is finding local processing facilities and ample quantities of locally-raised animals.

Figure 12. Italian dry salami hanging at River Bear American Meats. Denver, CO.

The meat industry does not suffer alone in its search for capital. Rana Foroohar of the *Financial Times* explains that, while America's financial system has doubled in size over the past forty years, only 15% of the assets are used for productive lending, such as to start a business (Pemberton, 2020). The rest is being used to buy and sell assets around the globe. Akin to Adam Smith's observations, Foroohar states that focusing the cumulative wealth of developed countries toward the carrying trade has caused slower growth in those countries.

The Longer the Chain, the Higher the Risks

Despite the risks, US policies and programs—export subsidies, trade pacts, strategic support of the WTO and IMF, monetary policy, government-backed export trade associations, federally funded upgrades to ports, etc.—forge ever-lengthening supply chains between US communities and their global suppliers. In the process, downtrodden loggers in Oregon berate the plethora of timber imported from Canada. Wyoming ranchers suffer at the hand of imported beef from Brazil. Wisconsin paper mills struggle to compete with producers from Venezuela and elsewhere. Far more companies, and their workers, continue to suffer across a nation of importing states, counties, and cities.

On the flipside, export crops such as timber and cattle from tropical regions often yield drastically lower income for locals than the harvest of non-timber forest products (NTFP) such as fruit, sap, latex, and berries (Grimes et al., 1994; Peters et al., 1989; Pinedo-Vasquez et al., 1992). While communities that integrate selective logging with NTFP extraction see an overall rise in production (Salick et al., 1995). Entrepreneurs in these regions have learned to manage disturbance in their favor, moving the successional dial toward the middle stage, where diversity and production are optimized.

At the level of an industry, sector, and nation, it is in the middle stages of succession where volatility may be moderated. To the contrary, dozens of severe crashes have rippled across the network of homogenized global market economies in the past century (Trefis Team, 2020), indicating high levels of volatility. A recent example is the 28% drop in US markets one month after the news of a global pandemic struck the US.

At a global scale, Stiglitz (2015) recognized an astounding 100 crashes since 1985, coinciding with a period of tremendous global market expansion. This includes the Great Recession, dubbed by some economists as the Great Trade Collapse of 2008 to 2009 (Novy & Taylor, 2020). Applying the concept of *uncertainty shock* to the global market economy, and drawing upon decades of US import and production data, Novy and Taylor created a model that explains why global trade is far more volatile than domestic trade. The volatility comes in the form of *second-moment* shocks, which produce extreme spikes in uncertainty among importers, in response to exogenous forces such as the sub-prime crisis, war, terrorism, changes in political parties, drastic shifts in oil markets, etc. In turn, global production declines significantly, as does the volume of international trade.

There are financial reasons why domestic firms cannot flip a switch and begin demanding product from domestic suppliers. To begin, domestic firms tied to the global market develop pricing strategies dependent on the cheapest global supplier. Even if the domestic manufacturer wanted to turn to a domestic parts supplier during a downturn, countries such as the US have lost their capacity to produce the required parts. Such was the case with the supply chain disruptions in the global lumber industry in the early 2020s, which caused great spikes in the cost of building materials. It can take years for an industry to restore its capacity to produce timber, semi-conductors, electric pumps, etc. In the interim, the global crisis often subsides.

Besides the impacts of volatility on workers, profitability, industry-wide inefficiencies, etc., there are higher level concerns over the volatility global trade tends to stimulate.

The Frail Link Between Trade, Energy, and Security

Despite the role foreign trade plays in undermining the productive labor and productive capacity of a nation over time, it is surprising so many economists and politicians view the expansion of foreign trade as essential to sustaining a nation's wealth. Perhaps, like early experiences with fertilizer, they believe if a little global trade is good, then more is better. Of course, applying too much nitrogen will destroy the crop. Unfortunately, the corrosive outcomes of foreign trade unfold slowly, unlike the impact of nitrogen on a field of wheat. And the lessons are more elusive. Or perhaps, when global economic tides are high, it is easier to dismiss the basic laws of complex self-regulating systems. Regardless, the US economy has increased its reliance on foreign trade in exchange for a weak productive capacity, low economic diversity, and a frail shield against in increasing mass of turbulent global forces.

America stands boldly in the afterglow of the greatest economic boom the world has ever experienced, with a meager 12% of its GDP attributed to agriculture and manufacturing. Real wages remain flat, and are likely to decline as the cost of living continues to rise and the wealth gap increases. All the while, proselytizers of a global market economy claim that increased foreign trade is essential to our prosperity, and the level of interdependence forged by global trade maintains peace on earth. They argue that two countries dependent upon one another for goods, services, debt, etc., wouldn't dare disrupt the peace. However, I know of no meaningful period in the history of global market capitalism that has enjoyed lasting peace as a result of trade. The Russia-Ukraine conflict of 2022 is the most recent example, with serious global implications.

Viewed under a broader historical lens, social tensions have defined the post-boom contractions of nearly all global superpowers (Arrighi, 2010;

Braudel, 1984; Cline, 2014; Smith, 2019). While the French Revolution, the American Revolution, the Opium Wars, and dozens of colonial revolts erupted at the height of the Industrial Revolution, culminating in the First World War. Soon after, WWII was incited largely by downturns in the German economy, hyperinflation in the midst of a global economic crash, and treaties that did not affect all parties equally. Repeated international unrest has lingered since WWII, including wars over the control of global energy supplies, and even regime-changing turmoil over fruit.

Historians such as Yuval Harari (2015) reflect on the relative peace on earth since WWII, and credit the global market economy for that peace. Harari does not ignore the increasing threats of terrorism, such as the Sept 11 attack on the World Trade Center, dozens of bombings throughout Europe, and hundreds of other terrorist attacks across the globe in the past eighty years. But those attacks, in his perspective, do not reflect a decline in peace. Harari also notes the tremendous rate of suicide and murder across modern nations (e.g., millions of deaths, far higher than the deaths resulting from war), yet those atrocities are also not accounted for in the ledger of peace.

Harari's perspective on peace also ignores the atrocities committed in, for instance, fruit-growing regions of Central America, which dominated the news in the '80s. The turmoil actually began boiling decades earlier, as global corporations began offering Central American countries exorbitant sums of capital, such as new railroads across lush tropical regions, in exchange for banana distribution rights to global markets (Livingstone, 2009). Politicians and capitalists in the export countries perceived a win, convinced that foreign trade would create far more value for their people than building strong domestic markets.

The United Fruit Company (UFCO) came to dominate the Central American fruit trade, converting export countries such as Guatemala, El Salvador, and Honduras into "banana republics." So exploitative were UFCOs efforts that wave after wave of revolts defined life throughout Central America for decades, to no avail. In 1954, UFCO lobbied the US government to engineer a coup to end a devastating Guatemalan revolution and install a more export-friendly military regime (Livingstone, 2009). Civil war consumed Guatemala for more than a generation, a tragic fate that befell several Central American countries.

In the heat of the Central American civil wars, United Brands Company—formerly UFCO—paid a US $2.5 million bribe to the Honduran Economics Minister in return for reduced export taxes (Hershey, 1976). Before the case was closed, the CEO of United Brands jumped out of his New York high rise office window, and Hondurans became embroiled in yet another military coup.

Another generation passed, with the foreign and carrying trades molding the Honduran economy to meet global rather than local needs. Today, hundreds of thousands of people continue fleeing Honduras and other destabilized Central American countries to America annually.

It would be easy to lay blame for such economic tragedies on corrupt government officials in export countries. But if there is a fact to be revealed by history, it may be that excessive global trade does not prevent, but rather stimulates the risk of corruption, social turmoil, suicide, drug abuse, homelessness, and even war. Regarding the social and economic tensions that lead to war, there is simply a lag between the cause of those tensions, and the effect.

As the world's single largest importer, the nature of trade in the US economy influences the stability and security of over 100 export-dependent countries across the globe. Recall that *secure*, used here, relates to a nation's ability to maintain a high productive capacity, which is tied to a nation's economic diversity and stability. A higher productive capacity engenders higher employment, more reliable food and medical supplies, military might, and other essential goods and services. Hence, to the extent increased foreign and carrying trades reduce a nation's productive capacity, the security of that nation is duly jeopardized.

The link between global trade, productive capacity, and security has never been clearer than it was in the wake of the COVID-19 pandemic. In response, politicians doubled down on the current model. As supply chains crumbled, the USDA made direct payments of over US $9 billion to US cattle, dairy, and hog producers (Dorning, 2020). Even before the 2020 harvest, the US doled out over US $16 billion to commodity farmers, corporations that are more dependent upon the strength of foreign markets than their own community. At the start of the fall harvest, another US $14 billion was earmarked for those same commodity producers (USDA, 2020b). All told, the US paid out a record US $46 billion in direct payments to farmers to ease the impact of the pandemic and trade disputes (Bunge, 2021).

At the same time, our family and friends gathered to purchase a side of Colorado grass-finished beef in the winter of 2020. But several of our favorite producers had experienced levels of demand that far outstripped their supplies. In essence, the century-long trend of subsidized industrial agriculture to meet the needs of global markets has rendered farmlands across US impoverished, with a diminished capacity to feed Americans absent continued cheap inputs.

The frail global supply chains revealed by COVID-19 went well beyond food, and were certainly not restricted to US consumers. A shortage of respirators and sterile medical swabs, alongside inadequate capacity in hospitals, jeopardized the health of citizens of all political stripes and income levels across the globe. The food and medical security of even the world's wealthiest capitalist nations had become undermined by the very system that had built their wealth.

The intractable relationship between foreign trade, energy security, and national security revealed itself again in 2022, with Russia's invasion of Ukraine. The US and its allies tried hobbling Russia with threats of sanctions: restricting oil refining technologies, exclusion from the SWIFT global payments system, halting export of semiconductors to Russia, etc. Anticipating such threats, Russia had spent decades building strong trade ties with China, and had stashed tremendous oil-generated wealth in Russian banks and elsewhere. Confidently, Russia then weaponized its oil reserves, by restricting oil exports—to stymie the growth of the US and its allies.

Struggling to mount a counter attack, America, the EU, the UK, Japan, and others grasped for India's hand as an additional ally against Russia. India, though, stood firmly on the sidelines. The threat of war was not India's concern. India's fear was that Russia would retaliate, by decreasing food supplies to India, who's domestic food-growing capacity is weak, relative to its 1.4 billion people.

In the midst of global turmoil, India's food system was tormented in spring 2022 with a record-breaking heatwave that struck Punjab, the "grain bowl" of India—equivalent to the breadbasket of America. The drought was expected to shrink grain harvests by about 25% of expected levels (Ghosal, 2022). India exports very little of its wheat, meaning that a 25 percent decline in harvest translates to a quarter less flour available to hungry citizens. This natural catastrophe came upon the heels of the pandemic, which left India's once-vast stocks of grain nearly emptied. India has no wiggle room.

The US offered to come to India's aid, promising to ship hundreds of thousands of tons of wheat across two vast oceans. President Truman made an even larger pledge in 1951—two million tons of grain—in hopes that India would align itself politically with the US against a growing threat of communism in Russia, Asia, Korea, and elsewhere (McMahon, 1987). Despite the offer, India remained economically and politically faithful to Russia and China. America's 2022 food pledge to India is poised to fail due to one element politics has no reign over. Severe drought also struck Kansas, America's top wheat growing state, threatening the 2022 harvest and, along with it, America's hopes that India would side with the West against the growing Russia-China threat (Plume, 2022).

It is our humanitarian duty to question if the co-dependency created by foreign trade is a guarantee of lasting peace. As future global fossil fuel markets increase in volatility and cost, driving the volatility and cost of all other global commodities, a more likely scenario is that foreign trade and exogenous energy will become powerful weapons against nations whose ability to meet their citizens' needs has been crippled. That is, those nations who have depleted their productive capacity. When the water, food, fuel, medicine, timber, clothing, and security you depend on are suddenly interrupted, and your productive capacity has eroded, what option is left but to revolt, flee, or support whichever tyrant promises to deliver those goods?

If foreign trade succeeds more often in creating unstable dependencies than sustaining a country's wealth and security, then how should the US and similar nations proceed? Should the socioeconomic pendulum swing toward complete isolationism? Of course not. Trade among neighboring economies and countries in times of need—drought, famine, civil unrest, pandemics, and the like—is downright humane. With history as our guide, I would argue global peace is ensured not by a system of global dependence, but by a system of economic independence. To be independent, a nation must restore its productive capacity. To the extent that nation produces excess goods, may that surplus benefit neighbors in times of need.

Clean Air and Water for Americans: Thanks to legislation or externalities?

America passed several acts in the '60s and '70s so that citizens could begin enjoying relatively clean air, high quality water, and untrammeled wilderness. But how much of the improved environmental conditions are due to the good work of those acts? Over the same period, US consumers have grown heavily dependent on imported goods from China, Taiwan, Honduras, and other countries with far fewer pollution regulations than the US. Hence, the pollution formerly created by US manufacturers to meet the demands of American consumers has been transferred to export countries around the globe.

A vicious downward cycle has materialized. The retail price Americans pay for imported products is lower than it would be if the environmental and social costs of production were accounted for by US manufacturers supplying those same products. The lower the price, the more we consume, contributing to more externalities in countries with low production costs.

That said, the solution is not to sever the foreign or carrying trade entirely. Such an action would breach the basic rules of self-regulating systems. And certainly, the US should not favor trade with, for instance, Britain over

China, China over Russia, or Canada over the EU. Such policies would simply amplify the rate and quantity of trade with other countries, stoke unproductive trade wars, or produce externalities elsewhere. Rather, America must develop a balance of trade that stimulates business diversity, strengthens its productive capacity, enhances economic stability, and internalizes the social and environmental externalities of consumption. Reflecting on the nature of resource transfers in ecosystems, the structure of such a system may appear obvious.

The Balanced Trade Triangle

There is at least one constant among the rise and fall of former global capitalist powers—Genoa, the Dutch, the British, and the US in transition. Each of them has championed policies ensuring a continual shift from domestic to foreign trade, and then to the carrying trade. In due time, global competition reared up against the very domestic industries that built the wealth of those capitalist superpowers. Profitability declined in those industries, creating a vicious feedback loop.

Industries were forced to produce even greater economies of scale, further reduce labor inputs, lobby for reduced pollution regulations, seek cheaper raw materials, or locate production facilities in cheaper labor markets. A recent example is Apple Computer, once thought of as America's largest corporation, which closed its last US factory in 2004 (Bosworth, 2012; Prince & Plank, 2012). Today, the US is nothing more than Apple's primary source for Research & Development, and their largest consumer base for products now made entirely from the productive labor of other countries.

The Balance of Domestic, Foreign, and Carrying Trades

The balance of economic trade shown in Figure 13 aligns, conceptually, with the resource transfer rules of self-regulating ecosystems. This balance of trade also reflects what Adam Smith and other economists have recognized as necessary to build and sustain the wealth of nations. The vast majority of trade consists of the home (domestic) trade. Greater than fifty percent of domestic production is generated by agriculture, manufacturing, and other productive industries. The foreign and carrying trades exist as a smaller fraction of the nation's collective wealth.

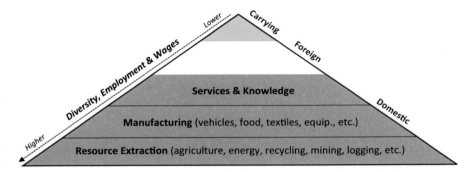

Figure 13. Balanced Trade Pyramid. The relative importance of the domestic, foreign, and carrying trade on diversity, employment, and wages. The greater a country's reliance on domestic trade, the greater the tendency for higher economic diversity, employment, wages, and stability.

Unlike the balanced trade pyramid, America's trade condition since the 1960s has been in the shape of a hot air balloon (Figure 14). The carrying and foreign trades have grown to dominate the top two thirds of the balloon, while domestic manufacturing, as a percentage of GDP, constitutes the ever-narrowing bottom, tapering down to the ropes. Dangling beneath is the agricultural industry, a miniscule basket of goods whose contribution to America's GDP does not exceed one percent. America's service and knowledge sectors have filled a greater volume of the balloon with each passing decade, fueled not by the productive labor of America but that of other countries.

Figure 14. Trade balloon, representing America's current global trade paradigm. Photo courtesy of Pexels.com

The spectrum of human reactions to a balanced trade pyramid is bracketed by three arguments. On one side, global market capitalists fervently argue against any restrictions on foreign trade, professing it will doom a nation's economic might. The poor around the world will suffer, etc. For perspective, those same arguments were waged during the passage of America's clean water, clean air, and endangered species acts. Long before that, global market capitalists claimed that abolishing slavery would destroy the US economy. Yet in the wake of such fear-soaked claims, America's GDP only rose.

On another side stands the historical perspectives of Marshall, Arrighi, and Braudel, whose views on balanced trade were mirrored by Schumpeter (1950) in *Capitalism, Socialism, and Democracy*. As Schumpeter wrote, "'restraints of trade'...may in the end produce not only steadier but greater expansion of total output than could be secured by an entirely uncontrolled onward rush [of global trade] that cannot fail to be studded with catastrophes." Similarly, during the Great Depression, Keynes (2017) promoted a national policy to achieve full employment via strong domestic production, which required a more favorable balance of trade among countries. In that same era, Hungarian-American economist Karl Polanyi referred to a self-regulating global market as a "stark utopia," which could not succeed for any length of time without destroying society and the natural world (Polanyi, 2011).

Finally, there are capitalists who argue that continued economic growth is not feasible without increased foreign trade. This argument not only ignores the physical limits of energy and other resources, but the capitalists waging it have fallen into a logic trap. If it is impossible for an economy to grow in the absence of continual increases in foreign trade, by extension the global market economy as an operational unit will run up against a natural limit. As of this writing, no new trade partners remain for the global market economy to tap into. The only way out of this predicament, then, is for global market capitalists to forge trade pacts with extraterrestrial partners.

Back on earth, an abundant number of economists and capitalists argue foreign trade is essential to maintaining an industry's comparative advantage—an argument that also has its delusions.

The Delusion of Comparative Advantages in a Global Market Economy

David Ricardo derived the theory of comparative advantage in the early 1800s (Encyclopaedia Britannica, 2018b), arguing that when an exporting country such as Venezuela produces a product such as paper more efficiently than an importing country (e.g., the USA), then the importing country ultimately benefits. Under this scenario, Americans spend less on paper—or lumber, iron, aluminum, washing machines, car parts, etc. As a result, consumers are left with more money to spend on other products, or to invest in the economy, thereby increasing America's GDP.

Ricardo's logic sounds reasonable. However, when the savings gained by one's comparative advantage are used to purchase more imported products, rather than more domestic products, the GDP of the importing nation is reduced commensurately. That is, the purchase of imported products supports the GDP of the country producing the products, not the GDP of the country that consumes those products. Some economists use accounting principles to show no decline in the importer-nation's GDP when a consumer there pays, for instance, US $35,000 for a car manufactured in Italy or Korea. However, the nation that produced that car (e.g., Korea or Italy) and then exported it to, say, America, also accounted for the US $35,000 in their GDP. From a global accounting standpoint, then, Global GDP is raised by US $70,000 from the production of a US $35,000 car. If you are confused by this math, have no fear; so are many economics professors, as well as the author of this book.

What is clear is that achieving a comparative advantage in a global market economy requires homogenization at a great scale, which places downward pressure on economic diversity. Over time, declining diversity jeopardizes economic stability, productive capacity, resilience, employment, profitability, and real wages. Low profit and wages translate to reduced spending power, which places downward pressure on domestic productivity.

The theory of comparative advantage is problematic for other reasons, such as its tendency to focus on a single product or industry without considering the broader socio-economic impacts. For instance, slavery was a key variable in the nineteenth-century British economy, providing abnormally cheap production at the time Ricardo was formulating his theory. This included the young American economy, where slave-produced cotton amassed abnormal degrees of wealth for a handful of global market capitalists, including those in New Orleans. But false pretenses—a fake comparative advantage—can endure only so long. By the turn of the twenty-first century, continual shifts in global markets left New Orleans with one of the highest poverty rates in the nation.

Land was also cheaper in the colonies that were supplying Britain with raw materials. At the same time, Britain had some of the cheapest coal reserves in Europe, and produced some of the worst environmental and social working conditions imaginable. The result, in theory, was a lower cost of living for consumers, and so a higher standard of living. That said, substantial disagreement exists over the impact the Industrial Revolution had on metrics such as standard of living and real wages for Britain's working class (de Zwart et al., 2014). From Thomas Piketty's analysis, European wages during the first six decades of the 19th century were as low as—or even lower—than in the previous few centuries (Piketty, 2014). The growth in productivity produced by the Industrial Revolution did not translate into higher real wages for laborers, according to Piketty, until the 1860s through 1870s. Shortly after, the Long Depression struck the globe.

What remains undebated is the fundamentally unequal social, environmental, and industrial contexts that exist across the global market economy. Trees grow faster in Venezuela than in Wisconsin or Washington, which cleared their old growth forests by the 1980s. Similarly, pollution regulations and labor costs are both lower in Latin American and Asian countries that produce increasing quantities of shirts, underwear, and pants for North Americans and Europeans.

To be clear, countries with cheap labor and land, and with fewer environmental and social regulations, have not forged a true comparative advantage. Those countries simply operate within a different SEI context than the US. While exported products are cheaper, such advantages are often offset by a rising cost of living not only for laborers of export-based industries, but for the citizens of import-based countries such as the US. It's a zero-sum game.

How Best to Degrade a True Comparative Advantage (and avoid its benefits)

A true comparative advantage for any industry or economy is gained not by securing the cheapest inputs from outside its economic border, but by discovering efficiencies of production within its SEI context. In other words, a paper mill in Wisconsin will attain a true comparative advantage over other domestic mills in the US when it discovers more efficient means of production, regardless of the labor costs, growing conditions, and the environmental and social values of the region. Stemming from such efficiencies are productivity gains, contributing positively to the nation's GDP without casting unwanted social and environmental externalities on unsuspecting citizens elsewhere.

In this light, I posit that the theory of comparative advantage is valid only among trading partners operating within the same SEI context. When trade occurs among countries with widely divergent SEI contexts, the tendency for

Is China Restoring its Balance of Trade?

For centuries China slept, disinterested in the carrying and foreign trades ballooning around them. Watching the booming Industrial Revolution unfold, the Ming and Qing Dynasties remained self-sufficient, maintaining a firm stance against foreign trade. China's staunch stance against global trade attracted the curious eyes of Adam Smith, Joseph Schumpeter, Fernand Braudel, Giovanni Arrighi, and others.

Eventually, Europe forced China's hand with the Opium Wars, granting France and Britain commercial privileges throughout China (Pletcher, 2020). Today, China is the globe's leading export-based economy, producing a vast spectrum of products the West has grown dependent upon. In response, China's per capita GDP climbed a hundred-fold since 1960, to US $9770 in 2018 (Trading Economics, 2020). For perspective, America's per capita GDP rose about twenty-fold over the same period.

China's raw GDP growth, like that of any nation, is not the answer to maintaining their position on the global stage. The answer is to *sustain* one's GDP and their productive capacity. Several factors suggest China's growth is unsustainable, which will ultimately undermine their 1.5 billion souls. To begin, China's agricultural output, relative to their population and GDP, declined significantly since the '70s (The Global Economy, 2020). China has developed a severe food trade deficit, as they import US $105 billion in food while exporting only US $60 billion (China Power Team, 2021). Much of those food imports originate in the US, whose capacity to grow food is shriveling, and whose desire to continue supplying China with food is waning. Meanwhile, China's reliance on exogenous energy has risen dramatically, placing them on the list of top petroleum importers. This explains China's tight bond with oil-rich Russia.

The laws of complex self-regulating systems are not on China's side. Resource transfers into and out of China, and excessive reliance on exogenous energy, place downward pressure on economic diversity, relative to their population and GDP. Diminished diversity, on top of an expanding gap between food production and population growth, leaves China at risk of volatile global forces.

One promising shift occurred in recent decades. The share of China's GDP derived from exports has been cut in half (Roach, 2018). Whether this decline was intentional, or the result of destructive competition from other countries, a trade rebalancing is occurring. Regardless, China has developed a national strategy to expand its domestic trade, to relieve the pressure of tariffs and other economic threats increasingly being aimed its way (US Congressional Research Service, 2019). China aims to manufacture 70% of the goods they consume by 2025.

exploitation exceeds any advantage the less developed country might otherwise gain from the exchange.

The US does produce some goods that reflect its true comparative advantage on the global stage, such as spacecraft, high-value machinery, integrated circuit boards, etc. Those products will naturally find global markets in countries that are unable to produce them, with the exchange benefiting both parties. But for US corn producers to compete globally requires subsidies, as labor and land costs in the US are higher than most other corn-producing regions of the world. Even with subsidies, tremendous exogenous energy is required to provide globally competitive yields. In response, soil fertility declines, rivers become polluted, wages and economic diversity dwindle, etc. The moment two countries with different SEI contexts begin trading similar goods, a race to the bottom begins. Competition becomes more destructive than constructive for those involved, and the quest for a true comparative advantage has been avoided.

Finally, the theory of comparative advantage ignores a few fundamental human conditions. Not everyone desires to work in the high tech or service industries that have come to dominate the US economy. While labor, as it turns out, is not that mobile across the country let alone across similar industries in the same state (Autor et al., 2021). And training is not a guaranteed solution to these issues. At least in the short-term, significant job losses and family disruptions occur at the hand of industries and economies attempting to gain a "comparative advantage" against one another in the global marketplace. Taking an alternative path, industries and countries that realize a *true* comparative advantage will yield longer-term benefits for workers and their communities.

The Truest Comparative Advantage

An infamous example of a true comparative advantage appeared on the global stage by means of Japanese automakers in the 1980s and 90s. The novel advantages of Japanese manufacturers were just beginning to seep into the American knowledge sector when I was studying business in San Diego. Among several jobs that scarcely paid the bills, I worked as a night guard at a robotic Sony plant, etching memories of the Japanese success story that endure today.

Japan's success goes far beyond robots. In the late 1980s, the three giant American automakers, GM, Ford, and Chrysler, were adamant Japanese automakers had an unfair advantage in the global marketplace. The American executives went so far as to believe a broader conspiracy was at play, threatening the very roots of American culture. In the 1995 book *Comeback*, detailing the collapse and reprisal of the American auto industry, Paul Ingrassia and Joseph White highlighted three common claims by US auto executives of the day. Japanese automakers used cheaper labor, the value of the yen was lower than the dollar, and a greater number of robots filled their plants. In short, they believed the Japanese system was rigged.

In a bold attempt to disprove American conspiracies, Honda broke ground in the US in Marysville, OH in 1982. Honda hired non-union workers and paid them union wages. Honda's aim was to prove to the world they could produce cars in America at the same low price as they could in Japan.

Emboldened up by Honda's success, Toyota began constructing their first US plant. Before the Toyota plant could even open its doors, however, ministers of the world's top industrial nations met in Paris to conspire against the Japanese. They agreed to drive down the value of the dollar, and push up the yen. Still, US automakers could not compete. So frustrated US auto executives began adding more robots to their plants—which were already twice the size and expense of their Japanese counterparts.

Time would reveal that a lack of robots on factory floors was also not the problem. Watching their global market share plummet, outraged US executives continued their finger-pointing at Japan's unfair playing field. And one by one, their concocted stories imploded.

Several more years passed before the big three carmakers would finally accept the facts. The true comparative advantage of Japanese car companies had nothing to do with robots, cheap labor, or the value of the yen. The Japanese were operating in the same SEI context as the Americans, where raw competition drove the redesign of Japanese manufacturing facilities to be more efficient.

The Japanese perfected the system of *just in time* (JIT) inventory to streamline production processes. A JIT inventory system demands every part arrive on the floor precisely when it is needed, which drives a chain reaction of improvements. Floor managers are required to adhere closely to tight assembly schedules, a goal that requires each factory line supervisor does the same. When an assembly line breaks down, workers are expected to fix it on the spot, not wait for a technician to arrive. Such systems require more skilled labor, translating to greater job diversity and higher levels of responsibility. Staff become an integral part of the operation, so are more accountable to its success. Nobody wants *their* production line to be the one falling behind schedule. As a result, JIT automotive plants are smaller, and more cars are produced with less capital.

Businesses and industries operating within the same SEI context continually apply competitive pressures on one another (e.g., Japanese and US automakers both operating in America), driving each toward true comparative advantages. That is, they apply constructive competition on one other. *Constructive Competition* produces an increase in economic diversity and net domestic productivity, via a more efficient use of resources. *Destructive competition* leads to declines in economic diversity and NDP, and often a decline in resource-use efficiency.

Constructive competition with Japanese automakers produced American-made cars with higher gas mileage and fewer maintenance needs. Destructive competition has resulted in the closure of hundreds of paper and grain mills in the US, leaving an incredible degree of physical infrastructure wasting away.

The Unbreakable Bonds Between Diversity, Energy, and Trade

In both economies and ecosystems, diversity, energy, and resource transfers (trade) form predictable bonds. Highly diverse systems can more efficiently extract usable energy and other endogenous resources from within their ecological or economic space, compared to low-diversity systems. Transferring exogenous energy into the system reduces that diversity. Diverse systems tend to have higher resistance and resilience to disturbance, and *net* productivity also tends to be greater. That productivity and diversity cannot occur without resource transfers within the system, which require energy.

Summarizing the past three chapters, I posit that transferring energy and physical resources *into*—or out of—an economy or ecosystem decreases its diversity. Systems with suppressed diversity have a lower capacity to capture and cycle resources, they are less resilient and resistant to disturbance, and they are less capable of maintaining other benefits described earlier. In our economy, those benefits cannot be sustained without restoring the foundational components of diversity, energy, and trade as one interrelated unit. Yet the restoration of these components is likely to be ineffective if we ignore a more fundamental question: At what scale should an economy exist?

SEVEN

SIZE MATTERS:
THE BASIC OPERATIONAL UNIT OF THE
GLOBAL MARKET ECONOMY

A debate has rippled across the centuries between those economists who view self-regulating markets as essential to economic growth and ever-increasing standards of living, versus those who view self-regulating markets as self-defeating. The confusion, I believe, stems from a fundamental ignorance that both extremes possess. That is, knowledge of the *scale* that a self-regulating economy must operate at in order to be highly functional.

The biosphere—the synergistic product of all life on earth—is continually growing. A clue to sustaining this growth is found in the emergent properties of a system. When various components become arranged and interconnected to form a new system, unique properties emerge. The unique properties of water, for instance, emerge only when hydrogen and oxygen bind together. With water's novel properties, coupled with earth's rotation, its distance from the sun, and so forth, cellular life emerged on the third planet from the sun.

Ascending the ladder of complexity, from cells to entire species, more novel properties emerge. At the level of an ecosystem, with innumerable individuals comprising thousands of species, the structure of system components actually shifts. Instead of essential parts being cells, organs, or a population of individuals, the foundational components of ecosystems (and economies) are less tangible: the diversity of species (and businesses), energy transfer between those diverse entities, and the exchange of material resources between them. When structured well, these foundational components bestow complex self-regulating systems with a degree of resilience and resistance that far exceeds that of the species (or businesses) comprising them. The system, as a unit, persists far longer than any individual within.

A critical issue many economists and ecologists have failed to grasp is the spatial scale at which an economy or ecosystem must exist, such that it can achieve ample degrees of resilience, resistance, NDP, etc. In other words, at what scale must an economy's foundational components be fully functional, so that it can flourish as a self-regulating system, and provide the social, environmental, and economic benefits thereof? Global, national, local, or some other scale?

The Basic Operational Unit of Complex Self-Regulating Systems

For a self-regulating system to persist, its components must be fully operational as a unit, capable of interacting with the system's external forces while maintaining key functions. Capra and Luisi, the authors of *The Systems View of Life*, use the term "operationally closed" to describe the various components of living systems. While I understand their rationale, I prefer the term *basic operational unit* to describe the various levels of organization within ecosystems and economies, for few living systems can persist when completely closed off from the greater systems in which they exist.

Basic operational units include organs, entire species (e.g., *Homo sapiens*), a given population of humans (e.g., the people of Scotland), or a specific individual within that population (e.g., Adam Smith). The economy of Scotland is also a basic operational unit, as is a heathland plant community in Scotland's countryside.

The Basic Operational Unit of Ecosystems

It is a fairly simple task to tease apart the basic operational units within a cell, lung, body, or species. It is far more challenging to fathom the basic operational units of ecosystems and economies. For clarity, an example from California's remote northern coastline may suffice, where a different form of skyscraper dominates the land.

Within a thirty-minute drive from the crashing waves, most people can easily witness a vast structural change from towering coastal redwood forests to the mixed evergreen-hardwood forests to the east. Naturally, a small degree of gene flow occurs between some plants in each forest type, despite the fact that plants cannot physically move. Instead, wind and wildlife transmit pollen and propagules for members of the plant world. Animals also migrate freely between each forest, mixing their genes with other populations along the way. Despite these genetic transfers, the dominant species and the structural diversity of each forest remains unique. Distinct environmental factors (e.g., precipitation, soils, temperature patterns, etc.) have shaped each forest differently. Each forest exists as a basic operational unit.

Besides their ability to persist over eons, amidst continual disturbance, complex ecosystems harbor other curious properties that distinguish them from lower order systems. Compared with less complex systems, such as the organs interacting within the human body, the survival of an ecosystem (e.g., the coastal redwood forest) depends much less on its interactions with adjacent ecosystems (e.g., other forests). There is a nuance to this property that may be clarified by another example.

Deserts by and large exist around thirty degrees north and south latitude, where the biosphere is extremely dry. Tropical rainforests exist primarily between the Tropics of Cancer and Capricorn—within 23.5 degrees of the equator—where the biosphere is extremely wet. If one attempted to erect a large enough wall around an entire desert or tropical forest, without interrupting its connection with the atmosphere, the walled ecosystem would persist for quite some time. That is, ecosystems exhibit a *complexity-persistence principle*: the more complex the system, the longer it can persist without a connection to adjacent systems of comparable complexity.

The high degree of persistence in ecosystems is not found in far simpler systems. If a doctor were to separate a patient's heart from their lungs, each component would fail immediately, and the patient would perish. Further up the complexity ladder, if all human beings were kept in isolation from one another, the species would soon go extinct.

The complexity-persistence principle also explains why the performance of one state's economy does not have a noticeable influence on the economy of adjacent states (Tran, 2011). That is, the "economic identity" of a given state is more influenced by its unique SEI context than that of an adjacent economy. Businesses will come and go over time, but the economy persists, just as species are continually evolving and going extinct, but the ecosystem persists.

Even the loss of a keystone predator such as the grey wolf in Rocky Mountain National Park does not spell doom for the entire system. Due to the complexity of the system, it merely shifts its identity under such a loss. Meadows may become drier, causing a shift to more drought-tolerant plant species, or the dominant plants may be more resistant to elk grazing. The diversity and net primary productivity of the meadow may decline, but the system does not perish.

I proposed earlier that the structure and interactions of an ecosystem's foundational components—diversity, energy, and trade—are responsible for its high degrees of resilience, resistance, and productive capacity. I further posit that economies and ecosystems exist at the same level of organization: complex self-regulating systems comprised of multiple communities. As such, the structure and functions of economies and ecosystems are influenced by the same foundational components, continually responding to the direction and magnitude of external forces.

Recall that each ecosystem, such as the coastal redwood forest, is nested within a larger system, such as the coast range. The coast range is nested within the northwestern forested mountains, which is nested in higher order systems—on up to the biosphere. While higher order ecosystems can persist independently from one another, the health of each ecosystem depends on the health of its lower order systems, just as the health of the human body depends on the health of its organs.

Similarly, the health and function of an economy depends on the health of the economies comprising it. Neither the global market economy nor the biosphere can function well if their lower order systems are functioning poorly. Only, the current global capitalistic model maximizes resource and energy transfers across economic borders at the expense of the diversity, resilience, and productive capacity of its basic operational units—national economies. In large countries such as the US, the basic operational units are the state and regional economies, most of which suffer the same fate as the national economies in which they are nested.

Economies are Nested Within Ecosystems

The productive capacity of an economy is dependent on that of its social, environmental, and industrial context. That is, every basic economic unit (i.e., regional economy) is unique with regards to the quantity and skill of its labor, cultural norms, and industrial infrastructure, all of which affect its productivity. An economy's productivity is similarly dependent on the quantity and diversity of natural resources available, as well as environmental factors such as weather, soil, and elevation. Stemming from this reality, we cannot ignore the fact that economies are nested within the surrounding ecosystems, and not the other way around (Figure 15).

Given this nested relationship, the net primary production (NPP) of ecosystems influences the net domestic production and the productive capacity of the economies within. For instance, the high productivity of tropical rainforests, with their abundant heat and water, is far greater than that of the arctic tundra. Yet deserts are dramatically lower producers than tropical forests, even though they are hotter. Water, not energy, is the limiting factor in the Chihuahuan Desert, which is why banana plantations are a rare site there.

A limiting factor of net primary productivity in ecosystems is the innovative traits of its primary producers—plants. In a cyclical manner, the system's environmental context drives those innovations necessary to extract as much usable energy, and hence material resources, as possible from the system. For instance, deserts persist amidst one of earth's harshest environments, where cacti and yucca evolved a novel means of photosynthesis: crassulacean acid metabolism (CAM). CAM allows many desert plants to exchange oxygen and carbon dioxide during the night, when heat stress is lowest. From this one evolutionary trait, water loss is minimized, and the efficiency with which cacti convert water and carbon dioxide into usable energy is increased.

Ascending the desert food chain, kangaroo rats have developed kidneys with excessively long loops of Henle, features that reabsorb water before it is excreted back into the desert as waste. These rodents are so efficient at extracting water out of each nibble of food, they can survive the scorching desert without ever lapping water from a puddle.

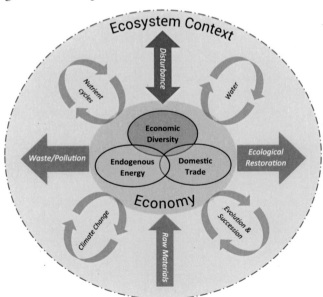

Figure 15. Economies are nested within ecosystems. Economies cannot consume more energy and resources than those ecosystems provide, without jeopardizing the ability of both systems to maintain their self-regulating qualities. Ecological restoration forms a balancing loop between economies and ecosystems, to maintain the productive capacity and resilience of each.

Defining the Basic Operational Unit of the Economy

Important questions remain. What should the shape and size of an economy's basic operational unit be, so that its productive capacity may be sustained without jeopardizing the ecosystems or social systems in which it is nested? In other words, how "local" should an economy be such that it can thrive upon the proper balance of diversity, energy, and trade? Is there some critical threshold of foreign trade that, if exceeded, jeopardizes the productive capacity of an economy, or impedes the primary goal, human fulfillment? Do ecosystems provide appropriate answers to such questions?

How Big is Too Big?

With respect to diversity, energy, and trade, collapsed empires do have at least one thing in common. They all exhibit similar expansionist architecture: concentrations of wealth and power via exogenous energy and other resource transfers far beyond their geopolitical centers. The resulting socio-economic system cannot be sustained amidst the constant threat of disturbances from within and without. A reduction in crop diversity and demise of regional soil resources put the Maya at high risk of drought. Oppression and famine in Rome led to revolt. The Incan Empire's ability to allocate resources to distant communities was undermined by political instability.

Long before the Incas and Romans, an expansive trade network of Bronze Age civilizations once flourished throughout eastern Europe, then collapsed in a historical blink of an eye. Drought had triggered famine and civil unrest, while frail trade ties quickly unraveled, draining the shallow prosperity. As historian Eric Cline of George Washington University reflected on the simultaneous collapse of Bronze Age civilizations (Cline, 2014), he surmised that the great kingdoms and empires of the era—Egyptians, Babylonians, Hittites, etc.—had undermined their self-reliance.

A "systems" answer to the repeated collapse of civilizations might be that high rates of exogenous energy and physical resource transfers (e.g., nutrients, raw materials, commercial goods, etc.) across economic borders causes abnormal concentrations of wealth, capital, natural resources, etc. into fewer hands. The transfer of resources *between* basic operational units—economic and political centers of various sizes—became greater than the transfer of resources *within* each operational unit. A critical threshold had been crossed.

In the process of capital accumulation, economic diversity declines—a lowered shield against a barrage of external forces. According to the structure and functions of ecosystems, the solution would be to restore our economy not as one homogenous global or national unit, but as a system of highly diverse regional economies, each responsible for producing and retaining the wealth and capital it creates.

To reiterate, the accumulation of capital itself is not the problem. Capital (i.e., biomass) accumulates naturally in all self-regulating systems. It is when resources (i.e., one form of capital) become concentrated into areas beyond their point of extraction that both economies—the one losing resources and the one where resources are being concentrated—become unstable. Furthermore, when capital concentrations result from maximizing a single foundational component, such as trade or energy, other system components and external forces must respond in ways that stimulate rather than moderate volatility. A rebalancing must occur.

From America's brief experiment with concentrating resources, by means of maximizing foreign trade and exogenous energy across multiple industries, volatility and collapse have dismantled regions larger than entire European countries. The 3,500-plus ghost towns across the US are a legacy of boom-bust cycles in mining, made possible by massive imports of coal, trees, food, finances, etc. from far outside the site of production and processing.

Abundant examples exist. High degrees of wood, food, financial, and other resource concentrations into remote subalpine mining centers such as Leadville, Colorado were driven by consumer demands far beyond the economic space where mineral extraction and processing occurred. In response, Leadville became—for a brief moment—one of the wealthiest cities in the world. The system collapsed soon after, its current population a fraction of what it once was. Similar boom-bust cycles ravaged the automobile industry (e.g., the seven-state Rust Belt). Repeated oil-and-gas booms and busts have occurred across the nation. The collapse of hundreds of grain mill and paper mill collapses in dozens of states across the US, and the impacts to those communities, are too easily forgotten. Or, such collapses go completely unnoticed by consumers in remote city centers; they may never question where the wheat for their baguette came from, or where the fiber for the bread bag originated.

Trade, Scale, and Instability in Colorado's Sugar Beet Industry

An unsung collapse in the US is that of its sugar beet plantations, which once employed tens of thousands of people along the Colorado Front Range. It was there, where nutrient poor soils and arid skies dominate rolling plains, that the tap-rooted sugar beet thrived. The sugar content of beets grown in the northern

Front Range was so high that locals dubbed the plant "White Gold," producing the highest income of any crop on the plains prior to WWI (Twitty, 2003).

Sugar beets were so productive that Colorado producers were competitive with cane sugar grown in the tropics. This attracted the attention of adventurous capitalists who could exploit the situation. As Twitty writes, Colorado's sugar industry "fell under control of a Sugar Trust, which quashed competition and formed an indomitable barrier to farmers seeking equitable returns for their efforts."

Sugar beets, fueled by growing global markets as much as profit-seeking trusts, sprang up in vast monocultures across the plains, only to suffer multiple epidemics, waves of tariffs, and trust-busting laws such as the Sherman Antitrust Act. Rampant boom-bust cycles were as unpredictable as the region's weather. Somehow, the Great Western Sugar Company maintained about fourteen factories in the South Platte Watershed. That is, until the Great Depression struck, igniting a federal battle between policies that would stimulate global free trade and those that would protect domestic industries from global free trade. Ultimately, DC promulgated a suite of measures, including price controls on each pound of sugar sold.

In the ensuing decades, the sugar beet industry faced a set of familiar forces—an era of great mechanization, facilitated by tremendous advances in transportation networks, refinements in farming technology, and cheap exogenous energy. The same forces that decimated farm diversity, paper mills, and auto manufacturers in the American heartland.

A wave of job losses rippled across the plains. The greatest technological advancements of the day could not save the sugar beet industry, now inept against the growing network of global sugar producers. US sugar producers continued to crumble even amidst America's monstrous post-World War II growth phase. Then came the rise of the Green Revolution. The last remaining sugar beet plant in Fort Collins closed its doors in 1960, as the nation witnessed the near extinction of an entire industry group—sugar beets. It was supplanted, in part, by a far thirstier crop—corn.

The collapse of the sugar beet industry is a poster-child for the interconnectedness of diversity, energy, and trade, and the malfunctioning of these components at the wrong scale. Domestically, demand for beet sugar became increasingly volatile as imported substitutes (e.g., cane sugar) became increasingly abundant. Agricultural diversity declined regionally. Turbulent weather patterns such as those responsible for the Dust Bowl devastated the low-diversity farmlands. Nationally, external forces (i.e., policy changes, technological advancements, investment capital, depressions, etc.) created additional volatility. Globally, forces such as cheap labor, competing species from different environmental contexts, and Cold War politics provided endless threats to the low-diversity landscape.

The instability of such a system is nearly guaranteed, and the ensuing social-economic-environmental degradation only hastened by exogenous energy and other resource transfers. Impacts include the dismantling of families, waves of business closures, homelessness, suicide, drug abuse, housing crashes, severe anxiety, and so on. Impacts that cannot be resolved until the foundational components of an economy are functioning correctly, and at the right scale.

The Free Economic Zone as a Basic Operational Unit

Before claiming something is "outside" an economy, its boundary must first be defined. If a clear picture of such an edge does not come to mind, that's because humans have been crossing equally fuzzy boundaries between ecosystems since our birth as a species. To further complicate matters, living systems exist at scales from the cell to the individual, the community to the ecosystem, and on up to the biosphere. Hence, it is difficult to know where the border exists between, say, a mixed grass prairie and a short-grass prairie, or between a lowland evergreen rainforest and a lower montane rainforest.

For those ecologists who are not stymied by blurry boundaries, they are free to delineate the borders of ecosystems—the biosphere's basic operational units, each of which exhibits a unique composition of species, precipitation patterns, net primary production, structural diversity, soil types, etc. Few resources are transferred across ecosystem borders. Each ecosystem must be fully operational as a unit, with ample levels of diversity and a high productive capacity, so as to maintain its self-regulating qualities—a stout shield in the face of external forces.

The Free Economic Zone

The basic operational unit of an economy is referred to herein as a free economic zone (FEZ). The structure and functioning of a free economic zone goes beyond the notion of, for instance, a manufacturing zone that receives special tax breaks. A free economic zone is capable of thriving independent from the global market economy, and is even distinct from the free economic zones of adjacent states. It is fully dependent on endogenous energy and other local resources, so as to engender the most diverse economic landscape possible within its SEI context. As such, the FEZ is tasked with sustaining the livelihoods of the communities within, reflecting their values and cultural norms while at the same time supporting those values. It is the economic space in which humans seek fulfillment, and where one's productive labor and ingenuity are essential to sustaining their community.

To clarify, a free economic zone is different from the concept of special economic zones, which have been used to support economic diversification (OECD/WTO, 2019) in developing countries, attract foreign investment, and alleviate large-scale unemployment. In some respects, the World Trade Organization and Organisation for Economic Co-operation and Development appear to be on the right track, by assisting developing countries in the creation of self-regulating economies. They embrace diversity as a key to economic growth, and support strategies such as transportation and communication corridors to facilitate a network of interconnected domestic economies.

However, the challenge with special economic zones has been their narrow focus on financial incentives (e.g., tax breaks, subsidies), expedited customs procedures, and other means of stimulating export sales rather than a highly functional domestic economy. As a result, special economic zones have a tendency to exploit a country's low-cost labor and limited natural resources, while perpetuating lax environmental protections (OECD/WTO, 2019).

To the contrary, a free economic zone is not structured around government interventions (e.g., tax breaks, subsidies, tariffs, etc.) that stimulate export-level production, but around an economy's endogenous energy, domestic trade, and economic diversity. While the exact boundary of any economy is best determined locally, one method is offered below: the watershed economy. To understand the rationale behind that method, some basic behavioral forces must be understood.

Long Supply Chains, Predictable Consumer Behaviors, and Natural Economic Boundaries

The natural size and shape of a free economic zone is influenced by predictable consumer behaviors in response to external forces. From the perspective of a free economic zone in, say, central Wisconsin, those external forces include shifts in federal policies and programs, a spike in Korean demand for steel or aluminum, the cost of wind power in Iowa, extreme weather in Nebraska, a thousand-foot-long container ship getting wedged in the Suez Canal, labor costs in Vietnam or Indonesia, thousands of striking dock workers on the west coast, the growth rate of trees in Venezuela, etc. The greater the distance between the point of production and consumption (i.e., the longer the supply chain), the greater the quantity of external forces acting on the costs of goods and services along the chain.

Uncertainty in the external forces acting on a supply chain creates *decision insecurity*, which stems from basic human psychology. The longer a supply chain, the more imperfect is the consumer's knowledge of production realities on the other end, or of the myriad disruptions that may occur along the way. The more imperfect is a consumer's knowledge, the greater their insecurity in making a purchase.

Imperfect knowledge also afflicts producers who cannot accurately predict the bottlenecks between multiple distributors and wholesalers of a desired product that must cross a patchwork of deserts, mountains, rivers, and oceans to reach the end consumer. More uncertainty weighs upon producers that rely on long supply chains of raw materials or component parts that are essential to, for instance, the oven or refrigerator they assemble. Yet more uncertainty strikes producers in the form of constantly-shifting consumer trends. Uncertainty among both producers and consumers results not only in financially inefficient processes, and in high material waste along supply chains, but in irrational consumer decisions. Decision insecurity during the COVID-19 pandemic led to rushes for pasta, toilet paper, ammunition, and other panic buying behaviors at the far end of very long supply chains.

The simple act of shortening supply chains between producers and consumers increases decision *certainty* at both ends, which fosters more efficient resource transfers throughout the supply chain, and leads to greater price stability. A free economic zone must be small enough that decision *security* remains high, and the fewest possible external forces impact the supply and cost of products and services within the FEZ.

Certainly, conditions such as decision insecurity and "short" supply chains are difficult to quantify, and vary according to the SEI context in question. Supply chains in a desert context may be longer than in a tropical context. Hence, a global rule does not exist for defining the size or shape of any FEZ. That said, the economic and ecological evidence provided earlier suggests that most free economic zones should be smaller than most nations, and even smaller than many large states or provinces.

The Watershed Economy

From the vantage point of the uncharted Colorado River, John Wesley Powell's 1869 exploration of the desert west returned with somber news for the young US government. The arid west was an unproductive landscape. As such, the

US should delineate states not based on geopolitical boundaries typical of the eastern US, but on watershed boundaries (Figure 16). The severe tribulations of Powell's expedition, and his descriptions of the untamed West, have been hailed in books such as *The Emerald Mile* (Fedarko, 2013) and *The Promise of the Grand Canyon: John Wesley Powell's Perilous Journey and His Vision for the American West* (Ross, 2018).

Powell's plea to define America's western states by watershed boundaries failed, but his vision remains. Coincidentally, Powell had envisioned California in about six separate states, similar to multiple California initiatives over the ensuing century. Despite the failure of those ballot initiatives, regional efforts such as the State of Jefferson and Cascadia remain strong.

Perhaps Powell's watershed vision may be more successfully applied not to the borders of states, but to the development of free economic zones within those states. A watershed is simply an area of land that gathers rain and snow-melt in a region, and channels it from ridgetops down into streams and rivers. Every square inch of land exists in a watershed. A few examples of watershed-defined economies could be the Upper Sacramento Economic Zone (CA), Upper Klamath Economic Zone (CA and OR), the Elkhorn River Economic Zone (NE), etc.

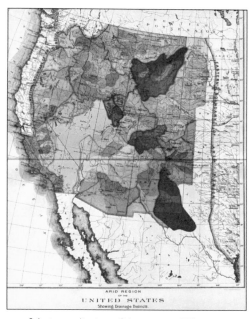

Figure 16. Powell's map of drainage districts of the western US, presented to the Senate in 1890. Credit: John Ross' Collection/Public domain.

In arid eastern Colorado, the South Platte watershed (Figure 17) exhibits a distinct SEI context with a multitude of bustling trade centers and budding economic diversity. This region is graced with ample river water, ore, timber, agricultural lands, and a thriving high-tech industry. The topography, geology, and climate of the South Platte Economic Zone provide the potential for a diverse energy economy, dominated by hydroelectric, biofuels, solar, and wind. Such a diverse energy economy could sustain abundant and diverse manufacturing industries, short-haul services, retail and professional services, high tech jobs, and more. The greatest distance between Denver—the financial capital of the South Platte Watershed—and any other town in the watershed, is about 150 miles. Most western states are in a similar situation as Colorado, with the potential to harbor several thriving economic zones, each comprised of multiple towns, counties, farming and extractive regions, and industrial centers.

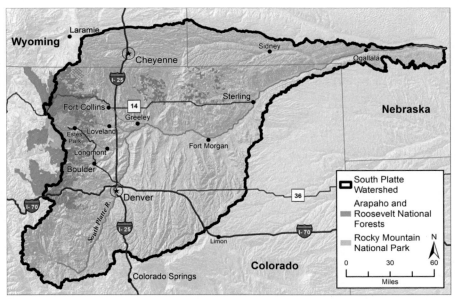

Figure 17. Potential South Platte Free Economic Zone, based on a 6th level Hydrologic Unit (USGS, 2020).

Delineating free economic zones by their watershed boundaries is different from the concept of Bioregionalism. Bioregionalism originated on America's West Coast by a group of environmentalists in the 1960s, as a means of protecting a regional ecosystem and its biotic components (Cato, 2017). Bioregions are flexible and ambiguous, and can include any landscape whose boundaries are determined by natural characteristics rather than human dictates (Sale, 2000). While bioregionalism may appear similar to a FEZ, bioregionalism lacks any consideration of the industrial context that is essential to a fully functioning economy.

Regardless the method a FEZ uses to define its boundary, every region is faced with a curious challenge. An aspiring entrepreneur who desires to, for instance, create a dairy operation to serve their local community, is faced with a harsh reality: Local consumers are currently networked into the global market economy. As long as local consumer decisions are tied to continual swings in global commodity prices, as well as the cheapest dairy products from around the globe, the entrepreneur's decision to build a local dairy business is fraught with uncertainty (i.e., risk). That uncertainty trickles up to investors, reflecting an immutable bond between the degree of decision certainty that exists in a business plan, and the amount of investment that business plan receives. That said, the "decision certainty-investment" process also operates in reverse. Consistent demand for local dairy products—in this example—generates greater certainty for the local entrepreneur, a condition that attracts investment.

Secession is Unnecessary
(Other means of establishing a free economic zone)

The boundary of any free economic zone is best refined according to the social, environmental, and industrial context in which it exists. Within the FEZ, resources must be focused on domestic—not global—trade, so that the production of goods can be more easily attained with endogenous energy sources, and peak diversity and NDP may be stimulated. Such actions do not require secession, altering state or county borders, or even unraveling the complexities of water law or other state and federal statutes. Rather, the geographic boundary of a FEZ could be established by simpler means, some of which are actually encouraged by the US Constitution and the Department of Commerce.

For those economic zones that span several counties within a state, or even multiple counties across state borders, the US Economic Development Administration (2019) has a formal process for developing economic development districts. The USEDA supports these districts with investments that generate sustainable job growth, while building strong and resilient regional economies. The Economic Development Administration recognizes the role diversity plays in attaining such resilience, but has yet to realize the role of endogenous energy and balanced trade in sustaining said diversity.

Should the communities of a free economic zone span several states, another legal tool is the *multi-jurisdictional economic compact*. The power of this tool draws on the compact clause of the US Constitution (Article I, Section 10, Clause 3), allowing states to enter into strategic compacts that facilitate cooperation, to the benefit of the public. One such example is the Colorado River Compact, which unifies the interests of California, New Mexico, Arizona, Colorado, Nevada, Utah, and Wyoming around one essential resource—water. So powerful is the Colorado River Compact that it has stood since 1922, enduring several depressions and recessions, the Dust Bowl, two world wars, etc.

If seven arid states can manage a century-long compact for something as contentious as water, certainly a handful of counties and cities can manage a multi-jurisdictional economic compact. In determining how large of a region an economic compact should encompass, it may be useful to ask how small would be too small.

How Small is Too Small?

An abundance of consumers know, intuitively, what economists have promoted for centuries: economies thrive when they embody multiple centers of production and trade. Regardless of a regional economy's SEI context, the rationale to incorporate multiple trading centers—cities, counties, industrial centers, agricultural regions, etc.—is supported by at least three economic principles.

First, larger bodies of trade (e.g., levels of automation necessary to meet the needs of an entire economy) are more financially efficient than smaller bodies of trade (e.g., artisan production). That is, large "bodies" can provide economies of scale necessary to more efficiently meet the needs of large populations and diverse consumer demands. This doesn't mean that artisan and non-artisan production cannot exist side by side. There are innumerable benefits of artisan production, the least of which is quality of products, ingenuity, and of course the fulfillment of the artisan.

Secondly, the more trade centers that exist in an economic space, the greater economic diversity can exist among them. But to be most effective, from a diversity standpoint, a high number of trade centers must not be stacked into a small economic space. When a network of trade centers exist across a broad geographic space (e.g., the entire South Platte watershed), rather than in a single local space (e.g., just Weld County, an agricultural production center in that same watershed), the total diversity of resources the economic zone can employ in production—labor, raw materials, energy, etc.—also increases.

For instance, twenty trade centers (e.g., a network of cities, counties, and industry groups) existing throughout the South Platte watershed is capable of generating more total economic diversity than could an economic zone comprised of three trade centers in one county. Ecologists observe the same pattern in nature. Resource diversity and environmental variability (i.e., heterogeneity) increase with landscape size, which drives species diversity (Huston, 1994).

Indeed, the variety of goods and services produced within an economy grows with its geographic extents—to a point. The further away the centers of production are from the points of consumption, the less control consumers have over the forces that impact the production and distribution of goods and services. That is, the risks to producers and consumers grow as the distance between trading centers increases.

Considering the relationships between trade, energy, and diversity in economies (and ecosystems), a nation built upon a diversity of free economic zones is more likely to sustain desirable social, economic, and environmental benefits than could one monolithic national economy bound to an inherently volatile global system. If this is true, how might society's knowledge of ecological restoration inform the process of economic restoration?

PART III

A Roadmap for Economic Restoration

EIGHT

EVOLUTION, SUCCESSION AND ECONOMIC RESTORATION

The prolific A.D. Bradshaw professed in 1987 that restoration is the acid test for our understanding of ecology. That is to say, in order to successfully restore an ecosystem, we must first know enough about its structure, and the functions of its parts. The aim of previous chapters was to outline that structure, and highlight key components and functions of ecosystems, so that we may better understand the process of economic restoration. But understanding is simply the first step. We must act, boldly, for it is only through attempts at economic restoration that the knowledge of our economy's structure, and the proper relationships among its parts, will be refined.

The underlying processes responsible for restoring a self-regulating economy—evolution and succession—have been illuminated by over a century of research (e.g., Bazzaz, 1979; Clements, 1936; Darwin, 1859; Cowles, 1899; Gleason, 1926; Grime, 1979; Odum, 1969; Tilman, 1985 and 1997; Weiner, 1994; Wilson, 1992). While ecological succession illuminates the critical role of disturbance in maintaining complex and productive systems, evolution plays an even more basic role. We need only apply this knowledge correctly, and at a regional scale, so that our economies may thrive in the face of continual global turbulence, rather than flail against its will.

Evolution's Role in Ecological & Economic Restoration

Evolution is the mechanism by which new species are formed, and is therefore a limiting factor in biological diversity. Importantly, evolution acts not upon the individual, but upon an entire population of individuals, and even on an entire community. That is, when an individual is graced by some genetically-derived advantage, such as black pigment, an opposable thumb, wings, fur, toxic skin,

163

or a crossed bill, its competitive edge remains meaningless unless that trait is transferred to its offspring.

Once an advantage is passed on to the next generation, the population has a chance to finetune the feature. When a sufficient number of generations passes, a new species is born. A species that, should it interbreed with a member of the unevolved population from which it sprang, could not produce viable offspring. Or, some hybrid would be formed, expressing traits of both parents. It is this slow steady march of evolution—not brute strength—that gave *Homo sapiens* a slight competitive edge over other hominids who tentatively stepped beyond the proverbial Garden of Eden to brave the sabertoothed landscape beyond. And from such risk came great reward.

Evolution, Niches, and Profit in Ecosystems

A vivid case of evolution is provided by Darwin's finches on the Galapagos Islands, nineteen volcanic specks of land lying 600 miles off the coast of Ecuador. This archipelago is where a single pair of black finches arrived long ago, blown off course by some distant storm and left to either die or evolve. Today, that original pair has split into seventeen new species, an evolutionary journey portrayed well by Jonathan Weiner in *The Beak of the Finch* (Weiner, 1994). On nearly every island, Darwin's finches exhibit a different set of features. Some use sticks as tools, to probe grubs from holes. Others have evolved excessively long and curved beaks, and the knowledge to utilize them in liberating energy-packed nectar from the deep recesses of similarly-shaped flowers. Yet others have developed mandibles like that of a grosbeak, large and powerful enough to crack the most durable island nut.

Convergent evolution has occurred among Darwin's finches, shaped by the environmental stressors of a remote desert landscape, requiring finches to develop traits of non-finches such as woodpeckers, grosbeaks, and honeycreepers, none of which exist there. And from ample geographic isolation, the gene pool of each evolved finch is protected well from genetic "pollution" by other finches.

Each island exists as a basic operational unit within the greater archipelago, its diversity growing with every new enterprising species that is profitable enough to expand its influence there. Yet as life continues evolving within the unique environmental context of each island, the system's boundaries remain permeable to the transfer of genetic knowledge from life beyond.

Darwin's finches are also the result of *geographic isolation*, a basic means of evolutionary pressure that arises when one population is physically separated from another. Evolution can also occur through the *reproductive isolation* of similar species occupying the same ecological space, such as the desert habitats of Isabela Island. Regardless of the evolutionary process, genetic variation within each population maintains genetic diversity within the entire species. Meanwhile, the processes of disturbance and succession are constantly at work within an ecosystem, applying necessary pressures on the evolutionary process, ensuring the most fit species are present at all times.

Evolution is also driven by the relentless interactions between predator, prey, and plant, which stimulate community-wide changes over time. This can begin with something as simple as the confusing pattern of black-n-white stripes created by a herd of Zebra racing across the Savanna. Or the profound advantage gained by those primates with opposable thumbs. The moment any species in an ecosystem evolves, seemingly insignificant shifts begin to unfold. The new species might fill a vacant niche, such as a stout-billed finch on an island with no woodpeckers. Competition between the woodpecker-like finch and other finches is minimized, or nonexistent. Alternatively, a new species of finch might evolve to more efficiently utilize a niche that is currently being used by other species. Competition is increased in this case, to the detriment of one or more species—at least in the short-term.

Cheetahs and leopards that hunt the same prey offer another example of competition within the same niche, top predators of various desert and tropical habitats. For instance, should a population of cheetah gain a competitive edge over a population of leopard in hunting a species of gazelle, the gazelle is pressured to evolve, as is the leopard. As it stands, leopards tend to hunt at night, and consume a wide range of prey. Cheetahs tend to hunt during the day, and tend to have a narrower diet. All the while, their ecosystem is continually responding to a great number of external forces, shaping the evolutionary pathway of all species within.

A truly earth-shattering example of evolution was the increase in pollinator habitats about 115 million years ago, during the rise of the angiosperms—earth's most colorful flowering plants. A complex set of evolutionary interactions unfolded as ecosystems across the globe became more brightly colored. Entirely new forms of coevolution arose, such as insect pollinators evolving together with insect-pollinated flowers. As the rampant creation, filling, and partitioning of niches spurred vicious feedback loops, novel forms of life emerged to enrich the ecosystems in which they exist. Edible fruits coevolved with fruit-eating birds and mammals, which distribute their seeds far from the fruitful tree. In response, system-wide changes provide evolutionary pressures for each species within.

As is the case between two species, competition between two businesses is never perfectly balanced. One business (or species) always gets a jump on the other in the greater competitive struggle of life. This competitive imbalance—the discovery of a new niche, or the enhanced ability to fulfill an existing one—is a driving force in the profitability of business. To the extent profit drives innovation, it can stimulate the evolution of entire industries, and eventually the evolution of an entire economy.

Should niches remain unfilled, species (businesses) would simply compete more fiercely with other species over existing niches, placing downward pressure on "profitability." Competition would therefore be more destructive than profitable. *Profit*, in this context, is a condition whereby the reserves of an individual or an entire community increase beyond the level needed to survive. In an ecosystem, profit is increased when a species—or a community of species—becomes more efficient at extracting resources from the system. For instance, the fat of an animal aids in its survival during lean times. While, throughout the growing season, plants store resources (e.g., starch), which may be drawn up to flower and set seed in the fall, or reserved for growth during drought years.

Economically speaking, increased profits are not only important to surviving lean years, but to support higher wages, invest in innovation and capital improvements, and building the wealth of a community. But the most enduring profiteer is not one who makes the most money on a single deal. It is the person whose ingenuity yields a product from the fewest resources, to a higher level of quality, or to fill a vacant niche, etc. Hence such capitalists bring greater value to the customer, industry, sector, and nation.

The Role of Knowledge and Technology in Economic Restoration

While the transfer of energy and other resources across borders puts downward pressure on diversity, the flow of information across borders is essential to maintaining highly functional systems. In ecosystems, information transfers occur in at least two forms: genetic transfers and shared knowledge. Genetic transfers between populations are so essential that severing those transfers can degrade a gene pool, such as the case with human inbreeding.

The survival of *Homo sapiens* and other species is also improved via *shared knowledge*. When a chimpanzee learns how to probe grubs out of a hole with a stick, that knowledge can be passed to its offspring, or to other populations, without requiring a transfer of genetic information. Shared knowledge can even be transferred across generations of chimps, or any other species, in a more nebulous fashion.

Hundreds of thousands of years have elapsed since humans first bent fire to our will, and I have found myself huddled around camps in the deep forests of the Rocky Mountains, pondering my warm attraction to the flames dancing above crackling logs. Might this sensation be a genetic imprint from our formative evolutionary days? Evolution is "conservative" in such regards, E.O. Wilson explains in *The Diversity of Life* (1992). That is to say, for a species to survive amidst a continuously uncertain future, it must conserve those physical and behavioral traits that ensured its survival in the past.

A species' complex set of behavioral traits has been described as its *epigenetic memory*. This includes a fear of snakes or spiders, our predilection for promontories, or our attraction to fire. At the level of an entire ecosystem, the collective epigenetic memory and knowledge base of thousands of species ensures the system's long-term survival—for one simple reason. Should a system fail to accumulate ample (and appropriate) knowledge to master its environment, it is doomed.

In any economy, ample exchange of useful knowledge across borders is essential to ensuring a highly functioning state in the face of continual disturbance. In *The Origin of Wealth: Evolution, Complexity, and the Radical Remaking of Economics* (Beinhocker, 2006), economic evolution transpires in three forms—physical technologies, social technologies, and business plans—with individual businesses serving as the enactors of economic evolution. External forces provide the selection pressure for businesses, who, in a self-regulating manner, devise strategies to maintain profitability in a constantly changing SEI context. In return, they may continue serving their consumers as efficiently as possible.

The global exchange of knowledge also flourishes by less obvious means such as tourism, which dates back to the Olympic Games in Greece, and earlier events, where tourists from around the globe were tantalized with a cornucopia of regional products. Similarly, the Italian Renaissance was a rich mingling of travelling artists and the leisure class, who would eventually return home with immense knowledge from distant cultures.

Prior to the Renaissance, the wild Champagne fairs of France were a "rendezvous for the whole of Europe," wrote Fernand Braudel (1984), creating a network of provincial markets from Champagne to Brie, where merchants from the Netherlands to Italy mingled for months. The exchange of goods amidst market stalls facilitated an exchange of human ingenuity and knowledge, inspiring traders to replicate that knowledge in their home economies. These regional fairs, coupled by a vast network of roads and rivers, were the precursor to the European world economy.

In light of the economic, social, and environmental challenges facing all countries, knowledge transfers via travel and trade may be more important today than any previous epoch of capitalism. Humanity must leverage its collective ingenuity across continents, toward those innovations necessary to ensure the long-term survival of the species. It is our genetic directive. We cannot fulfill that directive without protecting the ecosystems on which we rely.

Knowledge: A double-edged sword in economic restoration

There remains a barrier, however. One that is not surmounted by adding more information more quickly to our knowledge base. Adrift in today's over-information age, afflicted consumers are realizing that more information does not guarantee the transfer of knowledge. In fact, human behavior in the global market economy is being increasingly-manipulated by false information—the firehose of falsehood, fake news, the weaponization of social media platforms, etc.

All consumers succumb at times to invasive marketing campaigns, some of them so insidious to be dubbed *joy marketing*. The 2003 MacDonald's "I'm Lovin' It" commercial is but one example, where millions of unsuspecting burger lovers across the globe where firehosed with the pop vocals of Justin Timberlake in a single day. A decade later, marketing turned sinister, as in the case of Russia's "firehose of falsehood" strategy to annex Crimea, including a crushing mass of well-crafted—but reportedly false—broadcasts aimed at the electorate. Similar tactics have become commonplace in US elections, including those which lead to the deadly attack on the nation's capital in 2021. And pinpointing the culprit is becoming increasingly difficult.

Joy marketing and fake news is effective because, overwhelmingly, human beings often make decisions based not on logic, but emotion. This emotion includes the sensation derived by spreading alarming information, regardless if it's true. This helps to explain why fake news spreads faster than true stories on social media sites (Dizikes, 2018; Vosoughi et al., 2018). Specifically, the Dizikes study found that false news stories are seventy percent more likely to be shared on social media sites than true stories. False news is crated to be more alarming, stoking our emotions to the point that we cannot bottle them up inside. We must share it. Meanwhile, the true news remains obscured.

When emotion leads to the purchase of a taco, beer, or a cat, that's one thing. The moment human emotions, and the marketing campaigns that arouse them, undermine a nation's ability to wield knowledge to the benefit of humanity's long-term survival, a line has been crossed.

Modern media does have a bright side. Social media networks and the organization of online information can more easily connect consumers and producers working to restore their local and regional economies. Likewise, the ever-growing global knowledge base (e.g., energy-efficient machinery, biomimicry-based architectural designs, etc.) is more readily transferred across country borders today than in any previous generation.

Technology: A double-edged sword in economic restoration

The sharing of information and knowledge leads to innovation, which is essential to technological progress. Modern technology provides the means to more efficiently reap energy from dozens of renewable sources, reducing the need to burn trees or oil to power homes and businesses. At the same time, airplanes and highway systems provide a means to consume vast quantities of fossil fuel to ship food thousands of miles to communities whose own farmers are struggling to make ends meet. And what is progress worth, if our most important needs go unmet?

Alongside America's constantly-rising technological progress, citizens are experiencing historic levels of physiological stress, drug addiction, homelessness, chronic hypertension, and increasing rates of suicide, while an increasing mass of citizens are suffering from a litany of physical health issues. This progress has climbed right alongside America's GDP, while the life expectancy of Americans has actually dropped (Center for Disease Control and Prevention, 2017; Medina et al., 2020; Schwandt et al., 2021). That is, regardless—or due to—America's great technological progress and ever-climbing GDP, there has been a decrease in life expectancy and human fulfillment.

Misguided, technology is not the answer to our continued prosperity. For technology to serve as a useful tool in economic restoration, it must be capable of meeting the needs of a diverse citizenry, while protecting the social and environmental assets our economies require for survival.

The Pressure Cooker for Economic Evolution

Elected officials in DC, or any other nation, cannot create a shiny new sustainable economy overnight. Attempting to do so would violate everything we know of the structure, functions, and evolution of complex self-regulating systems. Rather, evolution unfolds over time in multiple directions to inject meaningful changes throughout an economy.

Evolution trickles up from the level of the business, into industry groups such as automobile manufacturing, dairy farming, renewable energy, etc. Evolution within industry groups then influences entire industries, such as transportation, agriculture, and energy. For example, the evolution of the regenerative agriculture movement is transpiring in many nations right now. This evolution, to be described later, began with entrepreneurial farmers and is now trickling up and spiderwebbing through an entire industry. And some critical drivers of that evolution, such as increasing energy and water costs, are becoming more intense.

As the greater agricultural industry evolves, additional pressure is applied at lower levels, such as the wheat industry group, safflower, free range chickens, hogs, grass finished beef, etc. This is *coevolution* at work: the mutual influence closely-related businesses or industry groups have on one another, to the benefit of both. In response, every new innovation within a given industry group puts competitive pressure on businesses within its industrial realm. This helps explain why General Mills is in early discussions with regenerative farmers to determine how best to deliver their customers with the nutrient dense foods yielded from organic-rich farmlands. For the message over the millennia has remained clear: evolve or die.

The energy industry is experiencing a similar evolutionary dynamism. New niches have been continuously filled and created over the past two decades as shifts in, for example, clean coal occur alongside the refinement and expansion of technologies such as high-efficiency wind farms, concentrating photovoltaic panels, electric vehicles, and heat-to-power technology. Evolution is occurring not simply via innovative products, but in the storage and distribution of endogenous energy sources. Rather quickly, the entire energy industry is evolving.

As with evolution of species within ecosystems, the transfer of favorable traits across business and economic boundaries is a basic means of economic evolution. And those economies that accumulate the most favorable traits are more likely to thrive in a future of increasing turmoil. But what drives this process?

The theory of *punctuated equilibrium* posits that the evolution of a species—even a group of species—occurs quickly, rather than gradually over time (Eldredge & Gould, 1972). This theory is widely supported by ecologists across the globe, who are discovering that environmental stressors are a primary driver for many "punctuated" evolutionary events (Hoffmann & Hercus, 2020). That is, environmental disturbances and stressors provide the *pressure* for evolutionary change, by favoring novel behavioral or physical traits that can coalesce into an entirely new species. A recent example is the resistance to herbicides that many species of weeds develop. To survive amidst an abrupt appearance of new stressors in the environment (e.g., chemical toxins), the population must evolve quickly. At a higher level of complexity, as North America travelled thousands of miles northward over the past 300 million years, its ecosystems shifted dramatically: from tropical to temperate. Monkeys were replaced by mastodons. Figs by firs. Orchids moved from the canopy to the ground.

Similarly, processes of disturbance and evolution have affected every national economy throughout history, demanding dramatic shifts in their structure and functions. While the 20th century has been relatively stable, the 21st century is expected to be rocked by significant stressors—volatility, uncertainty, anxiety, pressure—in the social, environmental, and industrial contexts of economies across the globe. Ample stress has already unleashed itself in the first quarter of this century, with supply chain disruptions in multiple industries, swings in wage structures in dozens of economies, tremendous shifts in the energy industry, a broad-scale re-examination of global market capitalism, etc. If Greenspan is correct, we can expect more "punctuated" economic events in the coming decades; a period of great economic turbulence that will favor new economic structures; not the industrial dinosaurs of the past.

The turbulence cannot be constrained, for it is essential to rebalancing an economy that has wandered off course. However, the impacts of such volatility might be greatly moderated, as evidenced by the work of restoration ecologists. And ecological succession is an essential guide to the restoration process.

Succession: An essential guide for economic restoration

To refresh, succession is the process of rebuilding structural and biological diversity, while rebuilding the *net* primary production of an ecosystem following disturbance. A bitter-sweet example of such disturbance is wildfires, which have grown all too familiar in communities across the Western US. At the most catastrophic level, wildfires scorch every tree in the forest, destroying innumerable niches while stripping soils of their fertility (Figure 18). Charred upright tree trunks tower above ash-covered earth, and the telltale crunching of charcoal beetles echo through a once green canopy. The forest icons most humans connect with—the trees—have vanished.

Figure 18. Scorched forest and charred elk in the East Troublesome Fire, which threatened water supplies for the Colorado-Big Thompson Project.

The successional clock begins the moment the flames are out. Informative to economic restoration, the large trees that existed prior to the fire are typically not the first plants to return to the scorched hillsides. Instead, fast-growing grasses and wildflowers—pioneer species—generate the bulk of the productivity in the early years following a wildfire. Pioneer plants have traits allowing them to take full advantage of the resources often liberated by a disturbance: light, water, nitrogen, etc. The below-ground buds of shrubs, protected while the fire raged above, may resprout next.

As the recovering community accumulates biomass, there is a trickle-up effect. The liberated resources are transferred to herbivore populations, followed by a spike in predators, etc. These animals deposit propagules from some green landscape beyond. All the while, a diversity of fungi, bacteria, and other biota blossoms in the soil. Slowly, trees take root in the charred landscape as the web of life becomes increasingly interlaced and tightened.

Mismanaging Succession for Low Productivity and Low Diversity

Disturbance is essential to creating new opportunities for businesses or species in economies and ecosystems, including access to resources that were unavailable prior to the disturbance. In a dense old-growth forest, or an overbuilt and homogenized industry, the majority of resources are largely unavailable to a greater diversity of faster growing species (or businesses), remaining "locked up" in the system. Counter to intuition, disturbances like a fire or hurricane (or supply chain disruption, sudden technological shift, recession) are necessary to remove the system's most dominant individuals, so that the entrapped resources may be liberated.

Staring down at the land from a helicopter's cockpit, we see a great patchwork of communities thriving across a forested region, each in a different stage of recovery from some past fire. Innumerable shades, shapes, and textures of greenery; all of it appealing to the eye. This patchwork, a matrix of successional stages, creates landscape level diversity, is as important to maintaining a resilient and productive ecosystem as it is to an economy. It may not be intuitive, but seemingly beneficial economic programs (e.g., government subsidies, bailouts, loan programs, etc.) tend to homogenize our economic landscapes, not diversify them. The result is akin to a forest that has not experienced fire or some other disturbance for far too long—one homogeneous block of greenery, awaiting a spark.

Recall that diversity and productivity are not constant throughout the successional process. Ecosystems tend to experience peaks in net primary productivity and diversity not in the late or early stages of succession, but in the middle stages. Here lies another discord between economies and ecosystems.

Economies such as the US, which have grown overly dependent on the global market economy, tend to experience the highest levels of productivity (i.e., in terms of GDP and market performance) not in the intermediate stages of succession, but just before a major disturbance such as a depression or crash. The roaring '20s predated the 1930s Great Depression; the booming '90s predated the 2002 dot-com crash; the record-breaking markets of the late twenty-teens predated the COVID-19 crash. Long before, the booming economy of the 1870s predated the global market recession—the Long Depression—of the 1880s and '90s.

America's high gross domestic productivity is accompanied by relatively low diversity, so lacks a natural buffer against disturbance. Using *net* domestic production as a measure of economic health, the US would soon discover it was not performing so well. To complicate matters, government interferences in response to economic disturbance—subsidies or bailouts of large industry—tend to not only slow the recovery, but jeopardize long-term growth.

Regardless of the mechanism, economies that accumulate capital at the expense of diversity are in essence pushing the system toward the "climax" end of the successional scale; to the right side of the successional graph. Signs of a climax economy are evident in America's ever-declining rate of per capita GDP, flat to declining real wages, the concentration of wealth in the fewest hands, and declining returns on investment in innovation.

Here's where it gets confusing. In some regards the US economy also appears stuck in the early stages of succession, with increasing frequencies of economic disturbance resulting in low diversity and low NDP. Early-successional ecosystems tend to have a lower capacity to harness and transfer resources than do mid- successional ecosystems (Crews, 2004; Odum, 1969). The early-successional economy cannot produce goods or services as efficiently as a mid-successional economy.

Several reasons may explain this apparent schism in the successional tendencies of the US economy. A barrage of government interference is continually reinforcing late-successional conditions. Policies and programs that stimulate foreign trade and exogenous energy transfers are creating more severe and frequent volatility than would otherwise be expected, a condition of early-successional systems. On both ends of the successional spectrum, economic diversity is low, due to exogenous resource transfers. Meanwhile, the global market economy concentrates the system's capital and wealth into the hands of fewer individuals—a late-successional condition.

Amidst this clash of successional tendencies, the global market economy, and those economies wedded to it, struggles to function as a monolithic top-down economy. The closest example in nature is a monoculture farm, which relies on continual exogenous inputs and maintenance to maintain its structure, and is thus not a self-regulating system. There, productivity is artificial.

America's Schism in Economic Succession

When volatility does strike, the policy playbook is to plow more subsidies and investments back into the existing system. Two recent cases of such policy come from the State of Wisconsin. One resulted in the investment of capital into a foreign business. The other proposed a bailout to an economically out-of-place papermill.

In the first case, Wisconsin senators pledged to provide US $4.8 billion in subsidies to the Taiwanese company FoxConn, who would then establish a technology center and flat-screen TV manufacturing facility in Wisconsin. Based on the number of jobs to be created, the agreement would cost Wisconsin taxpayers about $240,000 per job, whether or not those jobs could be sustained in the face of globally destructive competition. Regardless, the project received praise and support from the Trump administration, and represented the largest subsidy to a foreign firm in US history. To sweeten the deal, the federal government backed Governor Walker's efforts to slacken pollution regulations as they rolled out the red carpet for FoxConn.

Regardless if FoxConn ever meets its subsidy requirements, the Wisconsin economy would need to be thriving in order for its citizens to afford high-priced flat-screen TVs. This example leads to case number two, with a deeper history. For decades prior to FoxConn, the papermills of Wisconsin have been in serious decline. They have struggled to provide good-paying jobs to thousands of workers in the face of destructive competition from producers operating in radically different SEI contexts across the globe. Fast growing trees, low labor costs, and cheaper land in South American mills are examples of such competitive pressures.

In July of 2020, Missy Hughes, CEO of the Wisconsin Economic Development Corporation, explained to me how Wisconsin was considering subsidies to keep mills such as Verso Corp from going under. There is no doubt that every one of Verso's nine hundred jobs is critical to the communities where it operates. The political pressure for action is intense. However, the medicine of choice—subsidies and bailouts—are likely to jeopardize long-term job growth, productivity, profitability, and wages. Alternatives for WI papermills will be proposed in a later chapter, aimed at sustaining Wisconsin's productive capacity and jobs without demanding millions in subsidies. Based on the nature of self-regulating systems, these solutions not only aid in restoring an economy's productive capacity, but may provide a natural buffer against volatility.

Mismanaging Succession for Economic Instability and Volatility

Amidst America's successional aberrations, we have likely exceeded a threshold of capital accumulation. A threshold that, when crossed, further jeopardizes

NDP, wage growth, employment, resilience, and other intrinsic benefits of a self-regulating economy.

The evidence from ecosystems indicates that the overaccumulation of capital in a late-successional economic stage is a highly unstable condition with a higher probability of severe disturbances, while an early-successional stage is a more volatile state with a higher probability of minor disturbances. In short, America has built a monstrous house atop an unstable foundation. But the US did not stop there. It created an economic space around that foundation that grows only shakier over time.

Should the lessons from ecological succession be inadequate to inspire change, even conservative economists such as Milton Friedman have argued that government actions such as corporate subsidies and bailouts, which ensure the survival of large-scale businesses, are more likely to increase (not alleviate) the risks of economic instability. At the opposite end of the political spectrum, Joseph Stiglitz argues that the concentration of wealth—a condition of late-successional stages—depresses a nation's productivity.

Friedman and Stiglitz, despite political differences, might have both agreed with the following basic economic feedback loop. The higher the degree of financial transfers into an economy (e.g., investments into export-based production systems, exogenous energy projects, bailouts, subsidies, etc.), the greater the quantity of material transfers into and out of an economy. In turn, the system trends toward low diversity, as large homogenous scales of production are required to meet the demands of an export-based system. That same system monopolizes finite resources such as usable energy, physical resources, and investments that would otherwise be available to a diversity of smaller firms within that economic space.

From such homogenization, the system trends toward unstable and under employment, flat to decreasing real wages, lower profitability and growth, and ever-lengthening supply chains. These conditions represent a fundamentally unstable system, with low resistance and resilience to disturbance. Chronic stress and anxiety come to define life, contributing further to social unrest. A threshold is crossed whereby greater capital must be allocated to maintenance rather than growth. In response to, or even in the process of homogenization, NDP will decline.

Countless government actions, likely out of ignorance, are actually managing the successional stages of the US economy, only in a direction that is unproductive, toward the extreme ends of the spectrum rather than in the productive, diverse, and dynamically stable center. The silver lining is that government actions can guide economic succession, just as restoration practitioners guide ecological succession.

Managing Succession for Peak Diversity and Net Domestic Productivity

In designing a restoration project, ecologists use the process of succession to their advantage. Knowing that the mid-successional stages exhibit peak diversity and productivity, restoration treatments are designed to move the system to the center. By contrast, actions such as wildfire suppression push the successional stage far to the right, causing an abnormal accumulation of old trees at the expense of diversity and productivity. If there is a benefit to this strategy at all, it is only in the short term. Eventually a fire, disease, pine beetle epidemic, or other disturbances will escape the clutches of human control. And due to the abnormal concentration of biomass (i.e., trunks, twigs, and needles) existing at such a large scale, the results are catastrophic. Fire comes to consume the extreme mass of capital, and the successional clock is reset far back to the left side of the succession scale.

If government actions can push economic succession to the far right or left, strategic actions can also move it toward the middle (Figure 19). Based on the evidence from economics and ecology, such actions are likely to stimulate innovation, productivity, diversity, resource-use efficiency, stable employment, profitability, wage growth, and similar benefits. These intermediate stages of economic succession are where high degrees of *creative destruction* may be unleashed, along with surges in innovation and growth, as outdated business structures and processes are replaced by new structures and process (Schumpeter, 1950).

In the footsteps of Joseph Schumpeter, many economists today argue that creative destruction leads to efficiencies, while destroying old wealth and creating new wealth. In this light, actions that push the economic succession stage to the right stymie the process of creative destruction. In this late-successional stage, a threshold of capital accumulation can be exceeded, creating a higher degree of *destructive* competition among businesses as they struggle for fewer and fewer available resources. Beyond the threshold, NDP and diversity continually decline.

Succession, though, does not exist in a bubble, and scale matters. Economic succession must be managed not at the national or global level, but at the basic operational unit of an economy: the regional economy. It is in a regional economy, such as a free economic zone, where capital may be redirected away from ever-larger scales of production for the global market, and toward the restoration of a diverse domestic economy, structured to produce and recirculate wealth and resources locally.

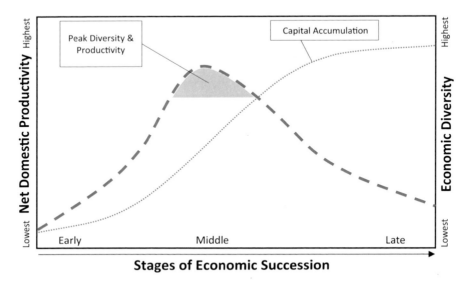

Figure 19. Threshold of economical succession and capital accumulation. A threshold of capital accumulation is crossed in the late stages of succession. Diversity and net domestic productivity decline with continued increases in capital accumulation, and vulnerability to external forces rises.

Establishing Thresholds of Regional, National, and Foreign Trade

The precise threshold of capital accumulation—beyond which the system's very capital becomes threatened, and volatility is exacerbated—will vary according to an economy's context. For instance, additions of water will have a more pronounced effect on productivity and diversity in a desert than in a tropical forest. Likewise, increased investment into technological progress (and hence productivity) yields diminishing returns in developed countries such as America, while they produce higher returns in less developed countries (Romer, 1994).

Defining the exact threshold of capital accumulation or resource transfers is further complicated by the fact that, over time, the system is continually evolving. Thresholds, should they be known, are continually moving. But we know what the trend must be. Based on the rules of complex self-regulating ecosystems, closer to 100% of an economy's capital, wealth, and resources must remain local. Closer to 100% of an economy's consumed goods must be produced within its economic boundary, not transferred there from beyond. And to the extent such a condition sustains a nation's productive capacity, that nation's seat around the table of global economic power may be secured.

The most efficient economies are structured as self-regulating systems, with capitalism as the primary driver of their efficiency. However, the role of government is to establish the rules and regulations necessary for its economy to function well—the rules of the game (Friedman, 1982). Exactly *how* government sets those rules and regulations is critical to an economy's success. Russia, for instance, suffered a critical fumble in its attempts at a free-market capitalist economy, for it ignored important legal and banking rules and regulations necessary to stymie corruption. While China is succeeding wildly in its global capitalist endeavors, despite its communist tendencies, but has done so at the expense of its productive capacity. Their tremendous GDP growth is also artificial.

China and America—and other nations, of course—have set policies to maximize global trade at the expense of their productive capacity, NDP, and the diversity of several important sectors, industries, and industry groups. Both countries have degraded their social and environmental conditions domestically, while producing similar impacts abroad via externalities. Importantly, the US, China, the European Union, and others have set an obvious precedent: trade can be managed.

Countries as expansive and resource-rich as America, China, Brazil, Argentina, etc., can promulgate policies to stimulate abundant trade at regional, state, and national levels. Trade policy is just one means. Another means is vis-à-vis the establishment of trade thresholds at local, state, and federal levels. In closer approximation to the resource transfer rules of ecosystems, these thresholds of trade are proposed:

- *Within a free economic zone*: A minimum of 70% of the goods and services consumed are produced within its economic space.

- *Within a state*: A minimum of 80% of the goods and services consumed are produced within the state's economic space.

- *The American economy*: A minimum of 90% of the goods and services consumed are produced within the national economic space. A maximum of ten percent of GDP is generated by global exports.

Capitalism, operating fully and freely within a national system of free economic zones, is essential to attaining the most efficient means of production and distribution within a country's regional, state, and national economies. In smaller countries, with far fewer resources than the US, similar thresholds may be established, though the basic operational unit may be an entire country, or a group of small countries with a similar SEI context. The European Union is one obvious example, as is the ten-member Association of Southeast Asian Nations. Of course, the EU and ASEAN economies have yet to set thresholds of foreign trade, as current policies are geared toward stimulating exports for the global market.

Trade thresholds must be accompanied by other actions, in order to reap the intrinsic benefits a self-regulating economy provides. Restoration actions must be focused toward those sectors and industries responsible for rebuild an economy's productive capacity (i.e., a nation's productive labor), such as agriculture, waste-to-resources, timber, renewable energy, manufacturing, etc. In the US and elsewhere, one industry in particular has already jumped on the restoration track—it merely needs some structural support.

NINE

RESTORING THE FOUNDATIONS OF AMERICA'S DOMESTIC ECONOMY: AGRICULTURE

An ecosystem is not restored the moment tried-and-true restoration treatments are applied. The dense green forest does not immediately return after seeding, nor does a broken bone heal the moment it is put in a cast. The doctor prescribes treatments, but the body does the healing. The restoration of any self-regulating system is a process, and the more complex a system is, the more important is the passage of time in producing the desired results.

In ecosystems, the restoration process begins with building the system's capacity to capture energy and nutrients, which increases with the diversity of vegetation. One might assume a schism exists, then, between ecosystems and economies with respect to restoration. While terrestrial ecosystems acquire nearly 100% of their usable energy from photosynthesis, trying to restore our economy by growing more plants would surely fail to meet the demands of an advanced economy like America. Right?

While pondering this, recall that the productive capacity of an economy relies on the enduring success of its domestic economy, which hinges on its productive labor. The industries responsible for maintaining that productive labor include agriculture, manufacturing, energy, waste-to-resources, and others. An economy's service industries (e.g., retail, entertainment, government, military, etc.) cannot be sustained for any meaningful length of time, except on the shoulders of an economy's productive industries.

Patterned after ecosystems, agriculture restoration is prioritized here as an initial step in the process of economic restoration. And we need not rely on the evidence of ecosystems alone to justify this. To claw their way out of chronic poverty, China prioritized the restoration of its agricultural industry as a first step in creating a market economy in the 1980s. In China's case, agricultural restoration meant privatization (Stiglitz, 2002), which led to increases in productivity, among other changes. By 2020, agriculture accounted for about 10% of China's GDP, which has grown faster than almost any other market economy.

Certainly, America's agricultural industry has enjoyed unprecedented high yields since the Green Revolution (i.e., high gross productivity), due to high inputs of fertilizer, water, and energy. However, gross productivity gains have occurred at the expense of America's natural soil fertility, thus decreasing the *net* productivity of farmlands from the Scott Valley of California to the Elkhorn Valley of Nebraska. Considering the estimated US $1.1 trillion cost of restoring fertility to the Corn Belt, which comprises less than a quarter of America's croplands, restoring the entire agricultural landscape of the US could run well over US $3 trillion. This is just the cost to incorporate compost into the soil, which may not even be feasible at the scale required.

Fortunately, more cost-effective means exist to restore America's agricultural landscapes, many of which can produce (not consume) taxes and resources along the way. But before discussing the restoration of America's agricultural industry, it may be informative to ask what exactly caused the death of Oakdale.

What Caused the Death of Oakdale?

Oakdale was the first town in the wooded hills and rich valleys of Antelope County, Nebraska, and for a brief yet prideful moment it was the county's political seat. Sadly, Oakdale was also the first town in the county to suffer a slow and certain economic death.

When you ask around town, or in neighboring Neligh—which "stole" the county seat from Oakdale—many will say it was the loss of the railroad that blew Oakdale its final kiss goodbye. Others believe it was the day the highway was built nearby, which shuttled the youth out of town faster than it could deliver them new opportunities. From personal observation, and through the lens of self-regulating ecosystems, here is what I have come to believe.

As the scale of agribusiness increased between 1940 and 1970, business diversity in Oakdale plummeted commensurately—if not logarithmically. The youth packed their bags, full of hopes and dreams better realized in a more diverse economy. And who's to blame them. When the landscape engulfing you for hundreds of miles in every direction is dominated by corn or corn-related business, your socio-economic prospects are duly squashed. If I were young in Oakdale, and the only industry staring me down was full of yellow kernels, I too would have fled. What's more, trombone players are no longer sought there, for the community band has long since perished (Figure 20).

I cannot help but feel deep sorrow for Oakdale and those left struggling to survive. Nestled among the embrace of oak-covered hills, a few creeks ripple through on their way to the Elkhorn River. Such a splendid setting cannot be manufactured. Why is Oakdale dying rather than thriving in America?

I believe the fatal blow was more of a slowly moving guillotine. Its blade was released the moment the town's collective drive became focused on an export-based economy—a vision sold to them as America grabbed the torch of global capitalist power from Britain. A better railway system. A larger mill. More consolidated and higher-yielding farms. Those aspirations were fueled by the growth of highway and interstate systems, the billowing farm subsidy program, and then the Green Revolution—an outgrowth of the post-war boom. It was capitalism on steroids.

Figure 20. Community band of Oakdale, Nebraska. Photo by John Giordanengo, of an original provided by the Antelope County Museum.

Slowly, wealth became concentrated in the next largest business. Then in the next largest town, Neligh, and then in Norfolk, and finally in the hands of Berkshire-Hathaway of Omaha, Nebraska, where investment moguls like Warren Buffett accumulate their wealth predominantly from the foreign and carrying trades—as far away from Oakdale as one can imagine.

Other external forces spelled Oakdale's doom, such as the cheap fossil fuels that made the Green Revolution and long-distance transportation possible. Some forces revealed themselves more insidiously, such as the redesign of locomotives. The moment engines could run on diesel rather than coal, maintenance needs plummeted. In turn, the pre-WWI national network of roundhouses—hubs for engine maintenance—became obsolete. And the roundhouse Oakdale so desperately fought for in the early 1900s succumbed to the blissful evolution of the energy industry.

Cumulative technological changes fueled ever-increasing scales of production, including grain milling operations. Oakdale operated the first flour mill in Antelope County, until Neligh developed a larger mill on the Elkhorn River. Both mills thrived from domestic demand alone, and were a financial boon to the region. That is, until long-haul trucking costs began declining at the end of WWII, making it cheaper to ship food across the nation and to distant ports (Ganzel, 2021).

After the war, food exports from the US climbed almost exponentially as lower-income nations replaced traditional staples like rice and potatoes with imported wheat-based products like bread (Ganzel, 2021). And farmers who once relied on the Oakdale and Neligh mills began shipping their grain as far away as Minneapolis, the home of General Mills. The Oakdale mill closed its doors permanently in the 1940s. The Neligh mill went extinct in 1950, and with it went the value-added revenue for local farmers. The diversity of the Oakdale and Neligh economies slid another step backward.

The next assault on Oakdale was delivered by the Green Revolution, fueled in part by cheap fossil fuels. For perspective, the cost of fossil fuel energy in the 1950s and 60s was US $1.81 per million BTUs, drastically lower than the US $5.50 per million BTUs in 2012 (Energy Information Administration, 2012, in real dollars). Petroleum-infused farms grew in size, and farm diversity took another astonishing hit. By the time the Green Revolution's vision was fully realized, five million American farms had vanished from the face of the economy.

To clarify, subsidies and bailouts of large agricultural corporations were complicit in killing Oakdale. Such resource transfers maintain artificially high production levels for targeted export industries, placing downward pressure on the value of equivalent farm products domestically. In effect, subsidies impede constructive competition, which would otherwise yield comparative advantages for farmers, via more efficient uses of energy, labor, water, and other resources. Instead, profitability, employment stability, wage growth, and economic stability are thwarted by the current system. Today, Oakdale is, for all intents and purposes, dead.

Colossal change is needed, lest the US agricultural industry and the towns that rely on its success suffer Oakdale's fate. Should the next revolution to strike America's heartland be of a different breed—one of domestic trade, farm diversification, and energy-neutral production—few, if any, global market forces will shake the pride of the brightest and hardest working people I have ever met, Nebraskans. Only, it will not be government bailouts and exogenous energy that restore Oakdale, as such efforts have already inflicted more harm than good. It will be the entrepreneurs of the land and the factory that restore their communities, and in the process restore an economy in which all of America can take pride.

Regenerative Agriculture and Its Allies

Gabe Brown, a straight-talking farmer from Bismarck, North Dakota is one such entrepreneur. In Gabe's talk, "Regenerative Agriculture: Details of a Profitable Journey," he reveals some emerging realities about *regenerative agriculture*. Through a strategy of increasing plant diversity, Gabe has vastly reduced inputs and maximized profits (Brown, 2020). Such a strategy is closely linked to the management of endogenous energy. The more diverse Gabe's farm is, the greater the total surface area of leaves—the solar panels of the plant world. With greater leaf area facing the sun, more energy can be captured. On the consumption side of the energy equation, Gabe's farm vastly reduces the need for tillage and irrigation, which decreases energy demands. From a strategy of diversity, he has become more profitable.

Gabe is not the first farmer to master the strategy. Farming methods that diversify landscapes and build soils are ancient. Modern farmers simply use different terms, such as regenerative agriculture, which is one means of sustainable farming (i.e., sustainable agriculture). In the comprehensive article, "Agricultural sustainability: concepts, principles and evidence," Jules Pretty (2008) uses the term *sustainable farming* to describe practices that make the best use of environmental goods and services without damaging those assets.

Other allies of sustainable agriculture include biodynamic, community based, eco-agriculture, agroecological, farm fresh, free range, low input, permaculture, etc. This diverse terminology reflects the myriad contexts in which agriculture exists. The term *regenerative agriculture* is more specific, requiring that plant diversity increases, and that soil health is rebuilt on farmlands.

Regardless of the terminology, methods such as regenerative agriculture are needed for one simple reason. Modern high-yield agriculture (i.e., conventional farming) has left in its wake vast regions of degraded soil. Modern agriculture's assault on soil fertility has been thoroughly outlined in the work of Pimentel et al. (1995), Ontl and Schulte (2012), Capra and Luisi (2016), Montgomery (2012), volumes of research conducted by the US Department of Agriculture (nrcs.usda.gov), and others. High-yield monocultures require annual tilling, which is the primary culprit of soil infertility. Soil fertility is built upon tiny fragments of organic matter that have taken centuries—even millennia—to build up in native (i.e., unbroken) soils. It is this organic matter that gave midwestern soils their deep black appearance, referred to as "black gold" by some farmers.

About 2.5 trillion tons of carbon is stored in earth's soils, comprising 80% of all terrestrial carbon on earth. This vastly exceeds the 560 billion tons stored above ground in plants and animals (Brady & Weil, 1996; Lal, 2004). Soils that are rich in organic matter not only increase their capacity to retain water and nutrients, but can better withstand the erosive forces of wind and water (Brady & Weil, 1996). Organic-rich soils can also require less nitrogen fertilizer to maintain yields, as compared to farms devoid of organic matter.

The great challenge of Green Revolution-style farming is its reliance on annual crops, which must be replanted from seed every year, and which live for just one season. In annual crops like corn, high applications of nitrogen stimulate more aboveground shoots, leaves, and seeds, relative to the amount of root mass. The difference is not trivial. Soils beneath our corn fields have about one fifth the amount of carbon than the soils of a diverse prairie (Dietzel, 2014). Quite insidiously, the microbes, fungi, and other soil biota responsible for consuming organic matter are stimulated by irrigation and nitrogen. Indirectly, then, the high irrigation and nitrogen infused farming systems destroy organic matter. Any soil carbon that does remain at the end of the growing season is further lost due to tillage and other monoculture farming practices.

In a vicious downward spiral, the more degraded the soil becomes, the more irrigation and nitrogen fertilizer are needed to maintain sufficient yield, a process that further degrades the soil's organic matter. Recall that one third of the US heartland has completely lost its organic rich topsoil, while over eight million acres of California's central valley have become degraded due to erosion, organic matter depletion, and salinity problems (Desai, 2018). This stark decline in soil fertility is more concerning when we consider the tremendous population growth that has occurred over the same period.

To think, soil erosion rates in most other countries are higher than in the US. Consider, for instance, the steep and misty alpine region of Malingua Pamba, Ecuador. It is not obvious why regions like Malingua Pamba are being farmed today, for it is no farmer's paradise. That is, until we understand that, like so many regions of South America and Central America, the choicest lowlands have been coopted to export fruit, cattle, palm oil, coconut products, petroleum, etc. Or to export cut flowers, coffee, and chocolate. In the process, untold thousands of rural farmers across the globe have been forced from their ancestral homelands by export-based corporations.

Displaced farmers have no options left but to farm the most marginal lands (Figure 21). There, they suffer not just economic hardship but rampant cultural decline as their children, like those of Oakdale, are lured away by distant economic opportunities. As soil and cultural decline spread across the rural landscapes of developing countries, greater demand is placed on imported food from America and elsewhere, where soil fertility continues to erode.

Figure 21. Eroding farmlands in the paramo regions of Ecuador, where erosion gullies undermine potable water supplies to rural farmers. Photo courtesy of Laura Backus.

Compensating for soil fertility losses and declining profitability, a plethora of software has been developed for farmers, along with improved mapping of soil chemistry and crop pests, more accurate soil moisture and weather predictions, etc. These innovations have no doubt helped modern farmers reduce the inputs required of large-scale monocultures. Yet fundamentally, such technology cannot reverse the impacts of declining farm diversity and soil organic matter. It can only attempt to compensate for such losses. At the same time, the fossil fuels essential to maintaining high yields have but one fate: to decline alongside a rising population. On the bright side, the same mechanisms that created America's soil-degrading agricultural system can operate in reverse.

Rebuilding Topsoil and Profitability

One of the most cost-effective steps to restoring the productive capacity of farmlands is to reverse the loss of topsoil. Primarily, this is accomplished through the planting of perennial crops, as well as other agricultural practices that dramatically reduce the need for tillage. Several organizations are dedicated to providing education to farmers on such methods, including Understanding Ag, the USDA Natural Resources Conservation Service, and other organizations across the nation and the globe.

Organic matter can be restored in depleted soils by basic methods such as cover cropping, crop rotation, compost and manure application, and a variety of rotational grazing systems. Such practices build biodiversity below the soil surface, while creating soil conditions that better receive and hold rainwater and nutrients. In turn, irrigation needs, pesticides, and energy demands tend to decline in concert, reducing costs for farmers while engendering abundant ecological and social benefits (Altieri, 2012; Capra & Luisi, 2014; Pretty, 2008). In a positive feedback loop, reductions in irrigation, nitrogen, and tillage have the benefit of minimizing declines in soil organic matter. Such feedback loops are critical to rebalancing the current resource-intensive agricultural system in favor of a self-regulating agroecosystem.

When the soil microbiome is rebuilt, and plant diversity is restored, net primary productivity rises. This rise in productivity is not trivial. Summarizing data from farms across the globe, Pretty (2008) found that farming practices that build soil organic matter produced yields up to 145% greater than conventional farming methods. The increased plant productivity translates to more resources being captured and transferred to chickens, honey bees, pigs, bison, and other consumers. For example, Gabe's five-thousand-acre farm produces about twenty food products, including six different animal products. There was a time when Gabe and his wife were over a million dollars in agricultural debt. As Gabe puts it, "it was diversity that got us out of the hole."

In addition to Gabe's practical experience, the research by LaCanne and Lundgren (2017) reveal that, on diverse farmlands, profitability is positively correlated not with yield, but with the organic content of soils. By taking advantage of a positive feedback loop, profitability has the potential to drive the restoration of soil organic matter in farmlands where fertility has been lost. However, regenerative agriculture and its allies will succeed only to the extent they make financial sense, and if those farms can nourish the hungry.

Farming for Nutrition, Not Calories

One crisp fall morning of 2020, I had a chance to sample some heirloom wheat from Moxie Bread Company, a small Colorado-based company with ancient roots. The crepes I made for breakfast were the best my 10-year-old daughter had ever tasted, at least from our kitchen. I can take little credit, for it does not require a skillful chef to solicit a delicious smile as much as it takes great ingredients.

Conventional agricultural practices have not only degraded the topsoil of US farmlands, but they have systematically suppressed the quality of ingredients (i.e., the nutritional value) filling the collective American pantry. A healthy human body requires *nutrient dense* foods, which are high in nutrients but relatively low in calories. Nutrient-dense foods have a high concentration of micronutrients and amino acids, the building blocks of protein, which is essential to a strong immune system.

Engineering a crop for high yield tends to result in low nutrient density. For instance, wheat varieties bred for high yields contain significantly less iron, magnesium, zinc, and other micronutrients as compared to historical varieties (Murphy et al., 2008). Similarly, conventional eggs provide lower nutrient density than eggs from pastured chickens (Brown, 2020). That such an inept agricultural system has persisted is baffling. The silver lining may be that, in response to changing consumer demands, great opportunities exist for companies such as Moxie to fulfill an entirely new market. Markets where people are not merely fed, they are nourished. And where farmers exchange subsidies for profits.

The Debate Over Organic, Sustainable, and Conventional Farming

It is important to differentiate organic farming from any form of sustainable farming, including regenerative agriculture. Organic farming does not by definition require a diverse landscape, or low-till operations. Rather, organic farming in the US is dominated by large-scale monocultures, scales necessary to supply national and global markets. This reality has stimulated academic debates over the energy inputs and crop yields between organic and conventional farming methods—an unfortunate diversion from meaningful progress in America's greater agricultural industry.

Ample evidence exists that conventional monoculture farms, infused with fossil fuel-derived fertilizers and herbicides, can produce more of a single crop (e.g., corn, rice, wheat) than can organic monoculture farms (Treu et al., 2017).

However, most studies of this nature examine only yields, while ignoring soil fertility losses, biodiversity loss, exogenous energy inputs, and other aspects of conventional farming (Pretty, 2008; van der Werf et al., 2020). That is, they ignore more important factors such as NDP and productive capacity.

Throwing the label "sustainable" on a system can be equally misleading, as exemplified by high-yield proponents such as Robert Paarlberg of Harvard's Sustainability Science Program. Paarlberg argues that modern agriculture is "better, because it uses low impact, 'precision' techniques that require less land, less energy, and fewer chemicals for every bushel produced. (Paarlberg, 2021a)" However, his article in the *Wall Street Journal*, "The Environmental Upside of Modern Farming," is full of false and misleading conclusions. For instance, Paarlberg states that conventional farms (i.e., high-yield and low-diversity farm) have become more efficient, because less irrigation water and fewer pesticides are being used than in previous decades.

Technically, Paarlberg is correct. However, he ignores the fact that the degraded soils of the high-yield systems hold less water than alternative systems such as regenerative agricultural, and require far more pesticides and herbicides than those systems. Using Paarlberg's logic, one can also claim that fewer people are dying today thanks to modern laser-guided missiles; therefore, we should wage more war.

Certainly, there have been some gains in modern agriculture that result in less water and fewer chemicals being applied today than seventy years ago. To be clear, Paarlberg is comparing modern agriculture (i.e., agriculture since the Green Revolution) to an already inefficient system (i.e., traditional monoculture farming), neither of which can maintain high yields without intensive irrigation, abundant fossil fuels, and a long list of other exogenous resources.

Paarlberg does highlight one important fact. In his 2021 article in the *Harvard Gazette*, he points out that about 80 percent of all organic sales in the US come from large scale monoculture farms, owned by conglomerates like ConAgra and Kellogg. Yet he maintains that high yield farms are the savior of humanity's food security needs.

For those champions of high-input and high-yield farming systems— organic or conventional—there are a few embarrassing details to consider. First, far more food is sent to US landfills today than before the Green Revolution (USDA, 2010). Second, America's current agricultural system (i.e., subsidies, exogenous energy, export focused, etc.) operates such that crops are tilled under when commodity prices decline far enough.

In short, much of the energy efficiencies claimed by proponents of high-yield agriculture are diminished by the system's inherent waste. The degraded soils of such a system have little capacity to capture and retain water and nitrogen, so require significant additions of both to prop up yields. The expenses related to those additions contribute to the fact that, since the Green Revolution, farmers have been receiving far less money in their pockets for every dollar of food purchased than earlier farmers (Center for Sustainable Systems, 2019). That is, high yield does not translate to high profitability, especially for smaller farms.

This reality demands that corporate farmers operate at giant scales for commodity markets, amassing small per-acre profits into one large profit. Alternatively, small-scale farmers can profit from niche markets while employing systems such as regenerative agriculture, which require fewer inputs.

Can Regenerative Agriculture Feed the World?

Before answering this question, let's put it into the context of conventional agriculture. Several studies suggest that, like the Second Agricultural Revolution, the Green Revolution did not actually translate to greater food security. For instance, the extensive literature review by Pingali (2012) reveals that, while overall calorie consumption has increased, dietary diversity has decreased for many poor people, and malnutrition has persisted. In some cases, Pingali found that traditional crops—sources of critical micronutrients such as iron, vitamin A, and zinc—were replaced by higher-value export crops, which tend to lack those micronutrients.

Furthermore, while energy-intensive monoculture systems can effectively maximize the yield of a single species per acre, the yield lasts only a few weeks. And that yield does not translate to more total food for humans per acre. For instance, the average cornfield has the potential to deliver over fifteen million calories per acre annually. That's enough to sustain fourteen people (Foley, 2013). However, only three million calories per year are actually consumed by people, mainly as dairy and meat products—enough to feed three people. The majority of sweet yellow kernels are instead exported, used to produce ethanol, manufactured into spoons and cups, or fed to domesticated animals, with a significant portion of the original energy lost along the way in support of their metabolic needs.

Modern agriculture is failing to meet the nutritional needs not only of developed nations such as the US, but of the world (FAO, 2019). For instance, in many countries experiencing rampant hunger issues, agricultural exports exceed imports (Lappé et al., 1998). In other words, many countries are net exporters of food, even while their population goes hungry. While Capra and Luisi, citing the work of Mulder-Sibanda et al. (2002), report that "…in the

Third World 78% of all malnourished children under five live in countries with food surpluses."

Besides the critical hunger concerns, there are basic economic concerns at stake for many food exporting countries dependent on modern agriculture. As stated earlier, the economics of high-yield farming demands higher application rates of fertilizer, herbicides, fungicides, insecticides, irrigation, and other inputs, all of which require exogenous energy (Pingali, 2012; Schnepf, 2004). In turn, food-exporting countries are more dependent on imported fuel, fertilizers, pesticides, and farm equipment to feed their citizens. As the costs of these inputs increase, or their supply becomes more volatile, the ability of those countries to feed their citizens becomes more costly and risky.

Single-minded solutions such as high-yield agriculture cannot resolve the food security concerns of any country. As a result, developing countries such as Mexico—the posterchild of the Green Revolution—are less self-sufficient now than they were prior to the Green Revolution. Even with its vast oil reserves, Mexico struggles to meet its own fertilizer and farm equipment demands, and many of its citizens flee to the US for jobs and a better life. This reality is playing out today for one simple reason: people were not the intended beneficiaries of the Green Revolution. Large-scale agricultural corporations were.

But can a system of diverse soil-building agricultural systems do any better? Can they fully nourish a population of eight or nine billion people? To help answer this question, let's begin with the most rudimentary Midwestern agricultural system: hundreds of species of plants producing carbohydrates and proteins in a tallgrass prairie, without reliance on fossil fuel. Data from The Prairie Power Project of Northern Iowa (Cambardella et al., 2016) revealed how a more diverse prairie produces far more carbohydrates than a less diverse plot of prairie. Similarly, a study in the journal *Nature* (Zuppinger-Dingley et al., 2014) reveals how diverse prairie communities can produce higher yields than monocultures.

Though these rudimentary agricultural systems produce fodder for domestic animals alone, they underscore a basic ecological reality: diverse communities sequester more energy than less diverse communities. The relationship between diversity, soil organic matter, and energy capture holds true for more complex farming systems, including the production of multiple crops in the same space.

The *three sisters* food system (i.e., corn, beans, and squash) that sustained the ancient Puebloans of the Americas is one well-understood example. Gabe Brown's diverse agricultural fields provide another example from the furthest northern latitudes of America. In tropical regions of the world, cultivating coconut, black pepper, cacao, and pineapple in the same field—in the same growing season—has been a long-standing tradition. Similarly, an incredible diversity of non-timber forest products (NTFPs) grown in the tropics harvest solar energy with several forest canopies in a single space, producing much higher economic value than grazing, swidden agriculture, logging, and other traditional agriculture (Grimes et al., 1994; Peters et al., 1989; Pinedo-Vasquez et al., 1992). Furthermore, integrating selective logging with NTFP extraction in tropical regions is known to increase overall production in those systems (Salick et al., 1995). In essence, the disturbance caused by selective logging helps to keep the system in a middle stage of succession.

Taken to the extreme, the Baranaja cropping system of the Himalayas produces twelve different crops in the same plot of land (Kala, 2010). Besides the high soil fertility and economic resilience these systems can produce, multi-cropping systems create jobs and more stable income streams throughout the growing season. Of course, the profitability of any farming system hinges on the strength of markets and the business acumen of the farmer. And in a future of decreasing fossil fuel reserves and an expanding human population, the most profitable agricultural system will likely be that which captures the most sun, while minimizing inputs.

Agricultural Restoration: Beyond the farm

A working definition of *agricultural restoration* is methods that increase the diversity, productive capacity, and profitability of farmlands. Such methods are similar to regenerative agriculture, with the exception that diversity must extend beyond the farm, to include regional farm diversity and a diversity of value-added agricultural products. Importantly, agricultural restoration must result in increased profitability for the farmer. Profitability attracts investment, and the system that receives investment will expand. Absent profit, the best restoration efforts will remain nothing more than a nice experiment.

Hundreds of farmers across America are working to restore the diversity and productive capacity of their local farmlands, for a few reasons. First, there is an age-old feedback loop inherent to complex self-regulating economies. People are demanding better food—more nutritious, tastier, and local foods. Second, the potential profitability of systems such as regenerative agriculture is attracting new entrants into the industry.

Besides the practical experience of farmers like Gabe Brown, a growing body of research backs up the claims of profitability. In a study of forty midwestern farms, LaCanne and Lundgren (2018) showed that farmers using regenerative farming experienced 78% higher profits over traditional corn production systems. There are a few key takeaways from their study that new entrants into agriculture should note. Farmers who build healthier soils are more profitable. Specifically, regenerative farms can thrive with fewer costly insecticides and fertilizers, for diverse fields harbor far fewer pests than monoculture fields. Finally, profitable farmers build diversified income streams, and market their products differently than conventional farmers.

Perhaps the ultimate reason for the local food renaissance is quite simple. We are social beings at our core, yearning to forge connections with one another. Local food production fuels that connection in ways unmatched by the crate of tomatoes and peppers shipped from thousands of miles beyond our community. The insecurity of those long supply chains for such a critical resource has struck a nerve for most Americans thanks in part to the recent pandemic.

Consumers have been making dozens of other connections between grossly unsustainable food production systems and the quality of their lives. This includes the high financial volatility of global food markets, the low resilience of monoculture landscapes, and the likely increases in weather-related uncertainties catalyzed by global climate change. Hence, agricultural restoration is perhaps the most profound economic achievement for any regional economy, producing a significant degree of opportunity for the entrepreneurial farmer.

For agricultural restoration to provide greater economic stability, enhance the productive capacity of an economy, increase profitability, and yield other socio-economic benefits, the following actions are needed, as a minimum:

• Increase the number and diversity of farms, which can lead to increased job diversity, greater productivity, and regional economic stability.

• Increase investment in applied research, to refine the knowledge and practice of diverse sustainable farming systems.

• Integrate sustainable farming systems with strong local and regional markets, building resilience in the face of year-to-year climatic and market variability, globally destructive competition, trade wars, and other external forces.

A Basic Path to a Restored Agricultural Landscape

In addition to the actions above, there are a few critical restoration steps that define agriculture's restoration path. First, regional economies must restore diversity to their agricultural landscapes, including timber, vegetables, grains, pasture, animal products, and other crops relevant to their SEI context. Second, the collective base of agricultural knowledge must be refined so that food production systems are capable of producing ample products from endogenous resources, rather than exogenous energy and other resource transfers from beyond the region. Third, Americans must dedicate themselves to building local and regional markets (i.e., demand) for regionally-produced agricultural products.

Precisely what those markets must deliver will vary depending on one's SEI context. In many regions of the American Midwest, the great distance to markets may require a large portion of farmlands be restored to prairie to support grass-fed beef, bison, pigs, chickens, and dairy. Wood fiber production may account for a larger portion of many midwestern landscapes, to feed regional paper mills and at the same time support mushroom production and a diversity of other products. Such a transformation would not only place upward pressure on profitability, but yield substantial watershed benefits, high levels of biodiversity, and increases in soil fertility.

Under other SEI contexts, a greater variety of grains such as wheat, rye, rice, and oats, will make the most economic and ecological sense. This could include heirloom and novel grain varieties, packed with greater nutrient density and the ability to be grown with fewer inputs. This work is underway at The Breadlab of Washington State University, and elsewhere. Where distances to markets are short, a diversity of vegetable crops and grains may define the agricultural landscape. Regardless of the context, a massive economic weight must be lifted from the American agricultural industry: Subsidies.

Can American Farmers Thrive Without Subsidies?

To stimulate agricultural restoration across America there is another force which must be reckoned with. This force is not China, the EU, nor climate change. It's a force from within: America's self-crippling farm policies. Besides the significant exogenous resources that are transferred into America's modern farms, subsidy programs have transferred about US $90 billion into those same farm systems between 1995 and 2010 alone (Foley, 2013). In the process, millions of farms have been dismantled.

American farm subsidies can be traced back to the first US farm bill, the Agricultural Adjustment act of 1933, which was established in the aftermath of the Dust Bowl—during the Great Depression—to address overproduction and falling commodity prices. It has since become a force for degrading the productive capacity of US farmlands and destroying diversity in the agricultural industry. To be clear, the US farm subsidy program does work for some; corporations that have amassed tens of thousands of acres of farmland to produce high-yield and low-diversity crops, and who lobby politicians in Washington DC to maintain the system.

The majority of subsidies are directed not to small farmers, but those with a net worth greater than US $2 million and incomes over US $200,000 (Riedl, 2007). In the process, overproduction is encouraged. The subsidized bounty is then exported, more often than not to feed China or fuel automobiles. Over time, corn genetics have been retooled around the global market economy, such that the vast majority of corn grown in the US today is not even edible to humans.

The farm bill would best serve the US today not by maintaining unnecessary subsidies, but by reconstituting the bill's post-depression aim: to sustain America's diverse and productive agricultural landscape. Certainly, countless industrial-scale capitalists will fight agricultural reform to the bitter end. But they are few in number, and can learn from the success of a country that bears the same name as its national fruit—the Kiwis.

A profound example of restored agricultural diversity and productivity comes from New Zealand, where government subsidies amounted to 40% of farm income in the 1970s (Ross & Edwards, 2012). Regardless of farmer protests, politicians were forced to act responsibly to a serious national budget crisis. New Zealand's farm subsidy program was ushered through fields of protesting farmers to the chopping block. By 1984, the farm subsidy program had vanished. Despite subsidy programs thriving in the US and the European Union—competitors of New Zealand farmers—the result was not as Kiwi farmers feared. As Ross and Edwards reported,

> When the subsidies were removed, it turned out to be a catalyst for productivity gains. New Zealand farmers cut costs, diversified their land use, sought nonfarm income, and developed new products. Farmers became more focused on pursuing activities that made good business sense. Official data supports on-the-ground evidence that New Zealand greatly improved its farming efficiency after the reforms. Measured agricultural productivity had been stagnant in the years prior to the reforms, but since the reforms productivity has grown substantially faster in agriculture than in the New Zealand economy as a whole.

The elimination of New Zealand's farm subsidies also led to reductions in fertilizer use, and lowered the cost of several other inputs that had essentially been "encouraged" by the subsidy programs.

If US politicians still doubt the power of a self-regulating economic system to resolve its own needs, they can take a clue from Italy. In the aftermath of the 2012 Modena earthquake, which rocked a critical industrial region of northern Italy, the leading producers of Parmigiano-Reggiano experienced a catastrophic blow. About 360,000 wheels of cheese—an estimated loss of about US $200 million—were damaged by the quake (Puno, 2017). Thankfully, the Italian government did not step in. Instead, world renowned chef Massimo Bottura, a native of the region, took his creativity out of the kitchen. Without government bailouts, Massimo worked with a cheese consortium to bring a classic Italian dish, cacio e pepe, to foodies around the world.

The plan worked flawlessly—there was a near immediate sale of every wheel of cheese to pasta lovers around the globe. Were such an incident to unfold in America, government intervention would have likely ensured a delivery of cheese not to the mouths of people, but to the bowels of landfills. It is doubtful the damaged cheese would have even been fed to hogs.

Would the elimination of farm subsidies in America yield similar results? Conservative politicians such as Dan Hill of Nebraska believe so, as do economists such as Milton Friedman, and countless others. But they're underselling the benefits. Based on the principles of self-regulating systems, and in light of the monstrous expanse of monocultures currently dominating the US, I would argue that eliminating farm subsidies would produce even greater benefits than what New Zealand witnessed. Benefits that would reach well beyond the farm, including: carbon sequestration, increased food quality, regional economic stability, and more stable regional employment.

Other Steps toward a Restored Agricultural Landscape

Even if America's political and capitalist elites lack the courage to end farm subsidies, there is great opportunity for change at the regional level. At the very least, the following avenues exist for local governments, community leaders, farmers, and business leaders to restore America's agricultural landscape:

Similar to the growing farm-to-table trend, create a table-to-farm program, delivering compost from urban centers to rebuild the soil fertility of local farms.

- Increase investment in research that focuses on the effectiveness of multi-cropping systems.

- Extend *sustainable* grazing practices to marginal agricultural lands, including America's Conservation Reserve Program (CRP) lands.

- Convert millions of acres of corn fields to prairie for a wide diversity of domestic animal production.

- Improve small farmer access to regional markets.

Beyond the local level, for the nation at large, there is a significant role for non-profits to play in building a stronger domestic marketplace for domestically grown food. In the early years of the Green Revolution, the non-profit Food Export Association of the Midwest USA was created in collaboration with thirteen state agricultural agencies and the USDA, with one mandate: to facilitate food exports to the world. Dozens of similar non-profits, with similar mandates, have been established across the US to promote food exports.

Countering the export-based mission of such non-profits are the Bread Bakers Guild of America, the Bread Lab (Washington), Arcadia Center for Food and Agriculture (Virginia), Institute for Local Self-Reliance, the National Sustainable Agricultural Coalition, and hundreds of other organizations across the US and the world. This trend toward restorative, resilient and nourishing local agricultural systems shows no sign of slowing. To multiply the impacts of those efforts, an abundance of organizations is needed to build domestic markets for domestic farm products.

Besides the tremendous niches remaining in food production, another path toward profitability for farmers is the *niche* remaining in value-added food products for regional markets. Such niches include milled flour, salami and sausage, baked goods, eggs, granola, cut flowers, etc., for local markets. Farmers and food manufacturers who serve local and regional markets not only have the potential to be more profitable, but they provide significantly higher wages for farm workers (Bauman et al., 2018 and 2019), and are less susceptible to national and global supply chain disruptions. As those businesses become more profitable, they also tend to grow in product diversity (Bauman et al., 2018). To the contrary, as food commodity production globally has exceeded global demand in recent decades, the prices that food commodity businesses receive have declined (Johansson, 2021).

There is a curious hurdle remaining for many small farmers, especially new entrants, to overcome: access to markets. Amidst a lavish fossil fuel and financially subsidized farming system, local farmer products struggle not simply to compete on grocery store shelves, but to reach the grocery store in the first place. In turn, the profound benefits of diverse farming systems go unrewarded by the current economic system. This conundrum underscores why agricultural restoration efforts must occur alongside other economic restoration efforts. Economic diversity must grow across all sectors at the regional level, alongside a dramatic increase in domestic energy production and a restored balance of trade. In doing so, additional opportunities arise for entrepreneurs and larger businesses to restore the productive capacity of our economies.

TEN

THE COEVOLUTION OF MANUFACTURING
AND WASTE-TO-RESOURCES

In ecological restoration, no treatment occurs in isolation, for the interactions between primary producers (vegetation), herbivores (deer), and other trophic levels (predators, decomposers, etc.) are constantly in motion. Should we ignore such interactions, and simply focus on sowing seeds, the herds of elk or rabbits may come through and destroy the seedlings, or a lack of soil fungi and bacteria may lead to a poorly functioning plant community. Sowing seeds without an understanding of the local climate or soils is also futile.

Likewise, economic restoration actions in any one industry or sector will influence, and be influenced by, shifts in other industries and sectors, all within an ever-evolving SEI context. When we understand the interactions, they can work in our favor. Agricultural restoration, for instance, will yield optimal benefits when integrated with the restoration of other regional industries, such as value-added foods (e.g., milled flour, dairy products, pies, and canned foods), energy, services, knowledge, transportation, and so forth. Through that integration, economic diversity emerges naturally, as do its benefits. The next few sections address a portion of this integration as it relates to manufacturing and waste-to-resources.

Slick Shifts in Manufacturing Systems

Much of the technology needed to restore the productive capacity of an economy, while protecting its social and environmental values, already exists. In 2002, *Cradle to Cradle: Remaking the Way We Make Things* by Braungart and McDonough shared a plethora of resource-efficient technology for the manufacturing sector. Two decades of technological breakthroughs have since transpired, and *Cradle to Cradle* remains an essential guidebook for the waste-to-resources sector. But to really thrive, this sector must coevolve with the manufacturing sector within a FEZ, so they may together make leaps in resource-use efficiency. To reiterate, resource-use efficiency is critical to the productive capacity and NDP of both ecosystems and economies, and increasing diversity is essential to attaining greater degrees of resource-use efficiency.

Many of the solutions showcased in *Cradle to Cradle* stem from the concept of *biomimicry*: the design of mechanical features and systems that mimic biological features and systems. Biomimicry has also been used to design energy efficient buildings, as well as porous surfaces in urban centers to reduce flooding and the pollution of waterways. More recently, biomimicry has gone as far as studying the architecture of the Javan cucumber seed to inform the design of tidal "kites" used in electric generation. Wave action or other slow-moving currents push the kite with great force, while its tether pulls relentlessly at a generator on the other end. It's like pulling the cord on a toy top, but the waves do the work. For endless inspiration, The Biomimicry Institute provides a clearinghouse of ground-breaking designs that span 21 countries and over 12,000 innovators.

Drawing upon ecosystems to inform the structure of an economy is simply biomimicry at a different scale, requiring innovation of not only products and features, but of systems that effectively integrate them across public and private sectors. Green Mountain Power of Vermont is one example. Their *Bring Your Own Device* (BYOD) program serves a wide variety of industrial and residential users. Interconnected users form a network of battery banks, vehicle chargers, and electric water heaters to store energy during off-peak periods when demand is low. During off-peak periods, when solar and wind are still producing electricity, excess energy is "banked" in the batteries of a wide range of personal devices. Users draw from those banks during periods of high demand, flattening out the peaks and valleys of energy consumption over time.

Similar systems are emerging around the globe, but at a snail's pace compared to the rampant evolution of technology itself. Yet a curious obstacle lies between the point of "wouldn't it be great if…" to "this is how we do business." That is, a lack of *need*—the mother of all inventions.

Need is suffocated when a regional economy becomes overly dependent on the global market economy. Government actions can also unknowingly stifle innovation and meaningful change. This includes bailouts and subsidies of corporations who employ wasteful irrigation systems, maintain inefficient energy systems, design throw-away products, etc.

Yet a beneficial irony has emerged during the expansion of global market capitalism. Abundant innovations have arisen to increase the manufacturing sector's ability to meet the needs of a free economic zone, without the titanic production scales demanded by global markets. These innovations include industrial efficiencies necessary to build (not destroy) the productive capacity of an economy.

Industrial Efficiencies via Symbiotic Relationships

Efficient economic and industrial systems stem from the ecological phenomenon of *symbiosis*: a biological bond between two species who expend less energy not by working in isolation, but by working together. The apple tree yields more fruit when bees pollinate its flowers. In return, the bee gains nectar to support the hive, and humans obtain honey.

Stretching the limits of symbiosis are the orchids, whose seeds—mere specks of dust—lack any endosperm (i.e., food reserves). This begs the question, how on earth do such orchid seedlings survive their first day on earth? In short, they don't. Not unless they are first infected by a host fungus, a particular species of fungus the orchid is utterly dependent on, like an infant to its mother. The fungus gains its nutrients and energy from decomposing plant matter, and feeds the germinating orchid from any excess. Why? Because the relationship will pay off in the long term. When the orchid matures, it provides nutrients for the fungus, so that it too may successfully reproduce.

And the cycle repeats, across countless species. In the process, diversity and net primary production in the jungle increase. Manufacturing industries have much to learn from the efficiencies of nature. This includes the means to producing a great diversity of products within a single manufacturing facility.

Agile Manufacturing Systems

While symbiotic relationships have their advantages, some of earth's most successful species are those that remain agile amidst an ever-changing ecological space. Dinosaurs are the classic case of a species that lacked the agility required to survive a rapidly changing environment. It was earth's smaller and "newer" species, such as mammals, that were agile enough to adapt. In doing so, humans rose to prominence as one of earth's most influential species.

Within a rapidly evolving economy, the business embracing a model of mass agility, not mass production, is more likely to endure. And the optimal structure of that business will be shaped by the context of its economic space. For instance, in a region where three hundred young children play make-pretend, a facility capable of manufacturing three million dolls is unnecessary. Hence, industries must be redesigned based on smaller production runs of a greater diversity of products for a regional—not global—market economy.

Such systems are not new; they evolved from the nineteenth century paradigm of flexible manufacturing. They simply go by a new name: *agile manufacturing* (Gunasekaran et al., 2019). By increasing their agility, manufacturers are able to produce a broad range of products with short lead times (Fliedner & Vokurka, 1997), arming them against the unpredictable needs of national and global consumers. In an economy crafted to fulfill regional (not global) consumer, labor, and energy demands, agile manufacturers have an even more important task. In order to produce a great diversity of products in a given space, they must involve more people on the factory floor.

Admittedly, when witnessing a factory floor of whirring robotic assembly lines producing thousands (or millions) of identical products, it's difficult to believe that involving more humans could yield more than one widget per shift. That might ring true without investment into the redesign of manufacturing facilities. But investment has begun to flow, in support of manufacturing systems that integrate human labor with redesigned workspaces, flexible factory floors, basic robotic tools, and even screwdrivers. Designed well, such integrated systems require less time to retool a factory floor when making the switch from product A (manufacturing snow shovels in November), to product B (manufacturing flower pots in March), to product C (manufacturing frisbees in June).

Pushing agile manufacturing to its limits, Australia's SAGE Automation does not produce a standard product. Instead, their factory floor has been designed for mass agility. The SAGE factory floor is full of assembly cells, each with its own mobile workbenches, electrical outlets, and a full set of tools and equipment (Figure 22). The cells can be reconfigured quickly to meet the needs of a new product line. SAGE's agile strategy is so successful they even meet the needs of consumers who demand Original Equipment Manufacturer (OEM) standards. Similar to diverse farmers, agile manufacturers receive the added benefit of a diversified revenue stream, which confers resilience to their business.

Fundamentally, agile manufacturing is profitable because it makes the most efficient use of fixed capital such as buildings, land, and equipment. Intel, for instance, uses knock-out holes in concrete ceilings to retool entire production floors for new orders. As the layout of the floor changes, holes are "knocked out" between factory floors, allowing for innumerable rearrangements of utilities, waste shoots, and other elements to generate the most efficient process imaginable.

Figure 22. SAGE Automation's advanced manufacturing facility, Adelaide, Australia. Photo courtesy of SAGE Automation.

Cooperatives

Cooperation is another form of system-wide innovation that confers a comparative advantage to participants. When compatible businesses share assets—labor, energy, land, information technology, equipment, distribution channels, etc.—each business can more efficiently meet production needs. These rudimentary efficiencies are a means to profitability, and at the level of an economy, a higher net domestic product. But rather than competing fiercely for said profit, co-operators form alliances within an entire supply network, integrating their operations across industries and sectors. And rather than focusing on the highest possible output of a single product, cooperation engenders solutions that yield greater efficiencies, higher quality, or both. The result is an interrelated web of producers and consumers, rather than a simple supply chain: extract, produce, consume, dispose.

Cooperatives (AKA co-ops) are the quintessential example of collaborative planning, and have been integral to the survival of small farm communities across America since the Industrial Revolution. In the *History of Cooperatives of the United States*, Pitman (2018) provides an excellent portrayal of the drivers and mechanisms of cooperatives. This includes shared capital, democratic management philosophies, cooperative loan and credit organizations, co-op marketing, etc. In response to the destruction of small trade guilds during the Industrial Revolution, cooperative efforts spread throughout Europe, and quickly grabbed the attention of US innovators. According to Pitman,

America's first cooperative was a mutual fire insurance company, founded in 1752 by none other than Benjamin Franklin.

More recently, cooperatives such as Organic Valley have forged innovative approaches to dairy and vegetable production at a national scale. In return, they have produced some of the highest revenues for some of the smallest American farmers. In an interview with Tripp Hughes and Elizabeth McMullen of Organic Valley (T. Hughes, personal communication, July 2020), I was able to garner a few elements of their cooperative success.

"Fundamentally," Tripp began, "co-ops are born out of market failure." For American farmers, this meant the US farm crisis of the 1980s, a time when the nation was struck with high oil prices, large debt levels, an overbuilt market in the wake of the Green Revolution, and a massive farm revenue bubble. The moment global demand sank, the overbuilt farming industry became "out of place" for even the most productive economy of the day, the US. In response, several Wisconsin farmers were forced to seek less conventional means to survive. This included cooperation, and rebuilding the strength of their domestic market.

Silently, another factor began to emerge, which was far beyond the grasp of conventional farmers. Rachel Carlson's *Silent Spring* stoked a global organic food movement. Standards such as the Organic Foods Production Act of 1990 began to materialize. In parallel, global demand for organic food rose sharply. Wisconsin farmers united around a mission of value-added food production. And CROPP Cooperative was born, the parent company of Organic Valley.

According to Tripp, there are some very simple reasons for Organic Valley's great success. Topping the list is their genuine support for their farmers, as well as the ability to gain market share through value-added products. From a history of cheese, Organic Valley now brings dozens of products to consumers, including milk, yogurt, butter, vegetables, whey powder, and eggs.

Organic Valley's product diversification strategy has increased farmer revenues substantially. For instance, the C weight (one hundred pounds of milk) for Organic Valley farmers in 2019 was US $30.25, whereas conventional farmers earned US $18.05. But there is something even more important to farmers than increased revenue. That is, price stability. "Conventional dairy swings high and low continuously, due to a number of global market forces," Tripp explained. Organic Valley provides more predictable revenue streams for farmers, creating the certainty they need to invest in new or improved operations.

"Co-ops will collapse," Tripp said frankly, "when the market failure that created them is resolved." This said, a peculiar challenge for organic dairy producers is their need for open rangelands. However, much of that space has been consumed by ethanol production, corn-fed beef operations dependent on fossil fuels, and the mass production of monoculture crops for export markets. As open prairie becomes increasingly converted to monocultures, housing developments, and a host of other uses, the cost of land rises, putting organic dairy producers at a huge disadvantage. Under such destructive forces, a more diverse technological toolbox is needed for dairy producers, OEM manufacturers, and a host of agile manufacturers, with which they can produce a better product more efficiently. In so doing, those producers have the capacity to adapt quickly to changing consumer demands while restoring the productive capacity of their economy.

Industrial and Ecological Clustering

Industrial clustering is a centuries-old form of cooperation. The strategy is simple: share resources (e.g., technology, skilled labor, supply chains, marketing resources, etc.) across a cluster of similar businesses in a region. In return, participants can more efficiently reach a broader market, drive innovation, and produce other benefits for participants. Knowledge sharing is significant within clusters.

Though industrial clusters have traditionally been focused on creating wealth via greater production levels for global markets (e.g., the leather cluster of Italy, the textile cluster of India, etc.), the concept can be molded to fulfill the needs of regional economies focused on domestic markets. Industrial clusters can include multiple businesses sharing shop space, renewable energy microgrids, communication technology, and other resources within the same industrial center or even the same building.

The bustling commissary kitchen is a prime example of a modified industrial cluster, where the simple act of sharing space allows locally-oriented businesses to produce a great variety of food products at a lower cost. The aggregate cost of the building, equipment, utilities, refrigeration space, etc. are not a burden to one entrepreneur, but is rather spread across multiple businesses. The key to a successful commissary is to utilize capital very efficiently.

Efficiencies are further facilitated by programs such as The Food Corridor, which provide kitchen owners and their entrepreneurial chefs with assistance in scheduling, billing, insurance, marketing, navigating complex health codes, etc.—a burden to entrepreneurs who could otherwise be hindered by such hurdles. Consumers win with a greater diversity of food at a lower cost. Commissaries can further facilitate efficiencies via shared food waste composting systems, pooling their demand into larger orders for local and regional farm produce, share endogenous energy systems, etc. Ultimately, chefs spend less time on administration and solving industrial design challenges, and more time nourishing their passion—cooking. This model can benefit a wide variety of locally-oriented manufacturers.

Ecological clustering is simply a modern brand of industrial clustering, and goes deeper than simply reducing expenses. In ecological clusters, all forms of waste must be reduced or even eliminated. Spearheaded by the Zero Emissions Research and Initiatives (ZERI), ecological clusters are built around compatible industries and businesses so that the wastes of one can more efficiently be consumed in the production processes of another (Pauli, 1998).

The purer the waste, such as organic fibers, heat, glass, metal, or plastics, the easier it is for ecological clusters to re-employ them in another production process. The more toxic the effluents, or the more difficult the wastes are to recycle (e.g., products that fuse plastic, metal, and paper), the greater the challenge to reincorporate those wastes into the production process. Some wastes are so complex, or so toxic, that the logical solution is to replace them entirely rather than create resource-intensive processes needed to reincorporate those wastes back into the resource stream.

A higher level of clustering is *industrial zoning*. This includes mixed-use zoning and other zoning systems already normalized across most economic landscapes of the world. Industrial zoning is becoming a tool to facilitate zero waste and energy-neutral manufacturing processes, while generating efficiencies in labor, transportation, and financial resources. This includes *vertical* solutions such as combining various residential and commercial needs in a single building. For instance, apartment complexes that design optimal spaces for bakeries, banks, restaurants, or clothing stores on the ground can reduce the cumulative housing and transportation costs of a city. Buildings that integrate greenhouses into vertical spaces generate not only food, but heat for the buildings with which they form an integral whole, while providing novel dining options for restaurants operating on the ground floor.

Mixed-use zoning also works at a *horizontal* scale, such as integrating light industrial businesses activities (e.g., machine shops, materials testing laboratories, etc.) with residential communities. The Uptown District of San Diego combines vertical and horizontal mixed-use development to balance economic, social, and environmental needs within the same community (Blackson, 2013). The benefits of mixed-use zoning go far beyond resource-use efficiency, to include the creation of more cohesive, diverse, and healthier communities, minimizing the need for automobiles, and lowering the cost of public services (Adams, 2021).

In concert, industrial zoning, ecological clustering, industrial clustering, cooperatives, agile manufacturing, etc. are patterned after the marvelous complexity of species interactions in ecosystems. Economies are complex self-regulating systems after all, where such a diversity of solutions are necessary for survival. What has stymied the development of complex regional economies is the exorbitant transfer of energy and physical resources into and out of them. In response, the most efficient solutions remain obscured, struggling to emerge from the din of the global market economy.

The Wasted Niche

So abundant are the species recycling resources in a forest that the diversity of fungi, bacteria, nematodes, and other soil life exceeds that of the plants and animals basking in the sunlit world above. Spoken plainly by mycologist Paul Stamets in the documentary *Fantastic Fungi* (Schwartzberg, 2019), such decomposers are the "digestive system of the earth." In the process of digesting the detritus of life, decomposers build soil fertility, raising the system's capacity to more efficiently harness resources.

Lacking a robust and diverse resource recycling (i.e., decomposition) sector, an economy is unlikely to meet its fullest potential, raise its productive capacity and NDP, attain energy neutrality, or expand its diversity. Here too, the forces of the global market economy have all but extinguished the need to capture and cycle the wastes of industry: chemical pollutants, metals, a growing diversity of plastics, excess heat, water, methane, furniture, and more. Even after sixty years of intensive recycling program development across the nation, despite great advances in GDP and technology, the US recycles and composts only 37% of its waste, with another 12% being diverted for energy production (Environmental Protection Agency, 2020). But this is an overestimate. A portion of America's recycled waste was actually sent to China and other overseas markets, where it may have wound up in landfills if it was too "dirty" to be recycled.

The moment China shut its doors to imported plastic, paper, and some metal waste in 2018, the US and similar countries discovered a harsh reality. America's waste-to-resources sector is dramatically undersized for the collective weight of its consumption. As of 2022 the US was still suffering the consequences of its overdependence on China as a dumping ground. For the entrepreneur, this translates to unimaginable opportunity in the waste-to-resources sector.

A thriving waste-to-resources sector produces abundant environmental and social benefits, the most common of which will be detailed in a later chapter. Less common benefits are showcased by—for instance—sewage treatment facilities that convert sludge into methane to attain energy neutrality (Maktabifard et al., 2020). Even less common, Spring Back Colorado Mattress Recycling provides much-needed job opportunities to former inmates, who experience lower recidivism rates while creating a variety of new products from difficult-to-recycle mattresses.

A free economic zone structured around endogenous energy and domestic trade does not see embrace the above solutions as simply a good idea, but as an essential means to increase their NDP and restore their productive capacity. That same regional economy, by necessity, would not expend energy to ship metal, paper, plastic, or other valuable resources across the world, or perhaps even across state lines, to feed industrial processes in some other economy.

The degree of business opportunity available in America's waste-to-resources sector is exemplified by the metal recycling industry group, systematically undermined by decades of US trade policy. Exorbitant exogenous energy is required to extract iron ore, convert it to ingots, ship the ingots to manufacturing centers, and then mold them into metal products. So backward is America's economic structure that hundreds of thousands of tons of steel rust away in fields and lots across America (Figure 23), while US industries import steel from the opposite end of the earth. In an energy-neutral economy, metal cannot be wasting away in landfills, agricultural fields, or industrial brownfields. It must re-enter the production cycle, creating regional jobs and reducing energy consumption in the process.

The same holds true for heat, an unavoidable waste product of all self-regulating systems, from the cell to the biosphere. In ecosystems and economies, energy may be employed to do immediate work, or it may be temporarily stored (e.g., fat, batteries, towers of molten salt, etc.) for future work. Either way, in the process of doing work, energy is lost from the system. In ecosystems, energy is lost—as heat—during a variety of metabolic processes necessary for growth, maintenance, and reproduction. Energy is also lost in the form of feces and other waste products.

In our economies, of course, heat and other energy losses can be greatly minimized by design. Heat pumps are one of the simplest means to reducing heat waste, and honey bees inform the basic design of those pumps. To survive cold winters and hot summers, honey bees employ various heating and cooling strategies to regulate their hives at an optimum temperature. Their bodies are intolerant of freezing temperatures, while their hives must be maintained below about 97 degrees Fahrenheit. Traditionally, honey bees have done this by creating their hives in tree hollows and other natural objects. In manufactured hives, honey bees use a sticky wax-like resin (propolis) to seal cracks and keep the heat in. This is just the beginning.

Figure 23. A fraction of the steel rusting into the American economic landscape, as global economic forces thwart steel's re-integration into the manufacturing industry.

When temperatures drop low enough, honey bees will form a compact cluster to reduce their collective surface area that is exposed to cold temperatures. In return, each bee expends less energy to keep warm. When temperatures warm, the cluster disperses, and the bees spend more time outside the hive where it is naturally cooler. Further, bees fan their wings in strategic locations around a hive, changing air circulation patterns that lead to energy-efficient cooling.

Beehive biomimicry is informing building designs so as to reduce the energy consumed in heating and cooling, while providing comfortable spaces for the human occupants (Jarimi et al., 2020). Rather than thousands of beating wings, window fans are used to draw cool outside air into a building space, while expelling warmer air. Similarly, the honey bee's clustering strategy informs the design of buffer zones around active living spaces (e.g., foyers), reducing the volume of air that needs to be heated or cooled. Buffer zones also help reduce heat loss to the outside world. Bees employ similar methods to not only maintain optimal temperatures, but to manage humidity in the hive, which in turn reduces mold while maintaining other benefits.

The more reliant an economy becomes on endogenous energy and domestic trade, the more efficiently it must utilize its domestic resources. A thriving waste-to-resources sector is essential to attaining that efficiency, and that efficiency is essential to building and maintaining an economy's productive capacity and NDP. But there is a less obvious economic benefit to restoring a thriving waste-to-resources sector, with roots in global military history.

Transforming Industrial Wastes into Productive Gains—Lessons from the military

In *The Long Twentieth Century*, Arrighi (2010) highlighted the financial gains realized by city-states who nationalized their military expenses in the early days of capitalism. Before that epic transition, the protection of a nation's economic interests—trade routes, centers of production, citizenry—required that city-states pay foreign mercenaries for protection. In essence, wealth that had been built by the productive labor of an economy was being spent on foreign guns for hire, diminishing one's GDP commensurately. This trend reversed when some city-states recognized that building their own military would convert a former drag on GDP (i.e., guns for hire) into an additional means of increasing GDP. Wealth was recirculated in the local economy.

Like the economic advantages realized by nations that "internalize" their military affairs, a thriving waste-to-resources sector transforms former economic expenses (i.e., the unproductive labor of storing, transporting, and landfilling waste) into additional means of production. In the process, environmental externalities associated with resource extraction, such as habitat degradation and pollution, are reduced, while business diversity and NDP increase. In the process, an economy that was once global and inflexible becomes agile by nature, more adaptable to the barrage of external forces, predicted to be even more volatile in the remainder of the 21st century.

Restoring an Industry's Comparative Advantage (The case of Wisconsin paper mills)

Some of America's earliest recycling efforts were mastered by its paper mills. While modern technology has allowed mills to improve their ability to efficiently transform local resources into paper, the opposite has occurred. Mills have suffered a fate similar to those US automotive and agricultural industries bound to the global market economy. Wisconsin's mills, which began their paper-producing journey by consuming rags, straw, and recycled paper to fill a growing demand for newspapers, have been especially hard hit.

Responding to the newsprint trend, mills erupted across America throughout the 1830s, together with a shift from rags and straw to virgin wood pulp (Wisconsin Historical Society, 2020). As local forests were cleared for pulp, Wisconsin mills migrated northward to more bountiful locations like Fox Valley, where Neenah Paper Company (now Kimberly Clark) rose to prominence. Incessant global demand for paper outpaced the growth rate of northern forests, forcing Neenah Paper and others to import wood from the Western US. In effect, Wisconsin mills began transferring global resource pressures to America's coastal mills, over a thousand miles away. In the process, west coast mills, enshrouded by thick timber, competed fiercely with Wisconsin mills. But the west's comparative advantages didn't last.

Paper mills began rising up through Canada's forest-rich landscapes, gaining a dominant share of the growing US paper market. To survive, Wisconsin mills were forced to diversify. Diversification, in this case, meant more product lines such as toilet paper and boxboard. The strategy worked, until even greater threats arose from abroad.

Europe, China, and South America had been building bigger mills, filled with faster papermaking machinery, to better meet the needs of a price-conscious global consumer. Dramatically lower costs of labor and land in China and South America made their mills even more destructive to US mills than were the Canadian mills. If those advantages lacked the potency to completely axe America's paper industry, trees grow more quickly in tropical regions of South America and China. Thus, the social, environmental, and industrial contexts of China and South America granted them an ability to produce paper cheaper than could the American mills. The Pulp and Paperworkers' Resource Council, who has tracked mill closures across the US since 1989, reported that over 500 paper and paper-related businesses have permanently closed or dramatically curtailed their operations.

Remarkably, the Wisconsin paper industry still generates US $18 billion in revenue and employs 30,000 people according to the Wisconsin Economic Development Corporation (WEDC, 2019). But wages begin at about US $17 per hour, and may reach US $20 per hour over time, which is lower than the real wages of the 1960s (in 2020 dollars, adjusted for inflation).

Low wages, coupled with relentless "triple shift" work required to survive destructive global pressures, have left mills scrambling to find labor. And though the highly varied work of modern US mills could attract workers with higher critical thinking skills (WEDC, 2019), the industry cannot afford those workers. In effect, global competition has placed downward pressure not only on wages, but on jobs that would be more fulfilling to the modern American workforce.

Other concerns abound, including labor shortages in the trucking industry, lack of access to trade professionals (e.g., electricians, pipefitters, instrumentation specialists, etc.), and the cost of regulations to address basic air pollution and water quality concerns. Finally, the lack of local fiber remains a problem, putting upward pressure on the cost of raw materials.

Wisconsin paper mills operate in a fundamentally different SEI context than their global competitors. The pollution of air and water, declining availability of trees, and the inhumane shift work required to keep Wisconsin's paper industry alive simply cannot be justified there, or in most regions of the US. American mills are in a global race to industrial extinction. And in a global market economy, paper will never be cheap enough.

Two traditional options exist. Mills can lower the costs of production (e.g., lower wages, attain cheaper raw materials, reduce pollution regulations, attain more efficient scales of production, etc.) to match that of their global competitors. Alternatively, mills can increase the costs of production to address the social and environmental expectations of American consumers. The latter, of course, cannot be sustained amidst a global marketplace. A favorable balance can never be struck between the desire for affordable paper and the desire for clean air—or clean water, habitat protection, humane working conditions, etc.—as long as American paper consumers and producers remain bound to the global marketplace.

But when we step back far enough to view the entire economic landscape of the Midwest, another alternative becomes visible. Millions of acres of subsidized corn fields that currently dominate the Midwest can produce much-needed fiber for mills. This includes poplar, which grows fast enough on Mark Shepard's diverse farm in La Farge, Wisconsin that the forest demands regular thinning lest it spread where it is unwanted. Mark's trees also support mushrooms for local markets, build soil fertility, improve water quality in the watershed, sustain birds and other wildlife, and diversify his income.

Considering the galactic scale of corn production across the Midwest, a conversion of even ten percent of those fields to poplars and other desirable tree species, where the environmental context is appropriate, could help fulfill the Midwest's fiber needs. And the excess heat generated by those mills, such as from timber drying operations, can warm nearby schools and office buildings, while various lumber waste can be transformed into ethanol, or blended with animal wastes to create high quality compost. In one Alaska community, the energy they gained from the waste of a nearby mill was estimated to save US $91,500 per year (Nicholls et al., 2004).

Another solution awaits to be rediscovered in the humble beginnings of Wisconsin's paper industry. America still generates a plethora of straw, rags, and waste paper, much of which enters landfills, or was once exported to China to become paper again. With minimal effort, much of that waste can be directed to domestic mills.

There is another solution, which many fear to even think let alone broach publicly. Given the current economic realities of the global paper industry, a painful question might be asked. Are there too many mills in Wisconsin for all of them to be economically viable? According to interviews in the 2019 WEDC report, some industry leaders admit so. In the midst of labor, trucking, and fiber shortages looming over the industry, mill closures would be healthy for the industry. Instead, according to Missy Hughes of the WEDC (M. Hughes, personal communication, July 2020), Wisconsin was poised to deliver an alternate strategy in 2020—to bailout mills. In the face of globally destructive competition, such bailouts are akin to treating coronary artery disease by prescribing more cheeseburgers.

Another difficult question remains. Should Wisconsin mills even try to compete at a global scale? Or should Wisconsin's remaining mills be retooled to better satisfy domestic needs, regional environmental concerns, and the expectations of local labor markets? If so, many industry leaders believe product innovations, such as replacing plastic goods with equivalent paper products, will aid in the transition.

Considering the long history of their paper mills, I have no doubt Wisconsin can maintain a thriving paper industry for years to come. Assuming, of course, the rules of a self-regulating economy are allowed to operate freely. Based on the drivers of profitability and capital accumulation in ecosystems, I offer the following alternatives, as a minimum, to restore a thriving paper industry in Wisconsin and elsewhere:

- Develop minimum content requirements for paper consumed by government facilities in Wisconsin and other states, which extends to government contractors. Verbiage such as "locally-produced paper required" is easily included in contract language.

- Partner with larger cooperatives, industries, and industry groups to instill those same local content standards for everyone they do business with. Organic Valley Food Cooperative is one large WI company that would likely back such an initiative.

• Create a "locally-sourced paper" campaign for consumers, touting the social and environmental benefits of local paper.

Certainly, the above strategy lacks the quick jolt of a bailout. Of course, the restoration of a productive and resilient economy is by definition a long-term process; a process that begins by restoring an economy's agricultural, manufacturing, and waste-to-resources industries. And in the restoration of those industries, the creation of an energy-neutral economy becomes feasible.

ELEVEN

CREATING AN ENERGY-NEUTRAL ECONOMY

So inefficient is the US economy that its per capita GDP, relative to the quantity of energy consumed, places it at number thirty out of 163 countries (World Bank, 2019, Table 3). Worse yet, the US is among the world's ten lowest performers in terms of the energy consumed to support its GDP (Enerdata, 2019). America earned this status thanks to its citizens who, on average, consume more energy in a year than the citizens of almost any other country. With renewable energy programs unfolding rampantly across dozens of nations, it is high time we ask if those programs alone are sufficient to meet our future energy needs. Or, will renewable energy goals fall short of what a self-regulating economy needs to thrive? Is 100% renewable energy even the right goal?

Beyond Renewable Energy

If all the energy consumed to produce and distribute an economy's goods and services was renewable, multiple benefits might rise—higher and more stable energy industry wages, cleaner air, etc. As it stands, though, the great bulk of America's energy is non-renewable, with fossil fuels accounting for the lion's share (Figure 24). The reason citizens of any country should care is elementary. Stemming from their current economic structure, the US and other nations will struggle to maintain a desirable NDP, productive capacity, standard of living, national security, and meet other basic needs in a future of diminishing fossil fuel supplies and more volatile energy costs. The turmoil in global energy markets that struck the entire globe when Russia invaded Ukraine in 2022 is but one incident in a long string of energy-related wars.

But change is in motion. The first two decades of the twenty-first century witnessed several American states taking baby steps toward energy independence, by setting alternative energy targets. Colorado broke ground with the first voter-approved renewable portfolio standard (RPS), requiring that a third of its electric utilities be supplied by renewable energy by the year 2020. Later, governor Jared Polis set a target for Colorado's largest energy utilities to acquire all of their electricity from clean energy sources by 2050.

It would seem that Colorado's great supply of solar, wind, and hydroelectric energy would make such targets a slam dunk. Yet, by 2020 only a quarter of

Table 3. Rank of per capita GDP on a unit energy basis. Partial list of countries included.

Rank	Country	Per capita GDP on unit energy basis	GDP in 2019* ($Trillions)	Population (2019, M)	Energy Use (2019)**
1	Switzerland	27.7	0.70	8.6	2960.1
2	Ireland	25.8	0.36	4.9	2819.9
3	Hong Kong	24.7	0.36	7.4	1970.5
4	Denmark	20.7	0.34	5.8	2816.6
5	Malta	17.4	0.01	0.4	1781.5
6	Luxembourg	16.4	0.07	0.6	6548.4
7	Israel	15.2	0.36	8.5	2777.9
8	United Kingdom	14.9	2.79	67.5	2764.0
9	Panama	14.2	0.07	4.2	1079.9
10	Italy	13.1	1.97	60.6	2481.8
11	Norway	12.9	0.40	5.4	5817.6
12	Austria	12.8	0.44	9.0	3800.3
13	Uruguay	12.1	0.06	3.5	1386.0
14	Japan	12.0	5.22	126.9	3428.6
15	Germany	12.0	3.82	83.5	3817.5
16	Netherlands	12.0	0.87	17.1	4233.0
17	Costa Rica	11.7	0.06	5.0	1023.0
18	Singapore	11.6	0.34	5.8	5121.8
19	Cyprus	11.5	0.02	1.2	1712.2
20	Spain	11.4	1.37	46.7	2571.3
21	France	11.1	2.67	65.1	3689.5
22	Sweden	10.7	0.55	10.0	5102.8
23	Mauritius	10.5	0.01	1.2	1111.4
24	Portugal	10.4	0.23	10.2	2131.7
25	Australia	10.1	1.39	25.2	5483.8
26	Dominican Republic	10.0	0.08	10.7	751.8
27	New Zealand	9.7	0.21	4.8	4444.7
28	Belgium	9.4	0.51	11.5	4687.8
29	Greece	9.3	0.21	10.5	2182.1
30	**United States**	9.1	20.41	329.1	6803.9
31	Colombia	8.7	0.32	50.3	724.0
32	Peru	8.5	0.22	32.5	790.2
33	Finland	8.1	0.26	5.5	5924.7

* Average of IMF and World Bank data
** International Energy Agency (2019 data, kg oil equivalent)

Colorado's total electrical demands were met by renewables. Even if Colorado does reach its 2050 target, the dynamics of a self-regulating economy underscore an uncomfortable truth: adding more renewables is not a guaranteed path to economic prosperity.

Energy Neutrality Defined

Based on the nature of energy production and flows in a self-regulating ecosystem, a self-regulating economy would be restructured such that the energy consumed at every point of production and consumption is generated at those same nodes. This is *energy neutrality*. Here too, small changes are being forged by nations across the globe, such as Norway, Germany, Sweden, Bhutan, New Zealand, and the UK. Even in the energy-intensive USA, a handful of cities—Montpelier, VT; Cambridge, MA; Bloomfield, IA; Georgetown, TX, etc.—have pledged to become energy neutral in the coming decades (Zero Energy Project, 2020). The details of such pledges beg to be revealed, however, so we may clearly differentiate energy neutrality from the actual energy goals those communities have set.

To begin, consider the difference between energy neutrality and *net zero*, which refers to balancing carbon exchange between an economy (or business) and the atmosphere. Energy neutrality also differs from a 100% renewable energy goal. As it turns out, many cities pledging to be energy neutral are simply aiming to acquire all of their energy from renewable sources in order to achieve net zero carbon conditions, lower their energy expenses, or attain other benefits. So renewable energy is acquired from anywhere possible. Hydro power from California may be cabled to New York City, while wind power from Iowa might end up in Minnesota, and their renewable energy goals can still be met. But those cities will be far from energy neutral.

Deeper structural changes are required for any economy to become energy neutral, reflecting the fact that energy cannot be created nor destroyed. Thus, 100% of an economy's energy requirements must be met not simply by renewable energy, but by endogenous energy—energy originating within one's economic border. The cascading effect of this one goal is that every business, residence, farm, and government building—every place where goods and services are produced—must generate enough energy to meet its own needs. And certainly, the benefits of such an economy could be net zero carbon emissions, resilience, increased job stability, or reduced energy expenses.

The Benefits of an Energy-Neutral Economy

The fear of economic catastrophe waged by many capitalists at the onset of America's environmental regulations of the 1960s and 70s never materialized. Social and environmental regulations did not put a stranglehold on GDP, nor impair anyone's quality of life. In fact, the opposite trend—higher GDP, cleaner air, and cleaner water—has occurred since the inception of the Clean Air Act, Clean Water Act, Endangered Species Act, etc.

America's transition to an energy-neutral economy will not wreak economic catastrophe, nor spoil the quality of life of its citizens. The more likely outcome is that energy neutrality will sustain both. And given energy's role as a foundational component, an energy-neutral economy may provide benefits far beyond what most of us typically imagine.

To begin, the risk of energy-related externalities is reduced as communities shorten their energy supply chains. A few current examples of energy-related externalities may suffice: social and environmental impacts of coal mining in Wyoming; contention over wind farms in the American Midwest; oil spills in Lago Agrio, Ecuador; and the 2010 Deep Horizon oil spill in the Gulf of Mexico. More recently, a gasoline tanker spilled over a thousand gallons of fuel into Colorado's Saint Vrain Creek in 2021, causing a large-scale fish kill and contaminating water just as farmers were drawing from the river for irrigation needs.

If this were an isolated incident, Coloradoans would have no cause for alarm. However, 55,000 barrels of oil and gas spills occurred in Colorado in 2019 alone (Center for Western Priorities, 2019). Tens of thousands more spills occur across the US every year. Likely, hundreds of thousands of accidental spills and discharges from wells, tanks, pipelines, and other conveyances across the globe occur annually, a large portion of which go unreported.

Environmental benefits aside, an energy-neutral economy provides several financial benefits. Just as nations achieve financial gains simply by internalizing their military and waste management expenses, so too may they make gains by supplanting exogenous energy (e.g., imported wind power, coal, petroleum, etc.) with endogenous energy production. In essence, by redirecting wealth (i.e., the surplus value of an economy's productive industries) toward domestic energy producers, rather than transferring that wealth to energy producers of another economy, GDP rises commensurately. Should domestic energy production be more expensive, this simply places pressure on the adoption of energy efficient technology, or acts as a stimulant for economic restructuring that would engender energy efficiency.

Besides the recirculation of domestically-derived wealth, broader benefits may result from energy neutrality. To begin, it is predicted that most nations will struggle to achieve an economic growth rate of even 1.2%—far below the average global growth rate over the past century—unless new sources of energy are discovered to replace fossil fuels (Piketty, 2014). That is, future productivity hinges on secure energy resources.

Furthermore, the creation of an energy-neutral economy would require significant and stable job growth throughout the energy industry. For instance, America's renewable energy industry group supports about two jobs for every job supported by the fossil fuel industry (US Department of Energy, 2020), per unit of energy produced. Another 2.4 million jobs are created by energy efficiency services and the construction of alternative energy facilities—more jobs than the fossil fuel and renewable energy groups combined. Importantly, renewable energy jobs pay about 25% higher wages than fossil fuel jobs (BW Research, 2020).

Regarding those businesses that implement energy-efficiency solutions, the cost savings are not trivial. For instance, over half the world's electricity is used to run motors, half of which power pumps and fans (Lovins, 2014). According to Amory Lovins, co-founder of the Rocky Mountain Institute, the energy consumed by motors can be cut in half simply by adopting existing innovations. The cost of integrating those innovations can pay for itself in about a year. Lovins's research indicates that US buildings can more than triple their productivity, per unit of energy consumed, with a cumulative saving of US $1.4 trillion. That estimate was made in 2010. Energy-efficiency technology is advancing so quickly that its adoption cannot keep pace, and the cost of energy is rising once again. Likely, the cost savings of modern energy-efficient technology are greater today than they were in 2010.

One family of energy technology advancing faster than its adoption is *combined heat and power*, and *waste heat to power* (i.e., recycled energy). These two systems are just beginning to gain favor in some US industries. By generating power on site, a business can more efficiently use the resulting heat loss—the unavoidable waste from energy production—to cool and warm its commercial spaces, or to meet other energy needs. These systems can cut energy consumption in half, compared to traditional energy systems, while avoiding energy losses that naturally occur as electricity travels through long transmission lines (Colorado Energy Office, 2019b).

Another recent energy-efficiency technology is the organic Rankine cycle (ORC) generator, which produces electricity from the heat lost during generation. An ORC generator uses fluids with very low boiling points—as low as

170 degrees Fahrenheit—to produce electricity (Thibedeau, 2019). ORC generators are similar to steam-powered generators, but use organic fluids instead of water.

The financing for energy-efficient systems is becoming more creative, such as power purchase agreements (PPAs). PPAs allow energy developers to own and operate an alternative energy system (e.g., ORC generator, solar array, etc.) that is installed on the grounds of participating businesses. The developer sells the power to a local utility at a fixed rate, and sells any remaining energy to the business that houses the alternative energy system. State agencies across the US provide a wide range of financing through programs such as Colorado's Green Colorado Credit Reserve. These programs incentivize private lenders to make capital improvement loans to businesses for energy efficiency and alternative energy projects.

Alternative energy solutions are not without their environmental downsides. For instance, the potentially toxic materials required of battery storage systems (e.g., lead, mercury, cadmium, etc.), when mishandled during the mining, manufacturing, distribution, and disposal process can cause environmental harm. More limiting, these rare materials are unavailable in many regional economies where batteries are a key component of the renewable energy system. Therefore, the essential materials of a battery must be imported.

Research on non-toxic battery storage is ongoing, with much room for ingenious tinkerers to make their mark. This includes not only technological innovation, but innovation in various social systems. For instance, energy utilities that charge variable rates depending on the timing of use have seen reductions in peak demand, which translates to reduced storage needs. An increasing number of communities around the world are using time-of-day pricing programs (e.g., adjusting the cost of electricity by season, day of the week, and by the hour. This is supply and demand economics at work; only, consumption decisions are facilitated by more accurate knowledge of supply. The timing of a community's peak demand hinges on their SEI context, which includes the type of endogenous energy system they have built. Yet regardless of context, strategic shifts in an economy's trade and diversity components must also occur for any community to reach the energy neutrality finish line.

The Friction between Diversity, Trade, and Energy Neutrality

A curious conundrum exists between energy, diversity, and trade in the US economy. America's productive capacity and NDP rests on its ability to capture and distribute energy as efficiently as possible within every regional economy. Economic diversity is a core means to achieving that efficiency. But like most developed countries, the US has enacted a litany of policies, pacts, and programs that result in great applications of exogenous energy at the expense of economic diversity, creating a vicious downward spiral.

To break the cycle, the most obvious shift would be to actually implement the plethora of energy-efficiency innovations already in existence—consuming less energy in the production and consumption of goods and services. An economy's remaining energy needs (i.e., after efficiency measures have been exhausted) must be met with endogenous sources at every node of production and consumption. This requires our economies employ not a single usable energy source, but a great diversity of sources. America's low-diversity energy system, with 80% of its energy supplied by fossil fuels (Figure 24), imparts

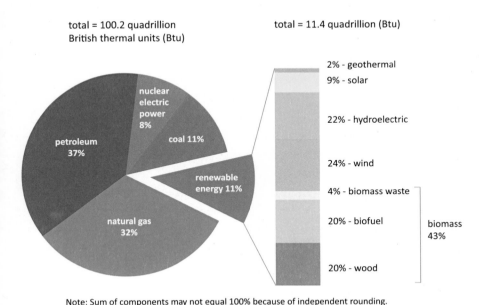

total = 100.2 quadrillion British thermal units (Btu)

total = 11.4 quadrillion (Btu)

2% - geothermal
9% - solar
22% - hydroelectric
24% - wind
4% - biomass waste ⎤
20% - biofuel   ⎟ biomass 43%
20% - wood   ⎦

nuclear electric power 8%
petroleum 37%
coal 11%
renewable energy 11%
natural gas 32%

Note: Sum of components may not equal 100% because of independent rounding.
Source: U.S. Energy Information Administration, Monthly Energy Review, Table 1.3 and 10.1, April 2020, preliminary data.

eia

Figure 24. U.S. Primary energy consumption by energy source, 2019.

equally low resilience and resistance to turbulent energy markets. The energy diversity of most nations is not much different (BP, 2021). Coupled with our low-diversity economic landscapes, this leaves tremendous ground to cover in building an energy-neutral economy.

A great diversity of renewable energy technologies—biodiesel, wind, solar, geothermal, biomethanol, hydroelectric—exist to meet energy demands in most regional economies across the world. However, technology is just one means by which diversity contributes to energy neutrality. Earlier, it was shown that more diverse farmlands capture greater amounts of energy and nutrients than less diverse farmlands. While a high-diversity economy is capable of consuming less energy and physical resources than a low-diversity economy, per unit of net primary production.

Regardless of an economy's technological prowess, or the energy-efficiencies gained through diversification, a prickly hurdle remains along the path to energy neutrality. For economic diversity to have a meaningful impact on energy neutrality, significant shifts in the balance of trade are required.

Transportation accounts for a whopping 30% of all energy consumed in the US (Energy Information Administration, 2020), and 90% of this is in the form of fossil fuels. Therefore, regional economies will struggle to attain energy neutrality until they achieve vast reductions in transportation. The most likely impact will come from shrinking the distance between producers and consumers.

At the high end of the inefficiency scale, Hawaii ships beef on 747s to the West Coast of the US, and then ships burgers and steaks back to the islands in refrigerated shipping containers. On average, the food on most American plates arrives after a thousand-mile journey across highways, railways, and cargo ships. The recycled steel and paper that is shipped from America and Europe across oceans (e.g., as far away as China, until 2018), only to be shipped back as finished products, is another example of gross energy inefficiencies associated with the global market economy. In total, about 60% of US products are imported, consuming tremendous exogenous energy simply in their transport.

Revolutionary economic change is needed before we can attain energy neutrality, providing boundless opportunity for entrepreneurs, urban and regional planners, and community leaders. Restoring the productive capacity of a region's agriculture and manufacturing sectors, to meet regional rather than global consumption needs, will shorten supply chains. In turn, the energy consumed in long-distance shipping will diminish. Furthermore, shorter supply chains place downward pressure on waste throughout the distribution system, translating to additional energy savings. Short supply chains also facilitate a thriving waste-to-resources sector, which reduces the energy consumed in the extraction, processing, and shipping of ore from distant mines to manufacturing centers, and from those centers to end consumers, which would otherwise be shipped back across oceans to a recycling facility, etc.

No doubt, some export-based manufacturing facilities can produce a given widget—car, refrigerator, shovel, bottle—more efficiently than a small regional manufacturer, due to their energy-efficient production lines. The critical factor in this discussion, however, is that the overall quantity of energy demanded by such an export-based business is not easily met with endogenous energy supplies.

There is a silver lining. Manufacturing facilities of all sizes, in every economic space, have ample room to increase their energy efficiency, without jeopardizing profitability. Amory Lovins's "Reinventing Fire" highlights some of the most advanced solutions, representing decades of research (Lovins, 2014). This peer-reviewed report is perhaps one of the most insightful works with regards to an energy-neutral economy. Lovins outlines a transformation of America's inefficient, aging, dirty, and insecure energy system into one of eloquent energy efficiency across all sectors. Similar to the profit motive of high-diversity low-input farming, profitability is a key driver for energy-efficient manufacturing. Driven by profit, the successful integration of energy-efficient technologies with an energy-wise economic structure is far less dependent on fickle politics. Such solutions are sustainable by design, not by mandate.

Vast opportunities exist not only in the successful adoption of physical technology by the public and private sectors (i.e., raw technological innovation), but in the integration of raw technological innovations with novel energy storage and distribution systems. The Green Mountain Project mentioned earlier is one example. Similarly, small-scale solar arrays, hydroelectric projects, and wind farms, coupled with modern microgrid technology, allow for the energy demands of cooperating neighborhoods or industry groups to be connected via a local energy network. Such cooperative solutions, "pooling" the demands of dozens of energy consumers into one larger energy project, provide financial efficiencies not attainable by individual businesses or residents operating their own small-scale system.

Is Energy Neutrality Feasible Without Restoring the Balance of Trade? (The case of New Belgium Brewing)

The challenge of attaining energy neutrality amidst America's current economic structure is epitomized by one of the nation's most sustainable businesses: New

Belgium Brewing. America's seventh largest brewery, New Belgium has made incredible strides in alternative energy, their Fort Collins facility sends less than 1% of their waste to landfills, and they have implemented some of the most progressive climate solutions in the nation.

New Belgium's on-site electricity generation (i.e., endogenous energy) comes in two forms. One is on-site generation in the form of solar photovoltaics, while a more novel form is anaerobic digestion, a biological process that breaks down organic waste—process water from brewing operations—in the absence of oxygen to create biogas, which is then converted to electricity (New Belgium, 2021). This is a great example of Combined Heat and Power (CHP) systems, which generate thermal energy to offset the energy consumed by natural gas-fired boilers or other on-site energy systems (Colorado Energy Office, 2019a). CHP is appropriate for a variety of energy intensive food and beverage manufacturers. New Belgium Brewing's CHP system not only reduces their total energy needs, but reduces electricity costs by about US $53,000 per year. Similarly, New Belgium's Ashville facility produces about sixty million BTUs of energy from biogas generation (Tuser, 2019).

New Belgium's energy efficiency gains are also stimulated by a self-imposed tax on every kilowatt hour of electricity they purchase. The dollars generated by this tax support energy efficiency and renewable energy solutions throughout their Fort Collins plant. From all these efforts, the Fort Collins plant meets about 12% of their total electricity demands with on-site generation, an incredible step in the direction toward energy neutrality.

Twelve percent is a lot. Yet, accounting for the energy used by its Fort Collins facility, which exports libations to dozens of states, New Belgium's most aggressive on-site energy production systems cannot keep pace with demand. They make up the difference by importing electricity from wind farms in Wyoming (Fort Collins Gov, 2021), far beyond Fort Collins's city limits, and even beyond the South Platte watershed. That is, about 88% of their energy is exogenous.

Fundamentally, manufacturing plants designed to meet the needs of national or global markets use far too much energy to be sustained by on-site—or even regional—energy sources. Those large-scale manufacturers have no choice but to concentrate energy from regions far beyond their production facilities. The high concentration of energy allows for the concentration of other resources, such as water, glass, aluminum, steel, hops, barley, financial capital, etc.

Certainly, large-scale production facilities can at times produce a unit of beer, or a unit of some other product, with less energy than a smaller producer can. However, such efficiencies often erode when accounting for the energy consumed in shipping, for instance, a heavy bottle of beer from Fort Collins to Minneapolis. To meet quality standards, that beer must also be refrigerated the entire distance.

Alternatively, when accounting for the energy consumed in the manufacture and installation of renewable energy systems, efficiency may increase by installing one large-scale system rather than several smaller-scale systems—whose total output is equal to the one larger system. The debate between the energy efficiencies of large- and small-scale systems, and the various solutions to resolve them, is outside the scope of this book. Besides, there is be a less technical solution to New Belgium's (or any company's) endogenous energy challenge.

Over two thousand homes in Fort Collins already have solar installations on their rooftops, with more installations happening quarterly. Through the city's net metering program, excess energy produced on rooftops can be fed directly into the grid. The financial cost and energy consumed to manufacture and install those systems, and update the city's electrical grid to integrate them, have already been expended. Should New Belgium, or any other business, pay homeowners to add a few more panels to their existing systems, the additional electricity generated helps offset that which is consumed in manufacturing processes. The incentive for homeowners providing the space for solar generation is simple. Energy produced beyond home consumption provides owners with a credit, reducing future energy bills. Of course, a cooler benefit may be that they are supporting the energy needs of their favorite restaurant or brewery.

Integrating Technical and Structural Innovations

Certainly, continual innovation will help advance endogenous energy solutions that bestow benefits to regional economies. This includes not only the adoption of ingenious technical solutions, but innovative structural changes. Ecological clustering, cooperatives, and agile manufacturing were highlighted earlier, which engender energy-efficiency simply by design. Through these symbiotic relationships, businesses may also pool their energy demands into one larger renewable energy system—a more cost-efficient means to attaining energy neutrality.

But it is the integration of technical and structural innovations that holds the greatest promise for attaining energy neutrality. For example, building one anaerobic digestion facility to serve a cluster of restaurants and breweries could allow for a more efficient conversion of organic wastes to biogas. Research on biogas and biodiesel production from organic wastes is ongoing, with significant progress in Europe (Bušić et al., 2018). However, there are often structural hurdles that prevent biogas and similar technologies from being most efficiently utilized.

Inadvertently, zoning rules may require a biogas digestor, for instance, to be located far from a food manufacturing and restaurant cluster, which means more energy will be consumed to ship food waste to the digestor. Innovative zoning, then, becomes another tool communities and regional economies may use to attain energy neutrality, by facilitating rather than thwarting system-wide energy efficiencies.

Regional and local governments can also help transform their economies to energy neutral states simply by setting targets. Even if the target is missed, the advances that occur along the way can be significant. Trade and energy-neutrality targets can also be set by industry, and be as effective as total quality management targets (zero defects), just-in-time inventory (zero inventory), and carbon neutrality goals. For instance, a company can develop a strategic plan to do 90% or more of their business in the South Platte economic zone, and meet all of their energy needs with energy produced there. At a federal level, targets may set into motion an energy-neutrality race similar to Kennedy's race to put an American on the moon.

When the resulting collage of innovation and structural changes reduces the exogenous energy required to meet the needs of a regional economy, the region gains one more step toward energy neutrality. Fossil fuels comprise the largest single industry in the world, and the US is their single largest consumer. By extension, an energy-neutral America will produce rippling effects across the globe.

The Unavoidable Link Between Energy Security and National Security

Global oil production is estimated to peak somewhere between 2025 and 2050 (Hirsch et al., 2005), then decline precipitously. While the exact date is under debate, as new fossil fuel reserves do arise over time, more important issues are at stake. As fossil fuel supplies begin to vanish, relative to growing demand, upward pressure will be place on the cost of all energy. Even before that day arrives, fossil fuel markets are likely to become volatile as nations begin scrambling to find suitable replacements to fossil fuel, waging the threat of war or sanctions (e.g., Russia, the US, the EU in 2022). Great uncertainty will ripple throughout related markets and supply chains, for no product moves without energy. In concert with this global uncertainty, the cost of all energy supplies may increase so rapidly that the cost of goods and services skyrockets, leading to serious inflation, such as the eight percent inflation in the US between 2021 and 2022.

A diverse and energy-neutral regional economy, thriving on ample domestic trade, provides a tremendous buffer to global market forces. That economy is decoupled from global commodity shocks, such as the price of oil or fertilizer. Further, local renewable energy and energy efficiency jobs are more likely to remain strong in the face of volatile global markets, knee-jerk national policies, or trade wars, all of which have plagued fossil fuel jobs across America for decades.

Ultimately, energy neutrality engenders economic security. Economic security is a prerequisite to national security (i.e., military strength), which hinges on one's productive capacity and NDP. In a vicious feedback loop, one's productive capacity and NDP are continually at risk in those nations that bind themselves to global fossil fuel markets and the cheap consumer products that fossil fuels produce and deliver.

The USA is a shining example. America's raw GDP is the highest on earth— as of this writing. However, that productivity is artificial; propped up by an abundance of relatively inexpensive fossil fuels, low-cost land and labor from around the globe, and a litany of social and environmental externalities cast upon cheap export-based communities with every purchase. The resulting costs of production are lower than what is otherwise feasible (i.e., should the endogenous energy, labor, land, and other costs of production reflect America's economic context rather than the context of supplier nations). The pressure on American industry to gain more fundamental efficiencies in production— not simply the financial efficiencies gained from a system of cheap imported materials—is duly relieved. The negative impacts of this system on America's productive capacity and NDP were outlined earlier, including degraded soil fertility, and a highly inefficient use of energy in meeting its production needs.

Energy security is a condition whereby the quantity of commercially available energy adequately meets consumer demands. Not only is the future energy security of the US dismal, but hundreds of communities across the nation have little to no energy production capacity at all. Communities that continue relying on state and federal governments to resolve their energy needs must take note. From countless failed wars in the Middle East, and tenuous negotiations between energy-poor countries over access to reserves in oil-rich countries, even the mighty US military is inadequate to secure an endless pipeline of exogenous energy to any citizen. In a vicious downward spiral, when the productive capacity of any nation erodes, its military might will be dragged down with it. Systemic change is paramount to our survival.

For US citizens, it is tempting to believe more nuclear power will secure our energy future, until we note three sobering truths. First, uranium reserves are a non-renewable resource. Based on consumption rates in the early decades of the twenty-first century, it is likely global uranium reserves will last another 135-250 years (Nuclear Energy Agency, 2020). This estimate is generous compared to others (Capra & Luisi, 2014). Of course, the best industry estimates are always questionable, due to the unpredictable nature of external forces such as changes in supply and demand for competing energy products, technological breakthroughs, global politics, etc.

Second, uranium reserves of the US are a fraction of the reserves of other countries, putting the US in a poor negotiating position in a tight energy future. Hence, the supply (i.e., the price) of nuclear energy to sustain the US economy will most likely grow more uncertain over time, at constant risk of external forces: trade barriers, global fluctuations in production and consumption patterns, political strife in uranium-producing countries, and so forth. Third, of course, is the issue of health and safety in the production, transportation, and disposal of nuclear materials.

A nation's energy security is attained not by investment in oil wars or any single alternative energy source, but through a strategic diversification of endogenous energy supplies. Until the nations of the world attain such a condition, the cost of energy must rise, alongside the price of nearly everything that consumers desire. This includes not simply the cost of food and shelter, but the cost of maintaining a strong military. In this light, national policies stimulating exogenous energy consumption and continued global trade are simply an attack on the security of the citizens those nations are charged with protecting.

Will the US Thrive or Collapse Without Fossil Fuels?

Most of us cannot grasp just how impactful exogenous energy has become to our daily lives until we ponder weaning ourselves from it. Modern labor-saving appliances, indoor lighting, multiple personal vehicles to shuttle us to the grocery store and back, fresh fruit delivered daily from thousands of miles away, water at the flick of the wrist, heat at the flip of a switch—little occurs in our daily routine that is not influenced by cheap fossil fuels or imported electricity from distant wind farms.

American homes consume between 800 kWh and 2,000 kWh of electricity per month, depending on their SEI context. Add to this the energy consumed by grocery stores, manufacturing facilities, retail outlets, personal vehicles, government buildings, commercial transportation, agriculture, the extraction and processing of raw materials, etc. Accounting for America's entire energy picture, annual consumption is closer to 80,000 kWh per person. To put this into perspective, global energy consumption is (on average) 30,000 kWh per person annually.

Would flipping the switch to an energy-neutral economy cause America's demise? In short, of course not. In fact, America's gross reliance on exogenous energy—mostly fossil fuels—is jeopardizing its future economic might. Of course, a great number of past global superpowers—the Roman Empire, the Maya civilization, northern Italian city-states, the Ottoman Empire, the Bronze Age Civilizations of Europe, and others—have suffered a similar fate. That is, the concentration of exogenous resources from distant lands into centers of wealth, followed by collapse, or at least a vast contraction to the detriment of their citizens.

Yet here America stands, its aggregate wealth higher than that of any previous superpower, and most of that wealth is concentrated into far fewer hands than any time before (Stiglitz, 2015). Considering America's prenatal-like reliance on exogenous energy, subsidies, bailouts, and imported resources from around the globe, is the US on the same trajectory as previous collapsed empires? That is, a path of ever-increasing energy and wealth concentrations at the expense of economic diversity, productive capacity, and stability?

I must answer no, for a few beneficial ironies have developed alongside the economic boom of the US and other developed economies. First, the extensive evolution of agricultural, industrial, and renewable energy technology has laid the groundwork for an unprecedented degree of business diversification and the efficient production of goods and services, relative to domestic energy supplies and the skill of labor. Today, the nations of earth have the potential to produce modern goods and services with less energy and physical resources than what was possible during any previous capitalist epoch.

Second, the democratic structure of governance, high degrees of connectivity between *domestic* trade centers, and vast natural resources of the US together provide an SEI context supportive of a highly functioning modern economy. Third, the borders of the world's most powerful and competitive nations— USA, China, Japan, the Association of Southeast Asian Nations, Russia, Great Britain, France, Italy, Germany, India, etc.—are relatively well set, each with similar advances in democratic governance (Harari, 2015). Coupled, these conditions allow highly functional free economic zones to thrive nearly anywhere on earth.

But can an economy as consumer-oriented as the US function as an assemblage of energy-neutral regional economies, and still satisfy its energy appetite? Based on the work of the National Renewable Energy Lab (NREL), renewable energy production can comfortably meet over two thirds of total electricity demands in the US by 2050, using existing technology (Hand et al., 2012). An important gap in the NREL study is the assumption that only a small portion of the current petroleum-powered transportation industry will be converted to electric-powered transportation. Should all transportation needs be powered by fossil-fuel-free electricity, a chasm will develop between the production and consumption of electricity. The best hope of closing that gap is for an economy to restore its balance of trade and vastly increase its economic diversity. Energy security will follow.

TWELVE

TRANSITIONS TO A RESTORED ECONOMY

In order to change an existing paradigm you do not struggle to try and change the problematic model. You create a new model and make the old one obsolete.

~ Buckminster Fuller

As a regional economy builds its capacity to efficiently capture and distribute resources, succession can follow myriad pathways, some more desirable than others. Fortunately, the process of succession is not left completely to the whims of nature. The experience of restoration ecologists suggests that succession can be assisted. In our economies, the practitioners, community leaders, entrepreneurs, consultants, CEOs, and politicians who develop restoration treatments to steer succession—toward the productive and diverse center—might be referred to as *restoration economists.*

Restoration economists may prescribe treatments, but the work is carried out by industry at local, regional, state, and national levels. there is also an overarching need for government to fill at those same levels. Milton Friedman, a rather conservative economist, understood that the role of government is to do something the market cannot do for itself—to determine, arbitrate, and enforce the rules of the game (Friedman, 1982). Friedman's stance implies that, with the rules of the game set, the reforms and innovations necessary to achieve economic restoration must be carried out by businesses—the basic units of economic diversity.

New Belgium Brewing's work is a notable example of progress in the brewing industry, as is Patagonia's work in the clothing industry. Long before those successes, paper and lumber mills developed waste-to-energy and recycling solutions that are the envy of modern environmentalists. More recently, Göss Brewing of Austria has built solutions that allow nearly half of their heating needs to be supplied by waste heat from a nearby sawmill (European Commission, 2016). Yet for such solutions to make meaningful economic

233

sense, a transition from a global to a national network of regional economies must occur in the US, the EU, the ASEAN, in Central America, and elsewhere.

Three Transition Models

The desire to form sustainable, self-regulating, self-reliant, resilient, self-sufficient, local, and regional (there are many terms in use) economies is nothing new. The aim of previous chapters was to outline the foundational economic components that must be managed well, and at the right scale, to most effectively guide our actions. And while the ultimate form of any free economic zone is a product of its SEI context, a few models are possible. One such model is already in the process of forming. It simply needs a collective nudge.

The Nested Economy

Within most states and regions of the US, or within any country, a complete shift to a free economic zone cannot occur overnight. Furthermore, there are some who fear a trade-off (real or perceived) between their quantity of life and their quality of life. In their minds, change must be witnessed before it is believed. In such cases, a *nested economy* within a larger county, region, or state may be the surest path forward.

A nested economy is nothing more than a local economy operating within the existing global market economy—parallel to it, if you will. It is a subset of the existing economy, the people of which are dedicated to restoring economic diversity, energy neutrality, and a balance of trade in their regional and local economic spaces. The nested economy is tasked with becoming a truly self-regulating economy and, in the process, making the old system obsolete. To reiterate, there is no need to secede from the nation, actively protest against the global market economy, nor form a new currency. More productive measures are needed.

A natural first step is to restore local and regional diversity to agricultural and food production industries. This diversification has begun across the US and other countries, in the form of community supported agriculture (CSAs), farmers markets, food cooperatives, in-season menus, and farm-to-table trends, etc.

Within a complex self-regulating system, however, no action exists in a vacuum. Actions must span sectors and industries to be effective. Diversifying a region's extractive and manufacturing industries must occur alongside restoration of its agriculture and retail industries. In concert, this blossoming of diversity allows for a more efficient use of energy and physical resources. These efficiencies are bound tightly with the productivity of endogenous energy and waste-to-resources industries, further facilitating the success of a regional economy. Yet it is not out of altruism that a regional network of businesses chooses to collaborate across industries and sectors; their ultimate success demands that they collaborate. The benefits of a diverse economy have been outlined: stronger real wages, higher employment, greater economic stability, resilience, etc.

Clean Slate

At the other end of the population spectrum, where a small region harbors just ten or even eighty thousand people, a clean slate approach may be feasible. The greater the current consumer support for local production and independence—the more likely a clean slate approach will succeed.

The State of Jefferson is one such US region ripe for a clean slate approach. Centered around Siskiyou County, California, Jefferson is blessed with abundant timber, ore, water, farmland, hydroelectric, geothermal, biomethane, and solar energy. Importantly, Jefferson harbors a healthy mix of rural and urban demographics that together could enrich the region with diversity. Ashland and Mt. Shasta support a thriving art community. Ingenuity abounds that, when integrated with the practical innovators and engineering-minded rural residents, creates a formula for raising the productive capacity, employment, wages, and other economic benefits for Jeffersonians. Recognizing this, the Jefferson Economic Development Institute (JEDI) has been working for decades to increase the economic well-being of people and communities, through business development and local wealth creation.

Cascadia in the Pacific Northwest is another independence movement. Hundreds of regions across the US exhibit similar demographics and socio-economic values as the State of Jefferson and Cascadia, while serious social movements in Scotland, Wales, Flanders, Catalonia, Quebec, and others have been rising throughout Europe and North America. As social tensions and wealth gaps continue rising across the globe, these independence movements will only strengthen, correcting an out-of-balance system that is struggling to operate at too great a scale.

The Donut Hole

From a birds-eye view, the ring of suburbs and rural areas surrounding a large metropolis can appear a greenish-brown donut, with a grey-green hole in the center. As the sun sets, the hole illuminates, dimming toward the fringes, where farm fields lay idle under the growing stars. The larger the city—San Francisco, Los Angeles, New York—the more challenging will be the restoration of a self-regulating economy. The concentration of wealth, not to mention the density of pavement and other infrastructure, may simply be too substantial to overcome.

The economic space of such metropoles has been the global market economy, rendering them vastly over-built for their regional SEI context, inviable without continual infusions from the globe. Travelling their subways and buses are humans who have grown so dependent on exogenous resources that meaningful change is difficult to imagine let alone secure.

In San Francisco, Los Angeles, or New York, is structural economic change possible without a collapse of the current system? Based on the economic past of similar metropoles, the answer is *possibly*. As described by Braudel (1984), the circle of towns and farmlands surrounding London were wildly productive during the Industrial Revolution. As Adam Smith portrayed the economic relationships in and around London and similar metropoles, he noted how the exchange of resources between town and country were essential for each of them to thrive. The modern American metropolis is no different. A free economic zone composed of, for instance, San Francisco and its encircling suburbs and rural areas, may produce similar economic benefits as those noted in London during the Industrial Revolution.

The economic success of local farmers in areas such as Sonoma, Gilroy, and Petaluma—communities on the fringe of San Francisco—is evidence a donut hole strategy might work. As with the nested economy, economic restoration in any metropolis must reach beyond the food and agricultural industries to include a great diversity of manufacturing industries, alternative energy, etc. As a transition strategy, the vast wealth of the financial metropolis laying at the center may be invested in economic restoration. As the productive capacity and wealth of the trading partners surrounding the metropolis builds, it becomes more probable that the restoration effects encroach inward. Might San Francisco restore a strong printing industry, or New York a diverse baking industry?

Planned Industrial Obsolescence

A community cannot simply kick out a behemoth manufacturing plant that has been exporting their resources, adopting innovations that require fewer jobs, or lobbying for dirtier air and water. But leveraging America's shared expectation for clean air and water, better paying and more fulfilling jobs, and other non-negotiable values, economic evolution might provide the necessary kick. How do we restore our regional economies so that, over time, the surviving industries are those where laborers work more like humans (not robots), where the restoration (not degradation) of their social and ecological values is prioritized, and where one can raise a family in the same town in which they were born and be greeted by greater (not worse) opportunities?

Stepping back far enough to observe America's entire economic landscape, we might witness something peculiar. The global forces of destructive competition, coupled with regional social and environmental forces, can conspire to forge meaningful change in a free economic zone. However, some form of economic judo is needed to catalyze such change.

Over the course of capitalism, industry has mastered the strategy of *planned product obsolescence*. That is, by design, corporations continually invent new products to replace old products. Or a product is designed to fail quickly so that another product can be sold to the customer. In turn, more refrigerators, for instance, can be sold to customers before they die.

Of course, planned product obsolescence can also lead to energy efficient appliances, enhanced recyclability, resource efficiency throughout the manufacturing process, etc. Though, considering the tremendous energy consumed to manufacture, deliver (e.g., from South Korea to Southern California), and dispose of a modern refrigerator, we must question if the energy savings gained by the new model outweigh the energy consumed in the production and disposal of the old model. Now consider the energy and materials consumed during the manufacture, shipping, and disposal of three or four obsolete refrigerators over the course of thirty or forty years.

Buckminster Fuller was a pioneering engineer and architect in the 1950s and '60s, earning him the Royal Gold Medal for Architecture by Queen Elizabeth II, among other accolades. As Fuller's philosophy evolved alongside the rise of planned product obsolescence, he took a clue from that strategy. Pondering planned product obsolescence at a higher level, Buckminster preached that the best way to create a new system is to make the old system obsolete.

The task is not to actively destroy the global market economy and the industries that comprise it, but to make them obsolete. The basic principle is "that which lacks utility will not be maintained." Human-built systems that are unmaintained have but one fate—to decay.

The process of industrial obsolescence is already underway via the diversification of regional agricultural and food industries. Small-scale heirloom wheat is being grown locally, milled locally, and baked into bread in the South Platte and other regions across America. Equivalent gains can spiderweb through the manufacturing sector, with the help of a few key catalysts. Consumer demand must be focused toward companies whose mission is to serve their regional economy rather than the global market economy. This includes demands for better working conditions, breathable air, drinkable water, better quality products, etc. Importantly, with every passing economic downturn, the process of creative destruction must be allowed to flourish, leaving the least innovative and most socially irresponsible companies with one fate: to wither. They must not receive bailouts. Together, such forces will conspire to make globally-oriented industry obsolete. This is planned industrial obsolescence, which may emerge naturally along the path of economic restoration.

Simple Steps Along the Path of Economic Restoration

There are several easy steps to economic restoration. Food security, water security, energy security, and resource security appear obvious. The case to restore diversity to a region's manufacturing and extractive industries, and strong system of domestic trade, has also been made clear. Yet for a FEZ to thrive, a spiderweb of connections must be forged between all nodes of production and consumption.

Adam Smith explained the synergy that emerges quite beautifully when "town and country" become an integral part of the same economic whole. Farm communities require tools, finished food products, home and business furnishings, and other town-made products, while the town would perish absent the products of the country (e.g., food, ore, timber, etc.). To the extent that rural communities and urban centers attain true comparative advantages, each will benefit the other, to the ultimate benefit of the consumer. The common interface of this mutual exchange is the regional marketplace.

The term *regional marketplace* is used here to reflect the sum of all goods and services produced in a regional economy. It is comprised of innumerable and ever-evolving retail shops—main street, digital storefronts, malls, etc. Retail shops are not simply where goods and services are rendered, but where some of our most basic human needs are nourished. Serving as pipelines for regional (not global) products, the regional marketplace is where communities show-case their collective creativity and productive capacity. It is where city dwellers connect with the work of farmers and artisans of the countryside, and where the value-added creations of the city (e.g., food products, tools, furnishings, etc.) are sought out by their rural counterparts. A thriving regional marketplace opens the door for a plethora of other restoration solutions.

Waste-to-Resources in the Regional Marketplace

A diverse regional marketplace can help strengthen the waste-to-resources sector. The examples are endless. For instance, rather than chasing down a representative from some far-off national headquarters to discuss food waste composting solutions for a restaurant or grocery store, the regional marketplace operates such that one local door is all that requires opening to start a dialogue. From that dialogue, the diverse regional marketplace can facilitate the restoration of soil fertility on nearby farms.

Modern composting facilities already serve as profitable wholesalers of soil amendments for surrounding farms. It is a matter of scale, ample participation by retailers and food manufacturers, and proximity to consumers that constrain the reach of compost as a restoration tool. Abundant food wastes—other than meat, dairy, coffee grounds, etc.—can also be efficiently utilized as feed for hog or chicken farms in the regional marketplace. In some cases, small shifts in regulations will facilitate the "waste-to-animals" industry group, or the success of anaerobic digestion facilities to convert organic wastes into biomethane and other biofuels.

With respect to plastics, chemicals, roofing materials, and other challenging wastes, the local marketplace may more efficiently reintegrate them into local manufacturing processes than the global market economy. For instance, it makes little energetic or economic sense to send used plastic bottles to China for recycling. Alternately, companies like American-born ByFusion PBC are upcycling a diversity of plastics into local building materials, while Twelve (formerly Opus 12) is working to transform CO_2 into a variety of fuels and chemicals.

While I was working in the recycling industry in the 1990s, industry representatives had been wrestling with the plastics industry for decades to make one simple change: alter labeling practices to facilitate higher recycling rates across the US. Immense efforts by hundreds of recycling industry staff across the nation were impotent against the multimillion-dollar green washing campaign waged by the global plastics lobby. Again in 2020, amidst rising concerns of plastic fragments piling up in oceans, a new generation of plastic lobbyists was poised to revive the old campaign.

I doubt the plastic industry's hollow campaign will succeed today. More likely, products such as the Ultimate Recyclable Cold-Drink Cup from Ball Corporation (Ball) will drive plastic cups to extinction. Ball's cup is "infinitely recyclable," and thin enough to reduce energy consumption throughout the manufacturing-shipping-consumption-recycling lifecycle. Of course, used aluminum cups must be recycled in order to beat plastics in the energy- and carbon-neutral claims.

The most efficient use of aluminum, paper, or "corn plastic" is facilitated when a diversity of industry is thriving within a regional—not global—marketplace. And when a region's SEI context—not the global context—dictates which type of cup fills concession stands, additional efficiencies may be gained. As bauxite reserves do not exist in Nebraska, corn-based cups (i.e., corn plastic) may be more energetically and economically sensible than aluminum cups at Husker football games. In a free economic zone, the most resource-efficient solutions must prevail. The fate of waste in such an economy is to serve as raw material for the manufacture of other products, not shipped to far-off landfills.

Curious hurdles do remain. To stimulate production of recycled products in the regional marketplace, the consumer must demand local products. Consider the case of Organic Valley, who aspires to keep dairy operations thriving in the same region where those dairy products are consumed. Volatility in demand for local dairy products stymies that goal. Such uncertainty creates risky for new entrants into the industry, knowing they will be competing with national and even global dairy producers (e.g., Canada) for shelf space in local supermarkets.

Federal action has not helped matters, as Canada and the US have been waging subsidy wars—and other artificial price support programs—for decades, aimed at stimulating cross-border trade of dairy products. Given DC's apparent lack of interest in trade policies that would confer strength to local dairy markets across the US, regional and state business leaders and politicians must take the reins.

Of course, demand for local dairy products must rise. When the consumer base grows closer to the producer base, more certainty exists in the marketplace. From such certainty, dairy producers, manufacturers of recycled products, or any other business can more readily secure local and regional investment. With investment secured, a community may then turn its attention to securing another critical resource.

Water Security

Not a single reader is ignorant of the role water plays in supporting life on earth. Yet economically booming regions such as the Front Range of Colorado—4.5 million people and growing—cannot sustain itself without water piped over the continental divide through a system of tunnels, pump stations, reservoirs, and canals. At each step along its journey, water is at risk of volatile energy markets, wildfires, and other disturbances. Farther down river, Los Angeles cannot support its vast citizenry without Colorado water. Somewhere in between lie three cactus-filled states, dotted with green lawns, swimming pools, and export-based commodity crops, tapping the Colorado River so dry it no longer meets its destiny—the Gulf of California.

Water scarcity remains so contentious in the Southwest that the century-old, seven-state Colorado River Compact made national news even during the 2019 trade wars, the COVID-19 pandemic, and again during the 2020 wild-fire season. Water managers and utilities are scrambling to find solutions within a river that is predicted to suffer historically low flows in coming decades as the Rocky Mountains—the source of that water—grow dryer and warmer. The implications for millions of people and thousands of businesses are obvious.

Drought is not a problem that is solved by building more dams and inviting more drinkers to the trough. Though farmers have traditionally consumed more water than their urban counterparts, the recent trend is for water to be prioritized for cities and industry. Urban water users have grown so voracious that they have helped craft Colorado's infamous "buy-and-dry" program, which allows cities to pay farmers who convert irrigated crops to non-irrigated uses, so that the farmer's shares of water can be diverted to the highest bidder. This program has caused the conversion of over one hundred and fifty thousand acres of agricultural land to non-agricultural uses, with six hundred thousand more acres to be lost in the coming decades (Colorado, 2019). Once the water is diverted to cities, a very small portion of it is used for drinking or growing food.

Simply giving water back to farmers does not resolve water insecurity issues, as farmers remain very heavy water users. In arid regions such as the western great plains, where fifteen inches of rain falls, and twenty-one inches evaporates into the sky every year, there is tremendous pressure for the farming and water industry to coevolve with the regional marketplace, simply to maintain adequate regional food supplies in a hotter and drier future.

This challenge isn't unique to Colorado. Even in the wetter farmlands of eastern Nebraska, which receive up to thirty inches of precipitation in a year, center pivots are required to generate financially viable yields of corn for global markets. At the same time, the soils of these high-yield farms are losing their capacity to receive and retain water. This, in turn, requires farmers to apply more water, often using center pivots that siphon water from beneath the ground. The vast Ogallala Aquifer—lying beneath a key seven-state agricultural region of the US, from South Dakota to Texas—is one such aquifer.

The Ogallala has subsided by fifteen feet on average, with some areas subsiding over 200 feet, according to US Geological Survey data (Taghvaeian et al., 2017). Just how many decades are needed to recharge the Ogallala to its historical high, via natural rainfall and river flows above the aquifer, is unknown. But it's not a quick process. Dramatic groundwater declines have occurred in several other aquifers across the west, demanding that farmers spend more hard-earned cash on electricity to pump water to the surface, further raising the cost of food. We can roll the dice, and hope energy costs will decline, but that is not the most obvious scenario.

Desert farmers around the globe have achieved vast water-use efficiencies, providing a clear message to US farmers: innovation can be used to their advantage. This translates to waves of opportunity for pioneering farmers, essential players in the battle for water security in America and elsewhere. Oddly, the greatest opportunities may not actually be in adopting the latest irrigation technology, but in restoring soil fertility, and in planting more drought-tolerant crops.

Water security can also be forged by crafting a new suite of water laws and policies to make obsolete those promoting waste. Conservation strategies are numerous: time-of-day pricing, water surcharges, and seasonally-adjusted rates, to name a few. Increased revenue from such strategies helps municipalities cover the full cost of owning and maintaining water infrastructure, and fund water conservation programs.

Relying on energy-intensive solutions, while tempting, is not a solution to water security. Take, for instance, desalinization: converting salt water to potable water via applications of exogenous energy. Saudi Arabia, whose aquifers continue to dry up, provides an important insight into the energy-water realities of a global marketplace. Desalinization plants have sprung up across Saudi Arabia in recent decades. Yet even Saudi Arabia's colossal fossil fuel reserves are inadequate to secure ample water for citizens, for the cost-effectiveness of desalinized water is utterly dependent on global energy markets. This scenario has driven Saudi Arabia—as well as Germany and others suffering their fate—to acquire farmland well beyond their borders to meet humanity's most basic need: food.

Energy Security

In a world with eight billion consumers, their very survival hinging on an abundance of non-renewable fossil fuels, energy security is the only path to lasting economic and personal security.

It is tempting to believe that energy and water security can be attained by raising our wealth. Countering this fallacy, the financial capital of the world, New York, has suffered multiple city-wide blackouts in the past half century, as has the world's energy capital, Houston. The energy grids of these wealthy cities are largely interconnected and centrally controlled, and rely on energy not only from the distant past (fossil fuels), but from distant lands. Natural gas is piped into New York from multiple states, as well as Canada, while electricity arrives from California—2,800 miles away. While Los Angeles depends on energy piped in from Houston, 1,500 miles away. This tenuous scenario explains why, when LA proposed a ban on natural gas in 2021, Texas lawmakers retaliated with federal legislation (HB-117) that would outlaw any county in the nation from following LA's lead.

On the opposite coast, New York has been shifting from coal to a diverse supply of solar, wind, and hydropower in recent decades, in an attempt to dissolve their dependency on exogenous energy. However, when New York's renewable energy originates in another state or country, it does not provide energy security. For example, Iowa's sixty square miles of wind farms generate energy for homes and industries far beyond the green cornfields where gigantic blades relentlessly spin. About a third of this energy is exported through long-term Power Purchase Agreements. Some of the remaining energy is used to power agricultural operations, only to be exported indirectly (i.e., as food products to China and elsewhere), or in the form of ethanol to meet transportation needs in other states.

This leaves Iowans supplementing their energy needs by burning coal, nearly 100% of which originates in Wyoming (Rock, 2020). As Wyoming continues cutting coal production and retiring power plants, upward pressure is placed on Iowa's energy costs. This places upward pressure on wind-generated electricity that is sold to New York.

Just how Iowa will develop future energy projects, and for whom, has become increasingly contentious. For instance, Iowa's exploration of utility-scale *solar* projects sparked a prickly debate between several counties and energy companies in the late twenty-teens. While the state legislature struggles to resolve the tension, the electricity from wind and solar are destined for the highest bidder—likely the financial capitals on the coasts.

No community can ensure their energy security via a strategy of exogenous energy reliance, and certainly not through a policy of continual energy export. The long-term needs of a region's industries, governments, and communities can only be secured through an endogenous energy strategy—energy neutrality. And a network of energy-neutral regions ensures the security of the nation in which they are nested.

The Water-Energy Nexus

The global water cycle as we know it would cease up without the sun's energy. Similarly, the water essential to sustaining our modern economies would stop flowing—or become so expensive as to produce nightmarish outcomes—without a reliable source of usable energy.

Water is so heavy, and such a great quantity is required for our survival, that about thirteen percent of America's total energy is used to treat, pump, and convey water to farms, industries, and homes (Copeland & Carter, 2017). In arid states like California, the amount of energy consumed to supply residents and industry with clean water is even higher.

In any nation, a water-wasteful economic structure speeds them toward a future of lower groundwater and reservoir levels, compounded by a drier and hotter future. In regions where soil fertility is depleted, more water is required simply to maintain current yields, let alone yields needed to feed a growing population. Under these scenarios, the amount of energy needed to grow and distribute food, keep us hydrated, and treat our sewage, must also rise. The resulting increase in energy demand places upward pressure on energy costs, which drives the cost of nearly all other consumer products.

There is an alternative course. The US, and other nations in their position, can dramatically reduce water consumption, relieving pressure on energy demands. The technology is available, and the desire for change across public and private sectors is growing quickly. Will the shift take place soon enough?

The Energy-Food Nexus

It is natural to feel pacified when food and water flow seamlessly into our homes from distant sources. It is equally comforting when renewable sources of wind power, solar, and ethanol arrive from far-flung agricultural regions to power our homes, shopping centers, offices, and cars. This holds true for the energy used to manufacture our food and drinks. An ever-growing number of social scientists, economists, ecologists, conservationists, agree that the future will not be so comfortable. The scarcer that energy becomes, and the more tightly bound our energy supplies are to national and global markets, the more volatile and costly energy will be. We cannot avoid the fact that energy is fundamental to producing and distributing everything we need. But we can direct where our energy originates.

An endogenous energy economy—not simply a renewable one—is as critical to food-growing regions as it is to food-consuming regions. A considerable amount of the wind power, solar power, ethanol, and other renewable energy currently generated in rural areas (e.g., Iowa, Nebraska, Wyoming) is exported to urban communities several counties away, and even to other states.

There is an intersection between food, energy, manufacturing, and trade. Ohio, as important to global food production as is Iowa, is also a significant global manufacturing center. As such, Ohio is among the top ten coal-consuming states in the US, and the fourth largest electricity consumer (Energy Information Administration, 2021b). Ohio has developed alternative energy and energy efficiency portfolio standards to help offset its colossal reliance on coal. But Ohio has created a problem that exists across the US and most developed countries. Ohio's energy demands cannot be met by its renewable energy capacity. The math doesn't add up.

The energy demands of global-scale manufacturing centers are simply too great to overcome with local renewable sources. Energy must be imported, so that resources from the globe can be concentrated in Ohio, manufactured into products, and then exported. Only, every unit of energy consumed by Ohio's export-based manufacturers is unavailable to producers who would like nothing more but to meet the needs of local consumers. Even if the Ohio legislature does multiply the state's mega wind and solar farms, ethanol production, and other renewable energy sources, the energy will be quickly consumed by the biggest energy consumers with the deepest pockets—not farmers.

In a future of volatile energy markets and ever-decreasing fossil fuel reserves, every unit of renewable energy generated in rural regions will be essential to pump water from aquifers, manufacturer fertilizer and compost, power farming equipment, process grain, transport food to regional consumers, and electrify rural communities. In the long term—the only term that matters—humanity has no option but to build an energy-neutral economy, which must coevolve with a shift toward regional manufacturing, agricultural restoration, and strategic increases in business diversity in all sectors. And fast money may aid in the process.

Fast Money and Strategic Investment

The *velocity of money* is a basic financial phenomenon that, managed well, can aid in creating a diverse and energy-neutral regional economy that is fully capable of meeting regional consumer needs. Velocity of money is a measure of how fast consumers spend money, and is equivalent to the number of times a dollar is used to purchase goods and services in a year. Economists regularly joust over the implications of slow versus high velocities of money, but is generally agreed that a high velocity of money is associated with high consumer confidence in the future. With confidence, a greater exchange of goods and services flows.

The circulation of resources in ecosystems may shed light on the role velocity of money plays in economic restoration. Imagine walking through the deep shade of a tropical forest, one of earth's most productive and diverse ecosystems. Witnessing a tropical forest floor riddled with severely decomposed leaves, casual observers and scientists alike have noted the great speed at which energy and nutrients are cycled through the production-consumption-decomposition lifecycle. Little of the biochemical energy and nutrients harnessed by a tropical jungle are stored in the soil or in roots. Instead, resources are quickly cycled and recycled through the system. In economic terms, the velocity of money is high in the jungle, coinciding with high diversity and net primary production.

In contrast, production and diversity are relatively low in America's alpine tundra, where storage of nutrients in the soil and in roots is high. For instance, the quantity of organic matter stored twelve inches below the alpine tundra on Mount Evans, Colorado has remained "locked up" for well over twelve thousand years (Tim Seastedt, personal communication, December 2020). The majority of organic carbon there resides not in the vegetation but in the soil, largely unworked by decomposers who would otherwise cycle nutrients for the community (Korner, 2003). This condition, coupled with the very short growing seasons and other environmental constraints, favors alpine plants that store large amounts of nutrients in their roots, slowly over time. This includes alpine avens and tobacco root, whose belowground biomass far exceeds their aboveground biomass (Figure 25). In economic terms, the velocity of money in alpine systems is far lower than in the tropics.

Environmental factors such as temperature, precipitation, solar angle, and the influence of glaciation events over time are also drivers of nutrient cycling rates, productivity, and resource allocations in ecosystems across the globe. Notwithstanding, the influence of nutrient cycling on net primary productivity is informative. And organic-rich soils capture and cycle more nutrients than

Figure 25. Resource allocations in alpine environments. Taproot of alpine avens (<u>Geum rossii</u>) on Mt. Elbert, Colorado. Where nutrient cycling is low, environmental stressors are high, and succes- sional processes are slow, the majority of the system's biomass (i.e., capital) is stored belowground.

soils devoid of organic matter. In the tallgrass prairie of Nebraska, for instance, when organic matter is eliminated from the soil, nutrient cycling often declines alongside the soil's water holding capacity. The system's productive capacity and net primary production diminish, thereby degrading the net domestic produc- tivity of Nebraska.

Adding organic matter to degraded prairie soils jumpstarts the nutrient cycling process and increases water-holding capacity, improving conditions for decomposers, which speeds up the successional process toward the more pro- ductive and diverse center. Economists and ecologists might agree, then, that for a self-regulating economy to restore its productive capacity, money (i.e., the medium of exchange for resources—goods and services) must be cycled quickly through an economy, and not stored in vaults and data servers.

At the same time, the notion of saving and spending can be taken to ex- tremes in a global market economy. At one extreme are those thriving on cheap imported products, only to amass a remarkable amount of wealth upon their death. At the other extreme are consumers so enthralled by the act of buying that they spend what they do not have, via credit, to purchase unprecedent- ed quantities of imported goods that, evidence shows, diminish their happi- ness. Personal savings rates in the US climbed as high as 17% in 1975. Savings reached a low of about 2% in 2005, coinciding with high levels of consumption stimulated by joy marketing. The purchasing frenzy subsided with the onset of the Great Recession.

The appropriate savings rate for a highly functional economy is debatable, and will certainly vary by region based on cultural values and social norms, as well as the greater cyclical nature of the economy. Less debatable is that higher savings translates to more capital for investors. However, the current structure of the global market economy requires that investors direct your savings (i.e., financial capital) to the most profitable ventures: those whose corporate wealth is not necessarily built on ensuring the economic health of any country. Alternatively, when local consumers spend money on domestic products there is no doubt where their money goes, regardless of how fast it is spent. In turn, the wealth of their economy is increased, all other factors being equal.

This said, some savings are needed to meet basic personal needs, such as to remain solvent over time, pay the mortgage, buy food and medicine should you lose your job, etc. Savings can fulfill a more overarching purpose: as strategic investments in innovation, restructuring an economy to facilitate energy neutrality, bolstering medical services, starting a new business, etc. Investment in the restoration of our regional economies. Domestic equity funds do exist in the US, to support domestic companies, but pale in comparison to global equity funds. A gaping niche exists in the availability of regional equity funds, community-based crowd funding, etc. to support companies focused on building the productive capacity, diversity, and health of their regional economy.

Dismantling our Perception of Bottomless Resources

The day I sat down to write this book, our global population was nearly seven billion. A decade later it reached nearly eight billion. Most of that growth occurred in China and India. To catch up, political pundit Matthew Yglesias calls for America to triple its population of heavy consumers in his book, *One Billion Americans* (Yglesias, 2020). Yglesias's call to action is for America to win the global economic race against China. His logic rests on one incomplete fact: the quantity of labor and the productivity of that labor are prerequisites to an economy's productive capacity. By simple math, then, increasing the quantity of labor automatically increases America's productive capacity. Yglesias's logic is similar to that of the global arms race, which led society to the brink of nuclear holocaust during the Cold War.

Yglesias ignores the basic means to increasing America's productive capacity, including an increase in the efficiency of production, innovation, entrepreneurship, political stability, etc. Yglesias also ignores a few inconvenient realities. America's ever-increasing GDP over the past half century has simply broadened the chasm between rich and poor. The wealth gap has stimulated a decrease in productivity, while at the same time diminishing America's productive capacity. Adding more people, history would inform us, will only hasten the decline, while doing little to ensure energy and water security, raise economic diversity, improve real wages, create more stable employment, and so forth.

Finally, Yglesias's twisted logic defies what a broad spectrum of economists, sociologists, and ecologists have come to agree on; resources are no doubt limited, and nations across the globe are running up against technological as well as environmental limits to population growth (Capra & Luisi, 2014; Greenspan, 2007; Spash, 2017). As the political backlash to China's one child policy could attest, including global outrage at the global trafficking of children that resulted, national legislation is not the solution to stemming population.

A more fundamental driver of growth was illuminated by Adam Smith long ago, and confirmed by biologists ever since. As long as resources are pumped into a self-regulating system, its participants (e.g., people, businesses, plants, bacteria, etc.) will expand to consume them. From basic supply-demand economics, it follows that the cost of housing, food, water, and other basic living expenses will increase with each additional consumer, alongside an increasing carbon footprint. Tripling America's population will simply raise the cost of living for all Americans, and most likely decrease their quality of life.

This said, a promising population trend has occurred in recent decades. The global growth rate has decreased from 2.2% per year to about 1.1% per year over the past fifty years (Roser et al., 2013). Even America's natural population growth rate and immigration rate have declined in the past decade according to U.S. Census Bureau data. Whether or not this trend holds, America's productive capacity will be best served not by adding more people and importing more resources, but by restoring its capacity to support the existing population with domestic resources. This requires Americans erase rather than nourish the delusion that global resources are a bottomless reserve.

THIRTEEN

THE FRINGE BENEFITS
OF ECONOMIC RESTORATION

Overshadowing the United Nations 1987 release of *Our Common Future*, which set targets for global sustainability, America's garbage barge made the headlines as it searched for a country that would accept its colossal cargo of waste. I was just graduating high school, and staring down a future in the trash business.

Nations of all shapes and sizes have since waged policies to reduce waste, increase alternative energy use, curtail greenhouse gas emissions, eliminate poverty, forge equality among a diverse citizenry, etc. Concurrently, non-profit organizations (NGOs), state and local municipalities, and corporations have launched countless programs in attempts to improve public health, address environmental degradation, reverse the trend of homelessness, squash drug and alcohol abuse, prevent suicide, and right other wrongs.

Pondering the litany of socio-environmental actions waged across the interconnected global economy is mind-numbing, not because of the monumental efforts taken, but because such efforts were needed in the first place. More numbing, because so many of these efforts struggle to yield lasting change, for they stem not only from an ill-structured economy, but from increasingly divisive politics. This includes Medicare, Medicaid, national education programs, and other programs that have had their heads on the political chopping block since their enactment.

Even America's Clean Water and Endangered Species Acts have suffered from rampant swings of state and national politics. America faced that very reality—again—during the writing of this book. It would be nothing short of irrational exuberance to believe such programs will not be hunted down by future presidents. A less obvious challenge is that NGOs around the globe succumb to fickle or inadequate philanthropic support, or the limited endurance of founders, staff, and volunteers. More subversive, various political elements wage false campaigns such as "recycling doesn't work." Should, by some miracle, the social and environmental programs be delivered fully, it is often due to tremendous inputs of energy, resources, labor, money, staying power, etc.—all of them increasingly threatened by a barrage of external forces.

In this light, America's most important social and environmental programs appear but Band-Aids atop a tumorous outgrowth. Their efficacy is akin to putting a new roof on a home whose foundation is crumbling. Rather than wage up-hill battles to forge lasting social, environmental, and economic change, how might our dearest benefits emerge naturally from a well-structured economy? Before answering, it may be helpful to examine the current tax-based benefits from a different angle.

The Self-Imposed Taxes of a Poorly-Structured Economy

Due to America's debilitating economic structure, a plethora of self-imposed "taxes" pervade the lives of us all. The word tax, here, implies a burden to personal, business, or economic systems. For instance, the simple act of acquiring clean water in our modern economies requires energy-intensive industrial processes such as tertiary water treatment facilities. The tens of millions of dollars of energy consumed monthly to send water over watershed divides to quickly growing populations is another example. Pumping water from aquifers hundreds of feet below the ground to produce high yield export crops, which by their very nature degrade the soil's ability to receive and hold moisture, is yet another example of a financial burden—a "tax" on the economy, nature, and society.

We may feel uncomfortable to think this, but other self-imposed taxes include physical fitness and mental wellness programs corporations provide for employees stuck in desk jobs. Or when employees pay out of pocket for a gym membership, sweat it out in Bikram yoga studios, etc. Largely, our current economic structure has created an expansive class of fitness-challenged humans. And when individual and corporate efforts fail to produce mental or physical well-being, governments—and individuals, and businesses—incur additional expenses to provide reactive healthcare. Or, health problems go untreated, leading to decreased productivity in the workplace, which deflates profitability.

In the aggregate, an economy's social and environmental taxes are tantamount to drags on a nation's gross and net domestic product. Self-imposed taxes are, in reality, maintenance costs. And as in ecosystems, maintenance costs increase as an economy slides toward a late-successional stage. This matters dearly, for every penny, watt, and second allocated toward maintenance is unavailable to restore the productive capacity of an economy. Alternatively, economic restoration directs capital to increase an economy's NDP and productive capacity, moving the succession dial toward the middle stages, not toward the late-successional stage.

Intrinsic Benefits of a Well-Structured Economy

Both the economic and ecology research indicate that values such as clean water, clean air, a high productive capacity, and resistance to disturbance increase with diversity. In our economies, increased diversity is correlated with wage growth, profitability, job stability, and other human values. In a self-regulating economy, the role of government, then, is to merely restore the structure of the economy; by setting the rules of the game, so that the system may efficiently do the work. Products of that work include an economy's intrinsic benefits.

Intrinsic benefits are those that arise naturally, rather than by mandate, when a region restores its economic foundation: economic diversity, endogenous energy reliance, and balanced trade. Such benefits are fringe, or free. Intrinsic benefits include food and water security, a high productive capacity, health and wellness, job creation and security, sustained profitability, resistance and resilience to disturbance—benefits requiring few if any exogenous inputs to persist.

It is tempting to place the benefits of economic restoration into distinct categories—economic, social, environmental. However, the complexity of an economy is such that any one benefit may fall into multiple categories. For instance, increased real wages is as much a social benefit as it is an economic benefit. Similarly, production efficiencies can yield equal benefits to the environment (e.g., decreased pollution and lower resource extraction rates per unit produced), to industry (e.g., reduced costs and increased profitability), and to society (e.g., cleaner water and air).

Moving forward, all of these benefits fall under the banner of *economic benefits*. The potential to deliver and sustain these economic benefits hinges on the nature of one's SEI context. And regardless of the SEI context in question, there are two basic factors that may be managed to restore and sustain economic benefits: the productive capacity of its land and the skill of its labor.

The productive capacity of any land stems from the quantity and quality of its water, soil, mineral deposits, and other natural resources. For instance, without any mineral or water rights, farmland in arid western Nebraska has a lower productive capacity—it is cheaper—than fertile farmland of eastern Nebraska, which receives ample rain. However, the productive capacity of both landscapes may be increased by the skill of labor (i.e., productivity, ingenuity, knowledge, etc.), which may be focused on the restoration of soil fertility.

America's globally-oriented economy has not only chipped away at the quantity and skill of labor in Nebraska, and elsewhere, but has steadily degraded the fertility of its land. Stemming from that degradation, the profitability of farmland per acre has dropped over time. Similar losses have occurred in manufacturing sectors across most regions of the US have—a steady decrease in skilled labor, diversity, and productive capacity. Restoring America's productive capacity across all sectors may yield not only social and environmental benefits, but a variety of financial benefits at regional and national levels.

Intrinsic Financial Benefits: Profitability

It is easy for an economist or ecologist to believe that diversity confers resilience to a system. But some intellectual arm-wrestling was required before I would believe that increased diversity could lead to increased profitability. I was visiting with Linda Nelson and Mike Larsen on their restored tallgrass prairie in southeast Minnesota when I became a true believer. It was a windless hot day in June 2020 as we stood amidst the waist-high grasses and wildflowers. Mike was sharing a story about the variable production of wild indigo (*Baptisia leucantha*) from year-to-year in the prairie, and the link between diversity and profit finally clicked.

The moment a species learns to exploit a niche better than any other species, or to more effectively share a niche with another species, several beneficial outcomes emerge. Less energy is required to secure food, water, shelter, and other resources. The tendency toward destructive competition between similar species is reduced, as constructive competition among them increases. In turn, energy that would have otherwise been spent fiercely competing is redirected to sustaining basic functions. The "profitability" of the individual has been improved, thus enhancing its potential for long-term growth and reproduction.

Less obvious, when a great diversity of profitable species exists in a community, more resources can be extracted and distributed throughout the whole system. In nature, such profit takes the form of excess fruit on a tree, which provides fodder for animals. In turn, those animals benefit the tree by distributing its seeds further across the landscape than if the tree were working alone. Profit also takes the form of surplus carbohydrates (i.e., beyond what is needed for growth and maintenance) stored in roots during productive years, and then made available for growth in future seasons. Profit also takes the form of the fat of a bear, the milk of a nursing elk, or the prodigious nectar of a honeysuckle. In each case the species has produced a surplus, beyond what is needed for growth and maintenance.

Excessive transfers of energy and physical resources into an economy—or into an ecosystem—tends to produce destructive competition, which often leads to decreased (not increased) profitability. Excessive resource transfers can also cause niches to go unfilled in the system receiving those transfers, such as the case with America's abysmal waste-to-resources, energy, and manufacturing industry diversity. Over time, declines in profitability and diversity lead to declines in NDP, and in a nation's productive capacity, as capital and wealth are concentrated into fewer hands.

Destructive competition can also occur in ecosystems when, for instance, humans suppress natural disturbance. A classic example is fire suppression in America's Western forests. In response, the forest becomes crowded and diversity declines. Destructive competition increases as trees of the same species struggle for resources. The result is visible even to the naked eye in the Black Hills of South Dakota (Figure 26). There, a century of fire suppression has caused abnormally high crowding of Ponderosa pine trees. The growth rate of each tree has slowed tremendously, as evidenced by very thin and tight annual growth rings. Each tree is left more vulnerable to disease and pests, while the overloaded fuel—high accumulation of capital or biomass—puts the entire forest at risk of severe wildfire.

It was not until park managers removed more than half of the trees that the degree of destructive competition in the forest became clear. Following eight decades of very slow growth, the diameter of the trees nearly doubled in just eight more years. That is, growth ballooned after thinning, as evidenced by the thicker growth rings.

Figure 26. A near doubling of growth is evident in the larger tree rings immediately after thinning an abnormally dense forest in the Black Hills of South Dakota.

To be clear, the Black Hills condition is human caused. Other cases of destructive competition certainly occur in nature, especially in systems where exogenous resources are transferred into the system, or where disturbances do not occur frequently enough, intensely enough, or at the right scale to stimulate diversity (Huston, 1995). In self-regulating ecosystems, the more typical condition is constructive (not destructive) competition between species in the same functional group: plants, insects, insect-eating birds, or top predators. As species compete for a fixed quantity of resources, or as they exploit new niches (i.e., to avoid destructive competition), a more efficient utilization of all resources in the system is attained. In turn, production and "profitability" is optimized for the entire community. Decomposers even employ surplus value from the aboveground community to build soil fertility belowground, further enhancing the productive capacity of the entire system.

No doubt a corporation can generate substantial profits, on a per unit basis, from large scales of production for a global marketplace. However, when the profit generated by each unit of available resources (e.g., acres of farmland, number of laborers, amount of energy, etc.) is lower, larger scales of production are required—more acres, larger manufacturing facility, etc.—to generate adequate profitability for the business. Should such a system turn ample profit, what is the cost? Has the global market system—increased exogenous energy and resource transfers to stimulate large scales of production and high concentrations of wealth—simply increased the population of at-risk humans? Humans and businesses who, like the ponderosa pine, will wage destructive competition between one another the more densely crowded they become, leaving each more vulnerable to a growing number of threats from within and without.

An entirely different economic model is within our grasp. A system that does not require continual subsidies and bailouts, exogenous energy inputs, and global resources transfers to maintain profitability or high net domestic productivity for a regional or national economy. A system that, by its very nature, does not funnel ever-increasing concentrations of wealth into fewer and fewer hands.

The Creation and Recirculation of Wealth

A basic definition of capital was provided earlier, which I will refine here as it relates to wealth. Piketty (2014), for convenience, equates wealth with capital, and defines capital as the total sum of non-labor assets that can be owned and traded. Therefore, wealth includes all forms of real property, financial assets such as savings, bonds, stocks, pension funds, etc., and professional forms of capital such as patents, equipment, industrial facilities, infrastructure, and so forth. Wealth, therefore, increases by amassing any form of capital.

The concentration of energy and physical resources from global to regional levels, as suggested previously, may be a fundamental driver of wealth into fewer hands. And as witnessed daily in the US since Ronald Reagan unleashed his 1981 plan for economic recovery, wealth does not trickle down. In fact, it has only trickled up in the US and other developed nations, alongside rising GDP. The fundamental reason for this is that the global market economy, and any economy bound to it, is not functioning according to the rules of a complex self-regulating system.

Ironically, the current economic model places not only the middle class and the poor at risk, but also the wealthy, for a poorly-structured economy yields an insidious byproduct. An increasing mass of evidence indicates that the rising income levels among the world's wealthiest people deflates rather than stimulates economic growth (Greenspan, 2007; Stiglitz, 2015). This is corroborated by evidence from self-regulating ecosystems, where resources such as carbohydrates, proteins, and nutrients—the system's wealth—are rarely concentrated among fewest number of individuals. Nor do resources trickle down. The net productivity of grass is not stimulated by an ever-increasing rise in the population of deer, nor the growth of the herd stimulated by adding more predators.

There is but one direction that resources trickle in a complex self-regulating system—up. This fate requires the bulk of an economy's wealth to be amassed among the greatest number of individuals, which requires wealth be built not at a global scale but at the basic operational unit of an economy, the regional economy. There, wealth is created and recirculated via many self-reinforcing mechanisms.

Diverse and thriving regional manufacturing industries stimulate demand for related services and products (e.g., resource extraction, retail, professional services, etc.), which places upward pressure on regional job creation. Job creation places upward pressure on wage growth. Employment stability also stems from economic diversity, as shown earlier. In concert, this set of labor conditions equates to more wealth being distributed to a greater number of workers, rather than being concentrated into fewer hands.

Local and regional wealth creation can also result simply by shifting the balance of trade in favor of the domestic economy, which shortens supply chains and reduces the number of intermediaries between producers and consumers. More profit remains in the local system. And from the unavoidable interactions of foundational components, an energy-neutral economy does not favor the concentration of resources from distant economies into local centers of production. In turn, economic restoration generates profits that are more likely to be recirculated locally rather than transferred to entities beyond one's economic border.

Positive feedback loops work in favor of local communities. Locally-owned businesses are more likely to invest profits within their community, as compared to national or global businesses operating in that community (Institute for Local Self-Reliance, 2003). This phenomenon stems from the greater *recirculation value*—the amount of a purchase that is re-spent in the local economy—provided by local businesses. A growing body of research shows the recirculation value of a dollar spent at locally owned business is far greater than when spent at big box stores, superstores, national or international retailers, or other chains (AMIBA, 2020; Cunningham & Houston, 2004).

A greater recirculation value not only places upward pressure on community-wide profit, wages, and benefits, but increases the demand local businesses place on local suppliers and professional services in the region. For example, it is far easier for a local restaurant to purchase local food and other supplies than it is for a global restaurant chain dependent on a rigid system of national and international suppliers. An increased recirculation value also stems from increased profitability of local businesses, which generate increased taxes for local and state government, and donations to local charities. The difference is not trivial. A study by Cunningham and Houston (2004) reveals that between 45 and 65% of the value of purchases made at independent businesses is recirculated locally. In contrast, the recirculation value of purchases made at chain stores is about 14% (AMIBA, 2020).

Less obvious, locally-owned businesses are more likely to hire professional services from within their community, such as accounting firms, legal firms, marketing firms, etc. Chain stores are more likely to employ those services at national or global offices, not in the communities where profits are generated, which partly explains why recirculation value is lower in communities dominated by chain stores.

A classic case is Wild Oats, a very popular health food store across North America in the 1990s. The staff of Wild Oats were housed in Boulder, CO, where they handled all the high-level accounting needs for their chain of stores across North America, including a string of Canadian stores. In essence, a good portion of the hard-earned cash Canadians were spending on food was leaving to support high-paying jobs in Boulder. Wild Oats was eventually bought out by Wholefoods, which was eventually swallowed up by Amazon. Where those accounting jobs are now is anyone's guess. Certainly, they do not reside in the communities where consumers are spending their money.

If about half of each dollar you spend at a local grocery store—or some other local shop—is recirculated locally, where does the other half go; the portion that is not recirculated locally? Why isn't, say, ninety percent of your local purchase recirculated? Much of the difference is accounted for by the fact that nearly all the goods sold at a local retail shop are manufactured outside the community. For every hundred dollars spent on a shirt, pair of shoes, skirt, or pound of cheese produced outside the community, a good portion of that is consumed by manufacturers as far away as China—or Bangladesh, or Indonesia—and by a series of distributors along the way, all of whom must be paid. When the value of your purchase is spread across so many corporations beyond your community, it should be no mystery why the retail wages within your community are so low.

But if Americans could grow and recirculate their wealth via the creation of strong regional and local economies, would they? According to Consumer Reports, yes. At least 80% of Americans prefer to buy products made in the US. And over 60% of Americans would pay more for those products, which helps explain why the great majority of US consumers prefer to patronize locally-owned businesses (Cunningham & Houston, 2004). The same trends ring true in Europe, where most shoppers prefer to shop locally (Brown & Bjoko, 2020).

To counter this, some consumers insist large chain stores are better positioned than small "mom-and-pop" retailers to offer healthcare to employees. The facts tell a different story. The high premiums of many corporate health programs are often cost-prohibitive to low-wage employees. In a study of Walmart, Home Depot, and Target employees, about 9,500 of them were receiving publicly funded health care—amounting to over US $12 million annually for taxpayers (Ridley & Associates, 2008). The Ridley and Associates report, and other studies, also reveals that big box stores tend to generate lower taxes for the cities where they operate, they increase demand for city services, and they provide lower wages and opportunities for career advancement. While other studies indicate that wages are, on average, slightly higher in big box stores, and the opportunity for a managerial job is greater. Despite the endless battle over data, retail wages remain relatively low in the US, and a store cannot be run by managers alone.

Some of the financial downfalls of big box stores are less obvious. Detailed earlier, an increasing number of large corporations—wealth concentration centers—are investing profits in foreign ventures, rather than in the country where they are legally established, or in those communities where their profits are generated. This trend explains, in part, why many domestic industries (e.g., the paper industry of Wisconsin) and businesses (e.g., River Bear Meats of Denver) struggle to attract the investment needed to upgrade facilities or increase marketing efforts.

By their very nature, fully functional regional economies require that resources be directed to regional and local businesses rather than concentrated in the hands of fewer large corporations. Production increases when more wealth is in the hands of middle- and lower-class citizens, for they consume the largest fraction of goods and services. This explains why the 2020-2021 stimulus checks were delivered to the largest consumer base of the US and Europe, and why an increase in minimum wages is desirable—to increase consumption, which stimulates production.

The above strategies suffer from chronic shortsightedness on several fronts. Without first restoring the foundational components of our regional economies, policies that stimulate consumption and raise minimum wages will forever be ineffectual, and likely counterproductive. When stimulus checks are spent on imported goods, GDP does not rise commensurately, and little to no progress is made toward restoring the productive capacity or NDP of the domestic economy. Rising labor costs in the US simply shifts production overseas, doing little for the NDP, productive capacity, resilience, or diversity of the home economy. High tech and service jobs are not immune to this phenomenon.

Furthermore, increasing wages drive affected industries to adopt innovations that reduce the demand for labor. For instance, big box stores have replaced thousands of retail jobs across the US with self-check-out stations. Under the current global economic model, rising labor costs stoke increases in the cost of living, due to inflation, which was at a historical high as of this printing. Ultimately, the laborer does not benefit. A favorable balance between labor demand, wages, production, consumption, and economic stability can never be attained via global market capitalism.

A progressive tax on the wealthiest citizens is also not a long-term solution. Fundamentally, an equitable distribution of resources (i.e., land, energy, wealth, and various natural resources) cannot be sustained within a system that favors the concentration of resources into large scales of production. As Thomas Piketty highlights, policies such as a progressive tax would require a high degree of international coordination, and would likely lack efficacy (Piketty, 2017).

Should a quick fix such as taxing the wealthy be promulgated, at least in the US, it would likely be undermined by the ever-shifting political landscape, or by the global landscape of interconnected wealthy capitalists. A more enduring strategy is to focus the production and consumption of goods and services at the regional and local level, concurrent with the diversification of businesses, industries, and sectors. In the process, other benefits may materialize.

Intrinsic Social Benefits

Through the success of The Little Bird Bakeshop in Colorado we open a window into the intrinsic benefits of an economy free of the global market. Forget for a second the great diversity of delectable treats produced at such bakeries. By their nature, local bakeries require a greater number of employees per product sold, and offer a high diversity of job tasks for workers, as compared to larger scale bakeries. Rather than employing only production bakers, a small shop requires front-of-counter staff, kitchen help, specialty skills such as cake decorating, and various other skills (Decker, 2019). These same local shops can play a key role in restoring the productive capacity of their regional economy.

Little Bird stuffs their ovens with a variety of locally grown ingredients, including heirloom wheat, sourced and milled by regional businesses such as Moxie Bread Company. In turn, industries across three different sectors are diversified and strengthened in the regional economy: agriculture, manufacturing, and retail. And what began as an owner's passion to bring customers a diversity of quality baked goods has, unknowingly, gone a few steps beyond (A. Corliss, personal communication, June 2021). Little Bird has strengthened the web of regional farmers and wheat millers.

Myriad social benefits emerge from a diverse web of regional businesses. To begin, the Moxie milling operation does not require three eight-hour shifts per day to meet regional consumer needs, for Moxie is not in a destructive competition with large-scale mills producing for the global market. Small businesses like Moxie operate within the bounds of their regional SEI context, a strategy that tends to provide more stable employment than many globally-oriented businesses (California Association of Business Brokers, 2015).

The history of grain mill closures is just one example of guaranteed job instability in the race to ever-increasing production scales. American mills have grown progressively larger and more concentrated over the past century. In the process, milling jobs succumb to destructive pressures of global forces (Figure 27), regardless of how many eight-hour shifts the largest mills require. When such a colossal mill closes, the trickle-down effect to the entire community is painful.

Figure 27. This H.D. Lee Flower Mill of Salina, Kansas (USA) closed in 2019, a strategic effort by ADM to concentrate operations into a higher capacity mill in Mendota, Illinois (USA). Similar closures were scheduled by ADM in Minneapolis and Chicago (KSAL, 2019).

The global market economy, when structured as an interdependent conglomeration of national economies, cannot resolve the social and environmental problems it naturally creates. Several examples were provided, including the steady increases in mental and physical health issues; the rise of homelessness; declining food and water security; ongoing toxic clean-up efforts in mine lands around the globe; pervasive decline in soil fertility, etc. These costs are tantamount to a self-imposed tax on individuals, families, communities, businesses, cities, states, and nations.

If these taxes are a natural byproduct of a global market economy, they are likely to dissolve by restoring our regional economies to achieve greater business diversity, energy-neutrality, and thriving domestic trade. This structural economic shift will demand a greater diversity of job tasks within the business community, which provides psychological benefits for employees as well as financial benefits. A worker who performs a greater diversity of tasks within a shift, or over a few days, is not only more satisfied, but their productivity rises (Staats & Gino, 2011). From such benefits flows a higher potential for profitability and wage growth. Might a more diverse and stable regional economy also alleviate the myriad mental and health maladies that have grown up alongside the global market economy? Will environmental benefits also result from regional economic restoration, to further enhance the social benefits?

Intrinsic Environmental Benefits

After making its infamous voyage from Long Island to Belize, and then back, the garbage barge of 1987 did find a port willing to accept its crappy cargo. That incident was but one testament to the legendary loads of waste America, and other developed nations, dump on unsuspecting countries daily via our collective blind spot for externalities.

Pondering the thousands of tons of trash and other pollutants consumers spew across the globe with every swipe of the credit card, it is difficult not to blink in stupefaction. Swipe. Dump. Swipe. Spew. At the same time, few Americans—currently enjoying relatively clean air, water, and land—could refrain from squirming in their chairs if asked to keep the byproducts of their consumption in their own backyards.

Certainly, managing the wastes of a global market economy appears a mountainous task. Yet for entrepreneurs, boundless opportunities arise in a regional economy, one that profits—rather than chokes—on the byproducts of its consumption. Here is one: Designing for energy neutrality and materials use efficiency throughout a product's life cycle (i.e., extraction, shipping, manufacturing, consumption, recycling) creates mouth-watering tasks for engineers and architects. In the process of bringing such solutions to market, entrepreneurs raise the diversity of their local economy. Lifecycle-based designs can also transform entire manufacturing processes and organizational structures so as to consume fewer resources.

The end result is not a reduction in the quality or quantity of goods and services rendered by the regional economy, but an increased capacity to sustain the quality of life of its citizenry. A classic example is manufacturing products from recycled content. Besides the social and environmental benefits, the recycling and re-use of waste creates upwards of thirty jobs for every one job created by landfilling that waste (Goldstein et al., 2011). Perhaps more importantly, in a free economic zone whose environmental context does not include ore, timber, or other raw materials, a thriving waste-to-resources sector is essential to supplying citizens with the diversity and quantity of products they demand.

As inferred by the role of decomposers in ecosystems, a thriving waste-to-resources sector improves the system's productive capacity and NDP, due to a more efficient use of energy, water, and other resources. Decades of research by the US Environmental Protection Agency and others (Goldstein et al., 2011) have shown that recycling aluminum cans and newspapers saves as enough energy to supply fifteen average-sized power plants each year, assuming the recycled materials are reincorporated into new products. Just one ton of recycled aluminum saves fourteen thousand kilowatt hours (kWh) of energy, the equivalent of nearly nine barrels of oil. The savings arise due to the tremendous energy that would otherwise be required to convert raw ore—bauxite—into ingots of aluminum.

Similar energy savings result with most recycled products. One ton of recycled office paper saves 4,100 kWh of energy, as compared to paper made from raw materials. Manufacturing one ton of recycled plastic saves 5,774 kWh of energy. One ton of recycled steel saves 642 kWh, while one ton of recycled glass cuts energy demand by 42 kWh. None of these savings takes into account the energy costs associated with shipping steel, for instance, from China to America. Further, the pollution generated and water consumed in the manufacturing of recycled products is typically lower than in products made from raw materials.

Tremendous innovation has arisen in the recycling industry since the voyage of the garbage barge. Yet for innovation to translate into a thriving waste-to-resources sector, the continual pipeline of cheap—globally subsidized—products that fill our lives must be replaced by a short circular pipeline of regional producers and consumers. Pollution prevention, workplace diversity, farm-to-table menus, or recycled products are not mere fads in a restored regional economy, nor taxes. They are simply byproducts, fringe benefits of a well-structured regional economy, along with water security, energy security, and job security.

Perennial Job Creation

It is imperative to have a proactive economic policy directed at promoting an economy that favours productive diversity and business creativity and makes it possible for jobs to be created and not cut. There is no poverty worse than that which takes away work and the dignity of work.

~ Pope Francis. Encyclical Letter Fratelli Tutti of the Holy Father Francis on Fraternity and Social Friendship, 2020.

To support Pope Francis's point, a final example of destructive competition and homogenization is worth exploring. Huffy Corporation was founded in

Dayton, Ohio amidst the global depression of the 1890s. They since became famous for making the Volkswagen of bikes, supporting thousands of solid American jobs. As global pressures built, Huffy began to diversify its operations, including the acquisition of Raleigh USA to gain access to retail shops across America. The strategy fell short.

To remain financially viable in an expanding global market economy, Huffy swallowed hard, and cut wages. But within America's SEI context, wages could be cut only so far. Huffy need to take more drastic steps. A century after its founding, Huffy initiated a wave of manufacturing plant closures across the US. By the mid-nineties, an eager American accomplice stepped up to close down Huffy's three remaining plants, bidding farewell to any remaining jobs: Walmart. Without blinking, Walmart made the impossible ask. Huffy must lower their prices, or Walmart would stop selling hundreds of thousands of their bikes across the globe.

No matter how efficient Huffy's domestic plants were, it couldn't be done. At the time, laborers in China were earning about US $0.31/hr (Adams et al., 2006; Yang et al., 2010), while US laborers earned $10-$16/hr (Bureau of Labor Statistics, 1995). If Huffy cared to survive, they needed to subcontract production of their bicycles overseas. Silently, the decline in US bike manufacturing jobs trickled "up" into the service industry, parts suppliers, raw materials, and other industries Huffy once supported.

But the reverse process also works. Restoring the productive capacity and diversity of American manufacturing industries drives the growth of other industries, such as mining, equipment, entertainment, retail, information technology, and consulting. To fulfill the employment needs of those regional and national industries, significant job growth must occur.

Tremendous job growth is also derived from the pursuit of an energy-neutral economy. The adoption and expansion of solar voltaic technology alone has created multiple niches in energy distribution and storage across the US. These new niches have in turn generated demand in manufacturing, construction, and service industries. New applications for inverters and converters have arisen, along with mounting designs for rooftops and solar arrays, battery manufacturing and recycling challenges—endless growth opportunities. Entirely new operational systems are on the verge of broad-scale acceptance, such as integrating solar farms with grazing and vegetable crops (i.e., agrivoltaics), which reduces irrigation needs and increases production of some crops. Innovation is arriving faster than its adoption.

Significant job growth must occur for these system components to be integrated into an economy. And to think, the energy industry has scarcely scratched the surface of innovation from just one reincarnated idea: capturing the sun. Improved applications of crystal silicon, thin film, and Passivated Emitter Rear Cell (PERC) technologies are just a few recent examples of innovations that reduce costs and/or increase the efficiency of solar energy (Kelly-Detwiler, 2019). The PERC technology gains its advantage by reflecting unabsorbed light back into the cell for a second chance to produce electricity.

Now consider the economic diversity and jobs that must be stimulated by an energy-neutral economy, one that is completely reliant on wind, micro-hydroelectric, wave power, passive solar, hydrogen fuel cells, methane and other biomass-derived fuels, and technologies yet to be envisioned. Each new technology requires specific technical and system integration needs—multipliers of jobs and economic diversity. Still, the potential for diversification in this one industry, and the jobs it can create and sustain, is difficult to grasp until we understand a few key facts.

- *Forget* for a moment that existing fossil fuel reserves cannot be replenished until long after our current reserves become economically unviable.

- *Recall* that the renewable energy industry creates two jobs for every one job created by the fossil fuel industry, while the energy efficiency industry creates more jobs than both of those industries combined.

- *Consider*, then, that renewables account for only twelve percent of all energy consumed in the US (EIA, 2021a), and eleven percent of global energy use (Ritchie & Roser, 2020). A transition to even fifty percent renewable energy would create millions of US jobs. Millions more jobs would be created by energy efficiency upgrades and business diversification required of an energy-neutral economy.

Perpetual growth in the renewable energy and energy efficiency industry groups is essential to maintaining the productive capacity of any nation. Furthermore, due to the interactions between an economy's foundational components, a synergy arises between the restoration of an energy-neutral economy, resource-use efficiency, and job creation. Stated earlier, the recycling and re-use of garbage creates up to thirty times more jobs than landfilling that waste, while vastly reducing energy demands throughout the production-consumption-recycling process. Similar job multipliers and energy efficiencies exist in diverse regenerative farming and agile manufacturing. Importantly, to the extent those jobs are supported by domestic demand, their vulnerability to global forces is deflated.

Affluence as a Byproduct of Economic Restoration

In 1930, the British economist John Maynard Keynes predicted that by the year 2030 his grandkids would be working a fifteen-hour work week, thanks to productivity increases caused by advances in technology and automation. That is, citizens would be more affluent, to the degree that affluence is epitomized by leisure time. If we had more leisure time, here is what Americans would do with it, according to the Pew Research Center (2008): The vast majority would pursue fulfilling hobbies, while about half of Americans would pursue a successful career, raise children, volunteer, or nourish their religious roots. Ironically, fewer than 13% of Americans actually care for the wealth generated by the current global market economy.

Yet here we collectively sit, nearly a century after Keynes's depression-era essay, reflecting on monumental GDP growth and technical progress, and affluence appears to be one thing citizens of our modern economies have been running from. In fact, citizens of the world's most advanced economies are laboring about twice as much as Keynes expected (OECD, 2021). If leisure really is the ultimate measure of affluence, we have been duped. And no, unemployment is not the brand of leisure Keynes had in mind.

Perhaps, to attain the abundant leisure Keynes was envisioning, it may be necessary to go back in time—not forward. In *Affluence without Abundance*, anthropologist James Suzman (2016) provides strong evidence that hunter-gatherers worked a mere seventeen hours a week to build and maintain their homes, feed their families, acquire water, and make clothes—however scantily clad they were. So skilled were our ancestors at acquiring essential resources that leisure time, not work, defined their daily routine. Based on the trends, it is doubtful citizens of a global market economy will ever realize the levels of affluence our ancestors took for granted.

Mindful of the ever-increasing cost of living and ever-shrinking leisure time that have transpired under the weight of global market capitalism, it is not a stretch of the imagination to believe affluence may be more easily attained in a system of self-regulating national economies, each of them sustained by multitudes of free economic zones. Modern technology certainly can support such a condition. Of course, how a community wields such technology, or how one enjoys the free time the system may provide, is best determined by the culture and values of the economic zone in question. Such is the nature of complex self-regulating systems.

Logs, Fire, and Water

The intrinsic benefits of economic restoration are illustrated well by the nature of wildfires in arid western states, from Colorado to California. Wildfire is on the rise in the west. In Colorado, the twenty largest fires on record were witnessed in the past twenty years. Fourteen of those fires erupted in the past decade. The three largest wildfires to ever strike Colorado occurred in 2020.

Besides the impacts to water quality for downstream communities, life-sanitizing fires closed several major transportation routes in 2020, including Interstate 70—a national trade artery running east to west. Landslides in the burn area closed I-70 multiple times throughout 2021. The monsoonal rains that struck after Colorado's High Park Fire a decade earlier produced similar churning floods of soil, rock, and charred logs. Miles of state highways and county roads were destroyed, and hundreds of public and private culverts and bridges were damaged. Farther downstream, water turned black with ash, forcing closures of intakes, clogging fish hatcheries, and interrupting manufacturing processes, sending water users scrambling for other sources (Figure 28).

Thankfully, communities ravaged by the High Park Fire were able to enjoy clean water from the Colorado-Big Thompson (CBT) project. Fighting gravity with great applications of energy, CBT water is pumped uphill daily on a trip from the other side of the continental divide through a system of tunnels, ditches, and pipes to the populous Front Range. Fortunately, that system of reservoirs, pipelines, and ditches—the back-up plan—routing water to Fort Collins was not impacted by the 2012 wildfires or their debris flows. Disaster was averted until eight years later, when the East Troublesome Creek fire of 2020 scorched nearly 193,000 forested acres upstream of CBT source reservoirs. That same year, the Cameron Peak Fire ravaged over 200,000 acres of forest watersheds above Fort Collins.

To think, Colorado's wildfires pale in comparison to those of California. In 2020 alone, about 4.2 million acres of California's watersheds burned. Come spring 2021, California was shaping up to be equally dry, with snowpack in many northern watersheds at less than four percent of the average (NRCS, 2021). By the end of the year, over 58,000 wildfires had ignited across the US, consuming over seven million acres of forests and grasslands (National Interagency Fire Center, 2021).

There is some evidence that extensive drought, and equally large fires, occurred in America's distant past. But there's a catch. Without resource-intensive and life-threatening firefighting efforts, recent wildfires would have likely been even more devastating.

Figure 28. Fish hatchery clogged with ash from the 2012 High Park Fire.

There is another catch, perhaps more insidious. Wildfire is essential to maintaining landscape level diversity in Western watersheds of the US. Only, similar to US policy aimed at minimizing the intensity of recessions and depressions, forest policy for the past ninety years has been directed at squelching fires—minimizing disturbance—in an attempt to keep catastrophe at bay. This assault on watershed health began during the Great Depression, when the US Forest Service promulgated the 10am rule. The rule mandated all forest fires be extinguished before 10:01am the day after smoke is spotted.

Unlike economic policies aimed at minimizing disturbance, fire suppression policies have been highly effective. An entire century has since passed, with loads of dead wood and dry needles silently building up beneath the green canopies above. Forests grew excessively dense, going unnoticed by the casual observer.

Congress did not act alone in its assault on watershed health, creating the largest expanse of overly dense forests in known history. Human populations slowly infiltrated the dense forests with roads, bridges, and flammable homes. This condition has vastly undermined the ability of local, state, and federal agencies to practice sound forest management—forest thinning, prescribed burning, selective logging—across large swaths of dense forest on the outskirts of population centers.

As a result, wildfires today burn at higher severity, more frequently, and over larger areas than any time in recorded history. When a wildfire rips through dense forest, it is not only harder to extinguish, but far more destructive than in a less dense forest. Additionally, the West's unnaturally dense forests harbor less diversity, and typically regrow more slowly after a fire than does a more diverse forest. With regards to socio-economic impacts, more dense forests also yield less water for downstream communities than their wilder and less dense selves (Saksa et al., 2020).

If the risks to life and water are not enough to motivate policy changes, the costs to property and society might grab one's attention. The 2012 High Park Fire hit society with nearly US $30 million dollars in firefighting costs alone. CalFire, a state-run entity, spends about US $2.5 billion a year to extinguish wildfires in California (Louie, 2020). Then there are the financial impacts to water, infrastructure, and homes, which can soar into hundreds of millions of dollars in the wake of a single fire. Even before the 2020 California fires had reached their fullest extent, scientists at Stanford University estimated the economic impacts to be US $10 billion (Louie, 2020).

Certainly, global climate change also bears some responsibility for the ever-rising scale and intensity of wildfires. But an even greater player may be the global market economy. While its forests burn, Colorado imports nearly 95% of its wood from Canada and other regions beyond its economic frontier. This curious scenario is created not only by the ill structure of diversity, energy, and trade throughout Canada and the US, but by Canada's heavy timber industry subsidies. Hence, timber imported by Coloradoans is cheaper than local timber, and externalities occur in watersheds across Canada and the US.

While suffering from the impacts of wildfire, Colorado's timber industry became nearly extinct at the turn of the century. By 2019, the industry could no longer supply ample lumber for new home construction. The industry's depressed productive capacity went untended for decades, until two fates arose in tandem. Housing and remodeling businesses began seeing a steep climb in demand, just as supply chain disruptions decreased timber supplies to Colorado. The cost of lumber nearly tripled (Chuang, 2021), and remained high in 2022. Colorado's timber industry remains so decrepit it can scarcely produce forest products to heat the homes built from imported lumber. Instead, Colorado's forests are left to be consumed by wildfire, sending carbon dioxide into the atmosphere. Meanwhile, Coloradoans—unknowingly—continue demanding that timber be imported from Canada on trains and trucks, which emit additional carbon dioxide into the atmosphere.

The Watershed Economy

By necessity, rather than mandate, an economy operating free of the global market must fully utilize local forest products to meet local consumer needs. In turn, multiple benefits emerge intrinsically. A reduction in the severity and extent of wildfires is one obvious benefit. Certainly, wildfire will eventually burn even the best managed watersheds, those in which forests are less dense and more diverse. However, the potential for devastating wildfires in well-managed watersheds is far lower, and those fires are far easier and cheaper to combat. Moreover, the ground below a thinned forest is dominated not by flammable dead twigs and needles, but a diversity of grasses, shrubs, and wildflowers.

Biologically diverse hillsides green up far more quickly after a wildfire, which leads to additional benefits. Grasses and wildflowers that flourish in a thinned forest provide forage not only for elk and honeybees, but cattle and horses, which may be employed in the process of forest thinning. Well-managed grazing not only increases biological diversity in the forest understory, but can reduce the risk of wildfire, by decreasing the amount of fine fuel (i.e., dried fine leaves of grass) on the ground. In the process of forest thinning, biomass energy is available to heat homes and businesses, which lowers the demand for exogenous energy. This is the *watershed economy*. It is a working watershed, rather than an idle watershed waiting for fire to consume it. The watershed economy raises economic and ecological values while suppressing the risks of fires and floods.

There is a benefits multiplier in a watershed economy. The timber businesses competing for local markets in the same free economic zone—the same SEI context—may do the work of restoring watershed health. Selective logging for dimensional lumber and secondary timber products (e.g., wood pellets, fence posts, chips, etc.) creates more domestic jobs, while supporting energy-neutrality, compared to an import-dependent economy.

Watershed economies produce other obvious benefits, such as reduced risks to life, property, and water supplies. Based on historic evidence, such basic benefits cannot be provided by the current top down, tax-based, self-defeating forest management approach: extensive fire suppression, followed by catastrophic wildfire, followed by tremendous costs to society, followed by exorbitant fire recovery efforts.

If there remains any doubt as to the feasibility and benefits of an economic approach to watershed management, America's western states can learn from those on the opposite coastline. At the turn of the century, New York City debated a wide range of solutions to secure quality water for a burgeoning population. Two options rose to the top, each with a radically different price tag. The cost of building and maintaining a physical water treatment plant was estimated at US $9 billion, in 2020 dollars. Alternatively, the costs of water-shed improvements would cost just US $1.9 billion. The cheaper alternative relied on economic activities such as regenerative farming, selective logging, river restoration, and other activities that improved ecological values while meeting watershed management goals.

The taxpayer-responsible solution was obvious: watershed restoration. Furthermore, by investing an additional US $500 million in water conservation efforts, New York eliminated the need to spend US $4 billion on new reservoirs and water delivery projects on the Hudson River. If the America's wealthiest financial center finds watershed restoration and water use efficiency to be in its best economic interest, it is self-evident that less wealthy regions will benefit from such solutions.

FOURTEEN

CLOSING THOUGHTS:
THE PATH OF MOST RESISTANCE

Having embarked on this book prior to the COVID-19 calamity—and the civil unrest following George Floyd Jr.'s death, the decade of catastrophic wildfire, the attack on the US capital, dramatic volatility in the global energy markets, China's ban on global trash imports, the retail employment struggles of 2020-2022, Russia's attack on Ukraine and the resulting global rise in gas prices—there was a sense of *déjà vu* as I edited this closing. Throughout our shared global economic history, developed countries of the world have followed the path of least resistance; a downhill pursuit of global trade and fossil fuel dependence. The result has been to weaken their resistance to, or even to stoke, turbulent domestic and global forces.

Economic restoration follows the opposite path; strengthening one's resistance to global and domestic turbulence, forging resilient economies in the process. The result is to secure our freedoms, offer greater opportunities for fulfillment, and sustain our quality of life.

The freedoms and other benefits that naturally emerge in a restored economy do not rise and fall according to the whims of the global market, or the never-ending political shifts across the globe. Rather, through an evolutionary pressure cooker of sorts, the bonds between economic diversity, energy neutrality, and domestic trade are continually refined and strengthened over time. In turn, the social, environmental, and economic values most communities desire are fortified rather than weakened with each passing drought, pandemic, supply chain disruption, and lightning strike. In the process, the current global market system has but one fate: to become obsolete. It will be replaced by a system of highly functional regional and national economies, should we choose.

The Illusion of Peace Provided by Global Market Capitalism

The false sense of security provided by global market capitalism is akin to the serenity of a dense green forest. The verdant canopy portrays a life of abundance, richness, and peace. In the eyes of a casual observer, the dense stand of trees appears healthy. It feels right to suppress fires there. Life and infrastructure are protected, as are forest products. To watch the capital of the system—the forest biomass—accumulate seems sensible, until a single spark ignites a blade of dry grass on the edge of a railroad. In minutes, the forest becomes enshrouded by flames hot enough to turn outbuildings into molten streams of metal and glass. The impacts can be as monstrous as they are morbid.

Centuries of gross trade imbalances and dependence on fossil fuels have built overly dense populations and degraded economic diversity across the US and abundant other countries. All the while, extreme concentrations of wealth and other resources have accumulated into ever fewer hands. The illusion of peace and abundance generated by the global market economy has coincided with relentless assaults on the very water and soil fertility required to sustain humanity's most basic needs.

It is a matter of time before one spark wreaks devastation to the US economy, and all those who have bound themselves to it. Yet global consumers are fire-hosed daily with the promise that global trade, the homogenization of industry, and subsidized standards of living can continue rising hand-in-hand—indefinitely. Countering the masses, Greenspan warned of several byproducts of global market capitalism that pose threats to the American Economy: widening income gaps, terrorism, global warming, stress and anxiety among market participants, and resurgent populism.

Greenspan and others recognize a peculiar conundrum in globalization. The higher America's standard of living, the greater will be the ensuing political unrest when that standard is decreased in the slightest. A fundamental paradox has arrived. The global market economy championed by developed countries must perpetually pacify their citizens. This is not possible without perpetually raising their perception of a quality life. Yet an increasing mass of Americans lack the wages necessary to cover the rent, buy food, pay medical bills, send kids to daycare or college, etc. The resulting levels of stress and anxiety not only impair one's health, but contribute to irrational exuberance, panic buying and selling, riotous will, and other market-destabilizing behaviors that economists of all stripes obsess over daily.

After leaving his decades-long post as Federal Reserve Chair, Greenspan admitted a personal fear, that atop the stress, income disparity, and anxiety Americans are experiencing, the cultural ties that bind society together will unravel (Greenspan, 2007). He further warned that disaffection and even large-scale violence would ensue, jeopardizing the basic civility necessary for any nation to persist.

The perfect storm has brewed. Civil unrest, burning forests, impoverished farmlands, and over-extraction of critical resources across the globe undermine our future survival. Meanwhile, pervasive joy marketing slogans inform us what to buy, where to live, how much money to save for retirement, the benefits of a global market economy, and on and on, *ad nauseum...*

Like wildfire in our forests, the risk of economic catastrophe has only grown under the banner of global market capitalism. The moment a nation's cheap exogenous energy is burned through, and the moment water and soil reserves are thoroughly depleted, the system will respond in kind. The intertwined societies of the Bronze Age, lacking adequate self-reliance, suffered such a fate. Only, the nations of the modern global market economy are perhaps more intertwined, and less self-reliant. Blind faith is required to believe a Bronze Age-like collapse will not repeat itself. Only, within the towering houses globalization has built, such a collapse has the potential to stoke a level of economic devastation beyond what humanity has ever witnessed.

Alternatively, our economies can follow the lead of earth's most resilient and resistant self-regulating systems. Choosing this path, we must restore the foundational components of our national and regional economies. As informed by the costs and benefits of restoring stagnant fuel-enriched watersheds, the costs of economic restoration pale in comparison to the alternative.

Resilience Through a Network of Regional Economies

The desire to form strong and resilient economies has become evident in the transition town movement, sustainability initiatives, and other efforts in thousands of communities across the globe. Many of these communities have set goals for renewable energy, waste reduction, social justice, etc. But to fulfill such goals, regional economies must set targets for economic independence from the global market economy, as no self-regulating system can persist on a model of continual resource depletion. Nor does soiling one's backyard with the industrial waste of an export-based economy engender fulfillment.

Self-sufficiency is another emerging trend, even in small towns like Evans, lying in the arid plains of eastern Colorado. Evans's self-sufficiency goals are backed by Colorado's Self-Sufficiency Standard, a product of the Colorado Center on Law and Policy. Self-Sufficiency Standards have sprung up in the great majority of US states, aimed at improving the livelihoods of low-income residents. This translates into job training, access to jobs, reduced spending, etc. However, self-sufficiency goals do not consider a regions ability to grow food, manufacture value-added products, attain water security, energy neutrality, etc. They are limited to the individual, regardless of the resilience or productive capacity of their surrounding economy.

Self-reliance is another modern movement, with equally challenged progress. Economic self-reliance (ESR) is an individual's ability to garner and hold economic resources in excess of their basic needs (Godfrey, 2008). ESR programs also aim to lift people out of poverty, while recognizing that an individual's self-reliance is closely tied to the success of their surrounding social systems. Recognizing the connections between our personal lives and the myriad systems we are nested within, we cannot escape the fact a sound economic model is essential to achieving self-reliance, sustainability, self-sufficiency, fulfillment, etc.

No doubt stop-gaps are needed to alleviate poverty, meet water and food security needs, fulfill basic educational needs, minimize our economy's impacts to the social and ecological fabric of the world, etc. But by definition stop-gaps have short reaches. This being said, the growing network of self-sufficiency and self-reliance advocates, transition towns, the State of Jefferson, and the independence movements of Scotland, Catalonia, and others represent a near universal value. That is, a collective vision for an economy that by its very nature provides for human fulfillment, without degrading the social and ecological context required for survival. The will is there. The question, then, is how should it be tapped? How do we turn the ship around, and at what cost?

America has begun turning the corner on watershed restoration. At federal, state, and local levels, some wildfires are left to burn freely, while prescribed fire is used as a tool to restore the health of watersheds. Forest thinning is becoming a preferred tool to reduce wildfire risk across Colorado and other western states. Regenerative agriculture is expanding quickly across dozens of US states. The mass of self-reliance, community resilience, sustainability, renewable energy, and similar initiatives continue their expansion across the US, dozens of nations across Europe, and countless other countries in Asia, Africa, Central and South America, Australia, and so on.

As an American, I believe the US—the single largest player around the table of global market capitalism—has the ability and the will to restore the foundations of its economy. And to the extent the hypotheses presented herein are justifiable, the restoration pathways are not difficult to design and implement. Restoration, in fact, may be deceivingly simple.

Now more than ever, the US and other nations have amassed ample wealth with which to invest in restoring economic diversity, attaining energy neutrality, and rebuilding the productive capacity of their domestic economies. Considering its global influence, the United States of America can take a leadership role in economic restoration, to demonstrate how a nation's essential economic, social, and ecological needs can be met into perpetuity, without jeopardizing those same needs in other countries. And through restoration, freedoms that have been systematically undermined by global market capitalism may be realized.

Declarations of Independence and Freedom

Milton Friedman described freedom as a delicate plant, whose greatest threat was the concentration of power. Friedman was referring to the concentration of *political* power, which he believed should be allocated to states or even local levels of government. Similarly, Adam Smith, Joseph Schumpeter, Joseph Stiglitz, and other economists have professed concentrations of *economic* power pose great threats to personal freedom. From the knowledge of ecosystem structure and function, I must agree. The more decentralized our economies, the greater the tendency for political and economic power to be distributed to local levels. By extension, greater freedoms may flourish.

The State of Jefferson

Several regions across the US are ripe for such a transformation. One of them resides in a state that stands above the rest with regards to change. If they were a sovereign nation, they would be the fifth largest economy in the world. That is, the unwieldy glamorous juggernaut we know as California. Where freedom is as contentious a word as is the word progressive.

Ever since California was admitted to the nation, its citizens have pondered dividing themselves into three, six, or even more manageable states. Perhaps intuitively, Californians understand that such a concentration of wealth and resources into so few hands runs counter to the structure of a complex self-regulating system. Silicon Valley's Tim Draper rekindled the debate in 2018 with a ballot initiative to chop California into six. Draper's initiative failed, but shed light on the influence smaller states and their economies should have on the freedom and prosperity of Americans.

Long before the Draper initiative, leaders from twenty-four rural counties in northern California and southern Oregon were laboring to build an independent State of Jefferson. Jefferson's political center is Siskiyou County, California, where advocates invoke Article IV, Section 3 of the United States Constitution, a provision guiding the legal division of an existing state. Underscoring the challenge Jeffersonians face, the last time division was approved by congress was 1863, when West Virginia split off from Virginia.

Today, the more difficult battle may not be getting congress to approve a new state, but the politics of the state in question. Draper's initiative to split California in six stoked ample intrastate debate, including a quite emotionally plea I received from an ex-resident of Siskiyou County in the run-up to the election. The young man echoed that which thousands of Southern Californians believe: Uniting California's poorest counties to create America's most impoverished state would be foolish.

This claim certainly appears logical on the surface. Digging deeper, though, the claim reveals a pervasive ignorance many Americans harbor regarding the enduring benefits smaller states and their economies can produce for citizens. Regurgitating something from the firehose, the ex-Jeffersonian further argued that such a small rural state would be incapable of governing itself without the tax-fed largesse of areas such as Los Angeles and San Francisco. On the flipside, rural residents of Jefferson are enraged their basic freedoms such as hunting should be controlled by liberals to the south.

Should we pause long enough to blow the socio-political fog away, a different picture materializes. The rationale for Jefferson far exceeds taxation without representation, hunting, dam removal, or any other hot button political issue. Pause a bit longer, and we may unearth the deeper concerns of Californians: ever-growing mental health issues and homelessness; a grossly unmanageable budget; an inefficient use of wealth; the catastrophic mismanagement of forests and watersheds; and an inept energy and water system—to name a few.

From the ever-deteriorating state of affairs in California, and America at large, it becomes clearer with each passing election that colossal top-down economies and governments cannot attain the intrinsic benefits of smaller governments and their regional economies. At the same time, the small state of Jefferson would do well to remember that building a thriving local economy is a prerequisite to strengthening its political base. After all, America's original colonies needed to create a thriving domestic economy declaring independence from the British Empire. That is, economic independence is a prerequisite to personal and political freedom.

Many Jeffersonians recognize it was Thomas Jefferson and his political peers who called upon the laws of nature in crafting the independent governance of the United States. Jefferson further understood the relationship between America's balance of trade and its independence. Regarding the role of a strong domestic economy in sustaining America's independence, Jefferson declared to Governor John Jay of New York in 1809 (Randall, 2015):

> *An equilibrium of agriculture, manufacture, and commerce, is currently become essential to our independence. Manufactures, sufficient for our own consumption (and no more). Commerce sufficient to carry the surplus produce of agriculture, beyond our consumption, to a market for exchanging it for articles we cannot raise (and no more). These are the true limits of manufacture and commerce. To go beyond is to increase our dependence on foreign nations, and our liability to war.*

Since the day Jefferson's memorial was erected, ecologists have continued to unveil the principles governing the structure and functions of complex self-regulating systems. Mindful of these principles, the first step for Jeffersonians may not be secession from California, but a declaration of independence from the global market economy. In so doing they may discover the freedom they so fervently seek, for the more dependent our communities are on the resources of other states, countries, and transnational corporations, the more control those entities have over our communities.

The State of Jefferson, or any community, can stay the course and be crushed by volatile forces of the global marketplace, or they can restore an economy capable of sidestepping those forces when they arrive. And in the process of restoration, a global assemblage of free economic zones will minimize the weight and volatility of external forces acting on every community.

Where the Power for Change Lies

Power follows money to the extent that money raises one's command over goods and services, according to Princeton's senior political scientist David Balwdwin (Baldwin, 1971). In Baldwin's view, that command stems from the concept of purchasing power, which is a subset of power. If Baldwin is correct, then the power for economic and political change is influenced by the ways in which we spend our money.

Yet there remains an insidious obstacle to overcome. A great challenge to the State of Jefferson and other independence movements is their insistence that the political right (or left) must prevail above the other. The resulting political machine produces masses of rhetoric far exceeding any efforts toward meaningful progress.

Listening to what the political right dreams of—independence, economic resilience, greater states' rights, freedom, America first—it is a shock to the senses that regions such as Jefferson have not already formed a free economic zone. Meanwhile, the political left yearns for renewable energy, locally grown organic produce, clean air and water, resilience, self-reliance, abundant open space, recycled products, etc. Jotting down the list of left and right values, it is comically clear those values would be best fulfilled not via the subsidies of a global market economy, but by restoring our regional economies based on the principles of earth's most complex self-regulating systems.

Forging meaningful economic change also requires bold leadership by small businesses, the basic units of economic diversity. No doubt some larger corporations have the potential to produce positive impacts within an economy by mandating recycled content paper, renewable energy, ethnic diversity, and zero waste policies. However, history has shown that such corporations have even greater potential to force companies like Huffy and Ford to ship jobs overseas, suppress the wages of shift workers, and lobby for decreased environmental protections. The power of such corporations is also wielded to stimulate federal subsidies and bailouts, spelling doom for towns like Oakdale, Nebraska or Detroit, Michigan. Similarly, it is not in the best interest of transnational brewing companies to break up their largest manufacturing centers in support of energy neutrality and thriving regional trade. Yet amidst the global market economy, there rests this hope.

Entrepreneurs: The backbone of economic restoration

Counter to intuition, the largest corporations of the world are in the minority. In the US, about 95% of all workers are either employees of small businesses or they are sole proprietors. This business community forges innovative solutions to local challenges, and is highly adaptable to an ever-changing social, environmental, and industrial context. Meaningful change will occur only by engaging the small business community and their workforce strategically, and by leveraging the collective purchasing power of their employees. Change further resides in a new generation of businesses who can deliver products and services with fewer resources, and through a community of entrepreneurs coalescing around one bottom-up mandate: economic restoration.

Successful entrepreneurs go into business to pursue a passion. Baking, growing vegetables, hog farming, making excellent salami, building the most energy-efficient cars, repairing those cars, accounting, making socks and beanies, rendering loans to small farmers, marketing, opening a grocery store, installing solar panels, constructing homes, building a better heat pump…the list is endless. And based on the behavioral statistics that abound, it is evident that the majority of entrepreneurs and their employees are content operating within their local economic space, building their community, and sustaining their businesses into perpetuity.

From an evolutionary sense, entrepreneurs are skilled in recognizing a vacant niche in their economy and jumping in fast, lest it be filled by another. In the process, they are not only fulfilled, but the entrepreneur delivers desirable products and services, while building greater resilience for their community. Entrepreneurs are an essential key to unlocking the power of economic restoration. From personal experience, starting a small business oriented toward a regional rather than global market economy is not a risky venture. Quite the opposite, it affords abundant freedom, security, stability, and fulfillment. From a network of such entrepreneurs, and the consumers supporting them, profound economic change is simply a matter of time. And economic restoration is the vehicle for that change.

The greatest economy is not some golden era of capitalism that lies behind us. It is that which lies ahead.

AFTERWARD

Basic Actions to Restore your Free Economic Zone

The passionate dialogue and inquiries following dozens of presentations on the topic of this book underscores the intense interest Americans have in restoring their local economies to better serve our communities and preserve the integrity of ecosystems we rely upon. Among the commentary, a consistent request has been for actions individuals and communities can take toward economic restoration. With those readers and audience members in mind, the following is provided, as a minimum, knowing that the best solutions will come from the community itself:

- Define the boundary of your regional economic space (e.g., free economic zone).
- Minimize transfers of energy and goods into/out of your economic space.
- Restore the productive capacity of agricultural and other resource extraction industries.
- Build a thriving waste-to-resources industry.
- Rebuild the manufacturing sector to meet local—not global—needs.
- Restore diversity in all sectors and industries in your regional economy.
- Maintain high recirculation value of money (spend it now, and on locally-produced goods and services).
- Build an endogenous energy economy. Strive for energy-neutrality.
- Start a small business to do any of the above.
- Support small businesses that do any of the above.
- Avoid buying any imported products, unless it's absolutely necessary and there is no local alternative.
- Teach more ecologic concepts to economics students.
- Teach more economic concepts to ecological students.

In addition, hundreds of books, articles, and other literature exist to learn more about recycling, composting, regenerative agriculture, starting a small business, alternative energy systems, ecological restoration, etc.

LITERATURE CITED

Acemoglu, D., De Feo, G., & De Luca, G.D. (2020). Weak States: Causes and Consequences of the Sicilian mafia. *Review of Economic Studies* 87, 537–581 (2020). doi:10.1093/restud/rdz009

Adams, F.G., Gangnes, B., & Shachmarove, Y. (2006). Why is China so Competitive? Measuring and Explaining China's Competitiveness, *The World Economy*, 29, 95–122.

Adams, T. (2021). *Mixed-Use Zoning*. Sustainable Development Code. https://sustainablecitycode.org/brief/mixed-use-zoning/

Ali, Y. (2020). *Direct Current Microgrids to Power Europe's Green Ambitions*. Microgrid Knowledge. https://microgridknowledge.com/direct-current-microgrids-europe/

Altieri, M. (2012). *The scaling-up of agroecology: spreading the hope for food sovereignty and resiliency*. Sociedad Cientifica Latinoamericana de Agroecologia. www.agroeco.org/scola

AMIBA. (2020, October 12). *The Local Multiplier Effect: How Independent Local Businesses help your Community Thrive*. American Independent Business Alliance. https://amiba.net/wp-content/uploads/2020/08/Local-multiplier-effect-whitepaper.pdf

Arrighi, G. (2010). *The Long Twentieth Century: Money, Power, and the Origins of our Time*. Verso Books.

Autor, D., Dorn, D., & Hanson, G.H. (2021, October). *On the Persistence of the China Shock*. National Bureau of Economic Research. Working Paper 29401. http://www.nber.org/papers/w29401. DOI 10.3386/w29401

Baker, N. (2017, August 25). *THE GREAT HUNGER - What was the Irish potato famine? How was Queen Victoria involved, how many people died and when did it happen?* The Sun. https://www.thesun.co.uk/news/4321971/irish-potato-famine-queen-victoria-death-toll-when/

Baldwin, D.A. (1971, August). Money and Power. *The Journal of Politics*, 33(3), 578-614.

Bauman, A. G., McFadden, D. T., & Jablonski, B.B.R. (2018). The financial performance implications of differential marketing strategies: Exploring farms that pursue local markets as a core competitive advantage. *Agricultural and Resource Economics Review*, 47(3), 477-504.

Bauman, A.G., Jablonski, B.B.R., & McFadden, D. T. (2019, July 21-23). *Exploring the Underlying Economics of Local Food Producers: Opportunities for Rural Economic Development*. Selected paper prepared for presentation at the 2019 Agricultural & Applied Economics Association Annual Meeting, Atlanta, GA.

Bazzaz, F.A. (1979). Physiological ecology of plant succession. *Annual Review of Ecology and Systematics*, 10, 351-371.

Bechtel, W. (2014, Dec 06). *Shipping Cattle to the Mainland*. Drovers. https://www.drovers.com/news/shipping-cattle-mainland

Beinhocker, E.D. (2006). *The Origin of Wealth: Evolution, Complexity, and the Radical Remaking of Economics*. Harvard Business Press.

Bivens, J. (2019). *Updated employment multipliers for the U.S. economy*. Economic Policy Institute. https://files.epi.org/pdf/160282.pdf

Blackson, H. (2013). *Don't Get Mixed Up on Mixed Use*. PlaceMakers. https://perma.cc/SPW9-Q3DH

Bogaard, A., Fraser, R., Heaton, T.H.E., … Stephan, E. (2013, July 30). Crop manuring and intensive land management by Europe's first farmers. *PNAS, 110* (31), 12589-12594. https://doi.org/10.1073/pnas.1305918110

Bosworth, B. (2012). *Conflicts in the U.S.-China Economic Relationship: Opposite Sides of the Same Coin?* The Brookings Institution. https://www.brookings.edu/wp-content/uploads/2016/06/20-china-us-economic-relationship-bosworth.pdf

BP. (2021). *Statistical Review of World Energy*. BP. https://www.bp.com/en/global/corporate/energy-economics/statistical-review-of-world-energy.html

Bradshaw, A.D. (1987). Restoration: an acid test for ecology. In Jordan, W.R., Gilpin, M.E., & Aber, J.D. (Eds.) *Restoration Ecology: A Synthetic Approach for Ecological Research* (pp. 23–30). Cambridge University Press.

Brady, N.C., & Weil, R.R. (1996). *The Nature and Properties of Soils* (11th ed.). Prentice-Hall, Inc.

Braudel, F. (1984). *Civilization and Capitalism, 15th-18th Century: The perspective of the world*. Harper & Row.

Brooks, A. (2013, December). A Formula for Happiness. *New York Times*. https://www.nytimes.com/2013/12/15/opinion/sunday/a-formula-for-happiness.html

Brown, G. (2020). *Regenerative Agriculture: Details of a Profitable Journey*. McHenry County College. https://www.mchenry.edu/cal/flyers/Forefront-Regenerative.pdf

Brown, A., & Bjoko, M. (2020, October 5). *Love For Local - Three In Four More Likely To Shop In Their Local Community Than A Year Ago*. Mastercard. https://www.mastercard.com/news/europe/en-uk/newsroom/press-releases/en-gb/2020/october/love-for-local/

Bunge, J. (2021, May 3). Farmers Want Help Cutting Emissions. *The Wall Street Journal*. https://www.wsj.com/public/resources/documents/cGCxEN8NFyxsGwhLV3IJ-WSJNewsPaper-5-3-2021.pdf

Bunge, J., & Maltais, K. (2020, April 27). Pork Industry, USDA Discuss Euthanizing Hogs After Coronavirus Closes Plants. *The Wall Street Journal*. https://www.wsj.com/articles/pork-industry-usda-discuss-euthanizing-hogs-after-coronavirus-closes-plants-11588015611

Bureau of Economic Analysis. (2019, April 22). US Department of Commerce, Bureau of Economic Analysis, *Industry Economic Accounts*. https://apps.bea.gov/iTable/index_industry_gdpIndy.cfm

Bureau of Economic Analysis. (2022, February 03). *Gross Domestic Product, Fourth Quarter and Year 2021* (Advance Estimate). US Department of Commerce, Bureau of Economic Analysis. https://www.bea.gov/data/gdp/gross-domestic-product

Bureau of Labor Statistics. (1995, August). *1995–1999 Annual Averages - Household Data - Tables from Employment and Earnings*. U.S. Department of Labor, Bureau of Labor Statistics. https://www.bls.gov/cps/cps_aa1995_1999.htm#weekearn

Bureau of Labor Statistics. (2020, May). *The Employment Situation — April 2020*. U.S. Department of Labor, Bureau of Labor Statistics. https://www.bls.gov/news.release/pdf/empsit.pdf

Bureau of Labor Statistics. (2022, April). *Table A-1. Current and real (constant 1982-1984 dollars) earnings for all employees on private nonfarm payrolls, seasonally adjusted.* U.S. Department of Labor, Bureau of Labor Statistics. https://www.bls.gov/news.release/realer.t01.htm

Bušić, A., Kundas, S., Morzak, G., Belskaya, H., … Šantek, B. (2018). Recent Trends in Biodiesel and Biogas Production. *Food technology and biotechnology*, 56(2), 152–173. https://doi.org/10.17113/ftb.56.02.18.5547

BW Research. (2020). Clean Jobs Better Jobs. *E2, Acore,* Celi. https://e2.org/wp-content/uploads/2020/10/Clean-Jobs-Better-Jobs.-October-2020.-E2-ACORE-CELI.pdf

Cadotte, M. (2013, May 13). *Productivity increases with species diversity, just as Darwin predicted.* ScienceDaily. www.sciencedaily.com/releases/2013/05/130513152830.htm

California Association of Business Brokers. (2015, July 7). *Baby Boomers: Incredible Numbers are Buying and Selling Businesses.* CABB. https://cabb.org/news/

Cambardella, C., Elgersma, K., Giddens, E., Myers, M., Sherrard, M. Smith, D. (2016). PRAIRIE POWER PROJECT Determining Maximum Sustainable Production of Biomass With a Mixture of Prairie Species. University of Northern Iowa, Tallgrass Prairie Center. https://tallgrassprairiecenter.org/sites/default/files/prairie_power_project_final_report_10-14-15.pdf

Capra, F., & Luisi, P.L. (2014). *The Systems View of Life: A Unifying Vision.* Cambridge University Press.

Cardinale, B.J., Wright, J.P., Cadotte, M.W., Carroll, I.T., Hector, A., Srivastava, D.S., Loreau, M., & Weis, J.J. (2007). Impacts of plant diversity on biomass production increase through time because of species complementarity. *PNAS, 104*(46), 18123–18128. https://www.pnas.org/content/pnas/104/46/18123.full.pdf

Carney, G.W., & J. McLellan. (2001). *The Federalist Papers.* Liberty Fund, Inc. The Gideon Edition.

Cato, M.S. (2017). The Bioregional Economy: Celebrating the local in production and consumption. In (ed.) Spash, C.L. *Routledge Handbook of Ecological Economics: Nature and Society.* Routledge.

Center for Disease Control and Prevention (2017, October 19). CDC *Reports Rising Rates of Drug Overdose Deaths in Rural Areas.* https://www.cdc.gov/media/releases/2017/p1019-rural-overdose-deaths.html

Center for Sustainable Systems. (2020, September). *U.S. Food System Factsheet.* Center for Sustainable Systems, University of Michigan. Pub. No. CSS01-06

Center for Western Priorities. (2019). 2019 Colorado Oil and Gas Spills Tracker. https://westernpriorities.org/issues/oil-gas-impacts/2019-colorado-oil-and-gas-spills-tracker/

China Power Team. (2017, January 25). *How is China Feeding its Population of 1.4 Billion?* China Power. Updated August 26, 2020. Accessed February 1, 2022. https://chinapower.csis.org/china-food-security/

Christensen, C. (1997). *The Innovator's Dilemma.* Harvard Business Review Press.

Chuang, T. (2021, April 29). *Record lumber prices are adding $35,000 to the sale price of a new home, further crunching Colorado's housing market.* The Colorado Sun. https://coloradosun.com/2021/04/29/lumber-prices-new-house-sales/

Clark, D.J. (2019, May 9). *Separating Truth from Myth in the So-Called 'Golden Age' of the Detroit Auto Industry.* https://www.smithsonianmag.com/history/separating-truth-myth-so-called-golden-age-detroit-auto-industry-180972139/

Clements, F. E. (1936). Nature and structure of the climax. *Journal of Ecology*, 24, 252-84 (1936).

Cline, E.H. (2014). *1177 B.C.: The Year Civilization Collapsed.* Princeton University Press.

Colorado, State of. (2019). *Colorado's Water Plan.* https://www.colorado.gov/pacific/cowaterplan/plan

Colorado Energy Office. (2019a). *Combined Heat and Power (CHP) at New Belgium Brewing.* Heat is Power. http://www.heatispower.org/wp-content/uploads/2019/03/CEO-CHP-New-Belgium-Flier-3-19-19.pdf

Colorado Energy Office. (2019b). *Combined Heat & Power (CHP): Efficient Generation of Electric Power & Thermal Energy.* Colorado Energy Office.

Colussi, J., Schnitkey, G., & Zulauf, C. (2022, March 17). *War in Ukraine and its Effect on Fertilizer Exports to Brazil and the U.S.* farmdoc daily. (12)34. Department of Agricultural and Consumer Economics, University of Illinois at Urbana-Champaign. https://farmdocdaily.illinois.edu

Copeland, C. & Carter, N. (2017, January 24). *Energy-Water Nexus: The Water Sector's Energy Use.* Congressional Research Service, 7-5700, R43200. www.crs.gov

Corby, S. (2019, November 18). *Who invented the first car and when was it made?* Cars Guide. https://www.carsguide.com.au/car-advice/who-invented-the-first-car-and-when-was-it-made-76976

Council of Economic Advisors. (2019, September). *The State of Homelessness in America.* The US Council of Economic Advisers. https://www.nhipdata.org/local/upload/file/The-State-of-Homelessness-in-America.pdf

Cowles, H. C. (1899). The ecological relations of the vegetation on the sand dunes of Lake Michigan. *Botanical Gazette*, 27, 95-117, 167-202, 281-308, 361-391.

Crews, T.A. (2004). Perennial crops and endogenous nutrient supplies. *Renewable Agriculture and Food Systems, 20*(1), 25–37.

Cunningham, M., & Houston, D. (2004). *The ANDERSONVILLE STUDY of Retail Economics.* Produced for the Andersonville Chamber of Commerce by Civic Economics. https://community-wealth.org/content/andersonville-study-retail-economics

Daly, H. (1991). *Steady State Economics* (2nd ed.). Island Press.

Darwin, C. (1859). *On the Origin of Species by Means of Natural Selection, or the Preservation of Favoured Races in the Struggle for Life.* John Murray.

Decker, F. (2019, March 6). *What Employees Do You Need for a Bakery?* Small Business – Chron.com. http://smallbusiness.chron.com/employees-need-bakery-35461.html

Desai, D. (2018, February 2). *Soil Conservation in California: An analysis of the Healthy Soils Initiative.* NYU Environmental Law Journal, Environmental Law Review Syndicate. https://www.nyuelj.org/category/scholarship/syndicate/page/2/

Desilver, D. (2018, August 7). *For most U.S. workers, real wages have barely budged in decades.* Pew Research Center. https://www.pewresearch.org/fact-tank/2018/08/07/for-most-us-workers-real-wages-have-barely-budged-for-decades/

Desilver, D. (2019, August 29). *10 Facts about American Workers.* Pew Research Center. https://www.pewresearch.org/fact-tank/2019/08/29/facts-about-american-workers/

de Zwart, P., van Leeuwen, B., & van Leeuwen-Li, J. (2014). *Real wages since 1820.* In van Zanden, J.L. et al. (Eds.), How Was Life?: Global Well-being since 1820. OECD Publishing. http://dx.doi.org/10.1787/9789264214262-8-en

Dietzel, R. 2014. A comparison of carbon storage potential in corn- and prairie-based agroecosystems. Dissertation. Iowa State University.

Dimico, A., Isopi, A., & Olsson, O. (2017). Origins of the Sicilian Mafia: The Market for Lemons. *The Journal of Economic History*, (77)4.

Dizik, A. (2016). Shopping a sale gives you the same feeling as getting high. BBC. https://www.bbc.com/worklife/article/20161123-shopping-a-sale-gives-you-the-same-feeling-as-getting-high

Dizikes, P. (2018, March 8). *On Twitter, false news travels faster than true stories: Research project finds humans, not bots, are primarily responsible for spread of misleading information.* MIT News Office. https://news.mit.edu/2018/study-twitter-false-news-travels-faster-true-stories-0308

Dohmen, B. (2014, September 4). *Carry Trade: The Multi-Trillion Dollar Hidden Market.* Forbes. https://www.forbes.com/sites/investor/2014/09/04/carry-trade-the-multi-trillion-dollar-hidden-market/#5eab45f84d91

Doolittle, A., Jones, A., Pope, L., Vorontsov, O., & Wray, J. (2013, December 12). *Industry Analysis: Baking Industry.* CSUS. https://www.csus.edu/indiv/h/hattonl/documents/BakeryIndustry.pdf

Dorning, M. (2020, April 17). *Trump Announces $19 Billion for Farmers.* Bloomberg. https://www.bloomberg.com/news/articles/2020-04-17/trump-announces-19-billion-aid-package-for-farmers

Dreibus, T. (2019). *Farmers got Older, Income Fell, Ag Census Shows.* Successful Farming. https://www.agriculture.com/news/business/farmers-got-older-income-fell-ag-census-data-shows

Duffin, E. (2021, January 7). *Distribution of net wealth in the United States from Q1 1990 to Q3 2020.* Statista. https://www.statista.com/statistics/299460/distribution-of-wealth-in-the-united-states/#statisticContainer

Economic Research Service. (2020, May 4). *Ag and Food Sectors and the Economy.* U.S. Department of Agriculture, Economic Research Service. https://www.ers.usda.gov/data-products/ag-and-food-statistics-charting-the-essentials/ag-and-food-sectors-and-the-economy/

Ekstrom, H. (2021). *Global lumber trade flows in the first half of 2021.* Cison, reporting data from Wood Resources International LLC. https://www.prnewswire.com/news-releases/the-record-high-lumber-prices-in-the-us-shifted-global-lumber-trade-flows-in-the-first-half-of-2021-301384506.html

Eldredge, N., & Gould, S.J. (1972). Punctuated equilibria: an alternative to phyletic gradualism. In T.J.M. Schopf, ed., *Models in Paleobiology.* San Francisco: Freeman Cooper. (pp. 82-115). Reprinted in N. Eldredge Time frames. Princeton Univ. Press (1985). (pp. 193-223).

Eliasson, G. (1991). Deregulation, Innovative Entry and Structural Diversity as a Source of Stable and Rapid Economic Growth. *Journal of Evolutionary Economics, 1*, 49–63.

Eliasson, G., Johansson, D., & Taymaz, E. (1995). Chapter VI: Firm Turnover and the Rate of Macro Economic Growth - simulating the macroeconomic effects of Schumpeterian creative destruction. In: Eliasson, G. (Ed.), *The Birth, the Life, and the Death of Firms: the role of Entrepreneurship, Creative Destruction and Conservative Institutions in a Growing and Experimentally Organized Economy*. Ratio (2005).

Emery, F. (1969). *Systems Thinking*. Penguin.

Encyclopaedia Britannica. (2018a, May 24). *Standard of Living*. Encyclopaedia Britannica. https://www.britannica.com/topic/standard-of-living

Encyclopaedia Britannica. (2018b, Oct 12). *Comparative Advantage*. Encyclopaedia Britannica. https://www.britannica.com/topic/comparative-advantage

Energy Information Administration. (2012). *Annual Energy Review*. Energy Information Administration. https://www.eia.gov/totalenergy/data/annual

Energy Information Administration. (2020). *Use of Energy Explained: Energy use for transportation*. Energy Information Administration. https://www.eia.gov/energyexplained/use-of-energy/transportation.php

Energy Information Administration. (2021a). *U.S. energy facts explained*. Energy Information Administration. https://www.eia.gov/energyexplained/us-energy-facts/

Energy Information Administration. (2021b). *Ohio: State Profile and Energy Estimates*. Energy Information Administration. https://www.eia.gov/state/?sid=OH

Enerdata. (2019). *Global Energy Statistical Yearbook 2019*. Enerdata. https://yearbook.enerdata.net/total-energy/world-consumption-statistics.html

Environmental Protection Agency. (2020, December). *Advancing Sustainable Materials Management: Facts and Figures Report*. US Environmental Protection Agency. https://www.epa.gov/facts-and-figures-about-materials-waste-and-recycling/advancing-sustainable-materials-management

European Commission. (2016). *The world's first CO2 neutral brewery*. European Commission. https://ec.europa.eu/energy/news/worlds-first-co2-neutral-brewery_en

FAO, IFAD, UNICEF, WFP and WHO. (2019). *The State of Food Security and Nutrition in the World 2019. Safeguarding against economic slowdowns and downturns*. Food and Agriculture Organization of the United Nations.

Fedarko, K. (2013). *The Emerald Mile: The Epic Story of the Fastest Ride in History Through the Heart of the Grand Canyon*. Simon & Schuster.

Felix, A. (2012). *Industrial Diversity, Growth, and Volatility in the Seven States of the Tenth District*. Federal Reserve Bank of Kansas City. https://www.kansascityfed.org/

Fliedner, G., & Vokurka, R.J. (1997). Agility: Competitive Weapon of the 1990s and Beyond. *Production and Inventory Management Journal, 38*(3), 19–24.

Foley, J. (2013). *It's Time to Rethink America's Corn System*. Scientific American. https://www.scientificamerican.com/article/time-to-rethink-corn

Fort Collins Gov. (2021, August 12). *Green Energy Program*. Fort Collins Utilities public information. https://www.fcgov.com/utilities/residential/renewables/green-energy/

Francis, Pope. (2020, October 2). *Encyclical Letter Fratelli Tutti of the Holy Father Francis on Fraternity and Social Friendship.* Libreria Editrice Vaticana. http://www.vatican.va/content/francesco/en/encyclicals/documents/papa-francesco_20201003_enciclica-fratelli-tutti.html.

Freund, A. (2018, October 29). *Fairtrade Tops $9 Billion in Global Sales for First Time on 8% Growth.* GlobeNewswire. https://www.globenewswire.com/news-release/2018/10/29/1638502/0/en/Fairtrade-Tops-9-Billion-in-Global-Sales-for-First-Time-on-8-Growth.html.

Friedman, M. (1982). *Capitalism and Freedom* (2nd ed.) The University of Chicago Press.

Gage, T.B, & DeWitte, S. (2009). What do we know about the agricultural demographic transition? *Current Anthropology, 50*(5), 649-55. doi:10.1086/605017

Galbraith, J.K. (2009). *The Great Crash 1929* (2nd edition). Houghton Mifflin Harcourt.

Ganzel, B. (2021). *Farming in the 1940s.* Wessels Living History Farm. https://livinghistoryfarm.org/farminginthe40s/money_09.html

Ghosal, A. (2022, April 29). *Heat wave scorches India's wheat crop, snags export plans.* AP News. https://apnews.com/article/russia-ukraine-science-business-india-global-trade-4d32889d982bf0a60396ff4ba817ca16.

Giaimo, C. (2015, October 14). *When the Western World Ran on Guano.* Atlas Obscura. https://www.atlasobscura.com/articles/when-the-western-world-ran-on-guano

Gleason, H.A. (1926). The individualistic concept of the plant association. *Bulletin of the Torrey Botanical Club, 53*, 7-26.

Godfrey, P.C. (2008). What is Economic Self-Reliance. *Journal of Microfinance / ESR Review, 10*(1, Article 3). https://scholarsarchive.byu.edu/cgi/viewcontent.cgi?article=1152&context=esr

Goldstein, J., Electris, C., & Morris, J. (2011). *More Jobs, Less Pollution: Growing the Recycling Economy in the U.S.* NRDC. https://www.nrdc.org/sites/default/files/glo_11111401a_0.pdf

Gough, C.M., Curtis, P.S., Hardiman, B.S., Scheuermann, C.M., & Bond-Lamberty, B. (2016). Disturbance, complexity, and succession of net ecosystem production in North America's temperate deciduous forests. *Ecosphere, 7*(6):e01375. 10.1002/ecs2.1375

Gould, E. (2020). *State of Working America Wages 2019: A story of slow, uneven, and unequal wage growth over the last 40 years.* Economic Policy Institute. https://www.epi.org/publication/swa-wages-2019/

Greenspan, A. (2007). *The Age of Turbulence.* Penguin Press.

Grime, J.P. (1979). *Plant strategies and vegetation processes.* John Wiley and Sons.

Grimes, A., Loomis, S., Jahnige, P., Burnham, M., Onthank, K., Alarcon, R., … Mendelsohn, R. (1994). Valuing the Rain Forest: The Economic Value of Nontimber Forest Products in Ecuador. *Ambio, 23*(7), 405-410.

Guglielmi, G. (2020, August 10). Why Beirut's ammonium nitrate blast was so devastating. *Nature.* https://doi.org/10.1038/d41586-020-02361-x

Gunasekaran, A., Yusuf, Y.Y., Adeleye, E.O., Papadopoulos, T., Kovvuri, D., & Geyi, D.G. (2019). Agile manufacturing: an evolutionary review of practices, *International Journal of Production Research,* (57),15-16, 5154-5174. https://doi.org/10.1080/00207543.2018.1530478

Haltiwanger, J.C., Jarmin, R.S., & Miranda, J. (2010, August). *Who Creates Jobs? Small vs. Large vs. Young.* NBER Working Paper no. 16300.

Hand, M.M., Baldwin, S., DeMeo, E., Reilly, J.M., Mai, T., Arent, D., … Sandor, D. (2012). *Renewable Electricity Futures Study* (4th ed.). National Renewable Energy Laboratory. NREL/ TP-6A20-52409. http://www.nrel.gov/analysis/re_futures/

Harari, Y. (2015). *Sapiens: A brief history of humankind.* Harper Perennial.

Hawken, P., Lovins, A., & Lovins, L.H. (1999). *Natural Capitalism: Creating the Next Industrial Revolution.* Little, Brown and Company.

Hernandez, R. (2018, August). *The fall of employment in the manufacturing sector.* U.S. Department of Labor, Bureau of Labor Statistics. https://www.bls.gov/opub/mlr/2018/ beyond-bls/the-fall-of-employment-in-the-manufacturing-sector.htm

Hershey, R.D. (1976, December 11). United Brands Bribe Called 'Aberration'. *New York Times.* https://www.nytimes.com/1976/12/11/archives/united-brands-bribe-called-aberration-inquiry-finds-the-agreement.html

Hirsch, R.L., Bezdek, R., & Wendling, R. (2005). Peaking of World Oil Production: Impacts, Mitigation, & Risk Management. National Energy Technology Laboratory. https://www.osti.gov/servlets/purl/939271

Hodapp, D., Hillebrand, H., and Striebel, M. (2019, January 14). "Unifying" the Concept of Resource Use Efficiency in Ecology. *Front. Ecol. Evol.* https://doi.org/10.3389/fevo.2018.00233

Hoffmann, A.A., & Hercus, M. J. (2020, March). Environmental Stress as an Evolutionary Force. *BioScience, 50*(3), 217–226. https://doi.org/10.1641/0006-3568(2000)050[0217:ESAA EF]2.3.CO;2

HRSA. (2020, December). *Behavioral Health Workforce Projections.* Health Resources and Services Administration. https://bhw.hrsa.gov/data-research/projecting-health-workforce-supply-demand/behavioral-health

Huston, M.A. (1995). *Biological diversity: the coexistence of species on changing landscapes.* Cambridge university press.

Ingrassia, P., & White, J.B. (1995). *Comeback: The Fall and Rise of the American Automobile Industry.* Touchstone, a trademark of Simon and Schuster Inc.

Institute for Local Self-Reliance. (2003, September). *The Economic Impact of Locally Owned Businesses vs. Chains A Case Study in Midcoast Maine.* Independent We Stand. https://www.independentwestand.org/wp-content/uploads/midcoaststudy-1.pdf

International Energy Agency. (2021). Japan 2021: *Energy Policy Review.* International Energy Agency. https://www.iea.org/reports/japan-2021

International Labour Organization. (1996, October 28). Globalization Changes the Face of Textile, Clothing and Footwear Industries. *ILO, 96*(33).

International Labour Organization. (2014, December 05). Wages in Asia and the Pacific: Dynamic but uneven progress. Global Wage Report 2014/2015, Asia and the Pacific Supplement. *ILO.* https://www.ilo.org/asia/publications/WCMS_325219/lang--en/index.htm

Jackson, K.J. (2019, December 16). *The U.S. Trade Deficit: An Overview.* Congressional Research Services, IF10619. https://crsreports.congress.gov

Jarimi, H., Tapia-Brito, E., & Riffat, S. (2020). A Review on Thermoregulation Techniques in Honey Bees' (Apis Mellifera) Beehive Microclimate and Its Similarities to the Heating and Cooling Management in Buildings. *Future Cities and Environment, 6*(1), 7, 1–8. DOI: https://doi.org/10.5334/fce.81

Johansson, R. (2021, July 29). *America's Farmers: Resilient Throughout the COVID Pandemic.* U.S. Department of Agriculture. https://www.usda.gov/media/blog/2020/09/24/americas-farmers-resilient-throughout-covid-pandemic

Kala, C.P. (2009). Status of an Indigenous Agro-Forestry System in Changing Climate: A Case Study of the Middle Himalayan Region of Tehri Garhwal, India. *Journal of Forest Science, 56*(8), 373–80. https://doi.org/10.17221/113/2009-jfs

Katz, D., & Kahn, R.L. (1969). Common Characteristics of Open Systems. In (ed.) Emery, F.E. *Systems Thinking.* Penguin Books, Ltd.

Kelly-Detwiler, P. (2019, September 26). Solar Technology Will Just Keep Getting Better: Here's Why. *Forbes* https://www.forbes.com/sites/peterdetwiler/2019/09/26/solar-technology-will-just-keep-getting-better-heres-why/?sh=28b56a617c6b

Keynes, J.M. (1930). Economic Possibilities for our Grandchildren. In *Essays in Persuasion.* Harcourt Brace, 358-373.

Keynes, J.M. (2017). The *General Theory of Employment, Interest, and Money.* Wadsworth Editions Limited. Ed. Tom Griffith. (Original work published in 1936).

Kira, T., & Shedei, T. (1967). Primary production and turnover of organic matter in different forest eco-systems of the Western Pacific. *Japanese Journal of Ecology, 17*, 70–87. DOI:10.18960/SEITAI.17.2_70

Kroeber, Theodora (1961). *Ishi in Two Worlds.* University of California Press.

Korner, C. (2003). *Alpine Plant Life: Functional Plant Ecology of High Mountain Ecosystems* (2nd ed.). Springer.

KSAL. (2019, April 25). *Salina ADM Flour Mill to Close.* KSAL. https://www.ksal.com/salina-adm-flour-mill-to-close/

Kurz, C., Li, G., & Vine, D.J. (2018). *Are Millennials Different?* Finance and Economics Discussion Series 2018-080. Washington: Board of Governors of the Federal Reserve System. https://doi.org/10.17016/FEDS.2018.080

LaCanne, C.E., & Lundgren, J.G. (2018). Regenerative agriculture: merging farming and natural resource conservation. *PeerJ.* 6:e4428; DOI 10.7717/peerj.4428

Lal, R. (2004). Soil carbon sequestration impact on global climate change and food security. *Science, 304*, 1623-1627.

Lappé, F.M., Collins, J., & Rosset, P. (1998). *World Hunger: Twelve Myths.* Grove Press.

Leach, A.J. (1909). *A History of Antelope County Nebraska: From its first settlement in 1868 to the close of the year 1883.* The Lakeside Press. R.R. Donnelley & Sons Company.

Livingstone, G. (2009). *America's Backyard: The United States and Latin America from the Monroe Doctrine to the War on Terror.* Zed Books.

Loranger, J., Violle, C. Shipley, B., Lavorel… & Garnier, E. (2016). Recasting the dynamic equilibrium model through a functional lens: the interplay of trait-based community assembly and climate. *Journal of Ecology, 104*, 781-791. doi: 10.1111/1365-2745.12536

Louie, D. (2020, October 9). *Damage from California's wildfires estimated at $10 billion, experts say.* ABC7news. https://abc7news.com/california-wildfires-cost-of-cal-fire-stanford-wildfire-research/6897462/

Lovett, G.M., Cole, J.J., & Pace, M.L. (2006). Is Net Ecosystem Production Equal to Ecosystem Carbon Accumulation? *Ecosystems, 9*, 152–155 DOI: 10.1007/s10021-005-0036-3.

Lotka, A.J. (1922a). Contributions to the energetics of evolution. *Proc. Natl. Acad. Sci. U.S.A.* 8 (6), 147–151.

Lotka, A.J. (1922b). Natural selection as a physical principle. *Proc. Natl. Acad. Sci. U.S.A., 8*(6), 151–154.

Lovins, A. (2014). *Reinventing Fire: Physics + Markets = Energy Solutions*. Rocky Mountain Institute. www.rmi.org.

Macrotrends. (2020a). *China Trade to GDP Ratio 1960-2020*. Macrotrends. https://www.macrotrends.net/countries/CHN/china/trade-gdp-ratio

Macrotrends. (2020b). *U.S. Per Capita GDP 1960-2021*. Macrotrends. https://www.macrotrends.net/countries/USA/united-states/gdp-per-capita

Macrotrends. (2021). *U.S. Net Migration Rate 1950-2021*. Macrotrends. https://www.macrotrends.net/countries/USA/united-states/net-migration

Maktabifard, M., Zaborowska, E., & Makinia, J. (2020). Energy neutrality versus carbon footprint minimization in municipal wastewater treatment plants. *Bioresource Technology*, 300. http://www.sciencedirect.com/science/article/pii/S0960852419318760

Maltais, K., & Wallace, J. (2020, March 30). Wheat and Rice Prices Surge in Coronavirus Lockdown. *The Wall Street Journal*. https://www.wsj.com/articles/wheat-and-rice-prices-surgein-coronavirus-lockdown-11585598044

Margolin, M. (1978). *The Ohlone Way: Indian life in the San Francisco-Monterey Bay Area*. Heyday Books. Berkeley, CA.

Marshall, A.M. (2011). *Industry and Trade: Two Volumes in One*. Cosimo Classics. (Original work published in 1919).

Marx, K. (2015). *Das Kapital, Volume I*. Progress Publishers. (Original work published in 1887 in English, 1867 in German).

McDonough, W., & Braungart, M. (2002). *Cradle to Cradle: Remaking the Way We Make Things*. North Point Press.

McMahon, R.J. (1987). Food as a Diplomatic Weapon: The India Wheat Loan of 1951. *Pacific Historical Review*. 56(3), 349-377. University of California Press. https://www.jstor.org/stable/3638663

McPhillips, D. (2018, October 10). U.S. Among Most Depressed Countries in the World. *US News*. https://www.usnews.com/news/best-countries/articles/2016-09-14/the-10-most-depressed-countries

Meadows, D.H, Meadows, D. L. Randers, J., & Behrens III, W.W. (1972). *The Limits to Growth*. Potomac Associates.

Medina, L., Sabo, S., & Vespa, J. (2020). *Living Longer: Historical and Projected Life Expectancy in the United States, 1960 to 2060*. US Department of Commerce, US Census Bureau. https://www.census.gov/content/dam/Census/library/publications/2020/demo/p25-1145.pdf

Microsoft Corp. (2013, August). *Reducing the Incidence and Cost of Work-related Musculoskeletal Disorders with Ergonomic Input Devices*. Microsoft Corp. https://webobjects.cdw.com/webobjects/media/pdf/CDWCA/Ergo_Whitepaper_June-2017.pdf.

Midolo, G., Alkemade, R., Schipper, A.M., Benítez—López, A., Perring, M.P., & De Vries, W. (2019). Impacts of nitrogen addition on plant species richness and abundance: A global meta—analysis. *Global Ecol Biogeogr, (28)*3, 398–413. https://doi.org/10.1111/geb.12856

Mokyr, J. (2020, February 4). *Great Famine*. Encyclopedia Britannica, Inc. https://www.britannica.com/event/Great-Famine-Irish-history

Montgomery, D. (2012). *Dirt: The Erosion of Civilizations*. University of California Press.

Mulder-Sibanda, M., Sibanda-Mulder, F.S., d'Alois, L., & Verna, D. (2002). Malnutrition in food surplus areas: Experience from nutritional surveillance for decentralized planning in Haiti. *Food and Nutrition Bulletin*, 23(3), 253-61.

Murphy, K.M., Reeves, P.G., & Jones, S.S. (2008). Relationship between yield and mineral nutrient concentrations is historical and modern spring wheat cultivars. *Euphytica*, (163) 381-390.

Murray, J. (2020, March 30). *What Products and Services are Subject to Sales Taxes?* The Balance: Small Business. https://www.thebalancesmb.com/what-products-and-services-are-subject-to-sales-tax-398764

National Academies of Sciences, Engineering, and Medicine. (2018). *Permanent Supportive Housing: Evaluating the Evidence for Improving Health Outcomes Among People Experiencing Chronic Homelessness*. The National Academies Press. https://doi.org/10.17226/25133

National Association of Manufacturers. (2020). *2019 United States Manufacturing Facts*. National Association of Manufacturers. https://www.nam.org/state-manufacturing-data/

National Coalition for the Homeless. (2009, July). *Why are People Homeless?* National Coalition for the Homeless. https://www.nationalhomeless.org/factsheets/why.html

National Interagency Fire Center. (2021, Sept 30). National Fire News. https://www.nifc.gov/fire-information/nfn

New Belgium. (2021). Climate: Our commitments. https://www.newbelgium.com/company/mission/climate/

Nicholls, D.L., J.I. Zerbe, R.D. Bergman, and P.M. Crimp. (2004). Use of Wood Energy for Lumber Drying and Community Heating in Southeast Alaska. US Department of Agriculture. General Technical Report FPL–GTR–152.

North, D. (1692). *Discourses Upon Trade*. (1907). The Johns Hopkins Press.

Novy, D., & Taylor, A.M. (2020). Trade and Uncertainty. *The Review of Economics and Statistics, 102*(4), 749–765. doi: https://doi.org/10.1162/rest_a_00885

NRCS. (2021, May 16). *Snow Drought Conditions*. National Integrated Drought Information System. US Department of Agriculture, Natural Resources Conservation Service. https://www.drought.gov/topics/snow-drought

Nuclear Energy Agency and International Atomic Energy Agency. (2019). Uranium 2018: Resources, Production and Demand. OECD Publishing. https://doi.org/10.1787/uranium-2018-en

Nuclear Energy Agency. (2020). *Uranium 2020: Resources, Production, and Demand*. NEA No. 7551. https://www.oecd-nea.org/jcms/pl_52718/uranium-2020-resources-production-and-demand

Numbeo. (2020). *Quality of Life Index 2020*. Numbeo. https://www.numbeo.com/quality-of-life/rankings_by_country.jsp

Odum, H.T. (1957). Trophic Structure and Productivity of Silver Springs, Florida. *Ecological Monographs*, (27)1, 55-112. https://doi.org/10.2307/1948571

Odum, E. P. (1969). Strategy of ecosystem development. *Science*, 164, 262–270.

Odum, H.T. (1973). Energy in Society: A Special Issue (1973) *Ambio*, 2(6), 220-227. https://www.jstor.org/stable/4312030

Odum, H.T. & Odum, B. (2003). Concepts and methods of ecological engineering. *Ecological Engineering*, 20, 339–361.

OECD/WTO. (2019). Economic Diversification—Lessons from Practice. In, *Aid for Trade at a Glance 2019: Economic Diversification and Empowerment*, pp 135-160. OECD Publishing. https://doi.org/10.1787/18ea27d8-en

OECD. (2021, August 21). *Hours Worked: Average annual hours actually worked*. OECD Employment and Labour Market Statistics (database). https://doi.org/10.1787/data-00303-en

Ontl, T.A., & Schulte, L.A. (2012). Soil Carbon Storage. *Nature Education Knowledge*, 3(10),35.

Organic Trade Association. (2020, May 25). *U.S. organic sales soar to new high of nearly $62 billion in 2020*. Globe Newswire. https://www.globenewswire.com/en/news-release/2021/05/25/2235699/0/en/U-S-organic-sales-soar-to-new-high-of-nearly-62-billion-in-2020.html

Paarlberg, R. (2021a). *The Environmental Upside of Modern Agriculture*. The Wall Street Journal. https://www.wsj.com/articles/the-environmental-upside-of-modern-farming-11612534962

Paarlberg, R. (2021b). *Only eat organic? You're paying too much, and it's not worth it, author says*. The Harvard Gazette. https://news.harvard.edu/gazette/story/2021/02/author-robert-paarlberg-argues-against-buying-organic/

Pauli, G. (1998). *Upsizing*. Sheffield: Greenleaf.

Pemberton, J. (2020). Director. *Capital in the Twenty-First Century*. https://www.amazon.com/gp/video/detail/ amzn1.dv.gti.24b96193-7f80-aa93-9256-a7d6bbb634a8?autoplay=1&ref_=atv_cf_strg_wb

Peters, C.M., Gentry, A.H., & Mendelsohn, R.O. (1989). Valuation of an Amazonian Rainforest. *Nature*, 339, 655-656 (1989).

Pew Research Center. (2008, April 30). *Who Wants to be Rich?* Pew Research Center, Social and Demographic Trends Project. https://www.pewsocialtrends.org/2008/04/30/who-wants-to-be-rich/

Phillips, M. (2001). *The Lochner Court, Myth and Reality: Substantive Due Process from the 1890s to the 1930s*. Praeger Publishers.

Piketty, T. (2014). *Capital in the Twenty-First Century*. Translated by Arthur Goldhammer. Harvard University Press.

Pimentel, D., Harvey, C., Resosudarmo, P., Sinclair, K., Kurz, D., McNair, M. ... Blair, R. (1995, February 24). Environmental and Economic Costs of Soil Erosion and Conservation Benefits. *Science*, 267(5201), 1117-1123.

Pimentel, B. (2006). Soil Erosion: A Food and Environmental Threat. *Environ Dev Sustain*, 8, 119–137. https://doi.org/10.1007/s10668-005-1262-8

Pinedo-Vasquez, M., Zarin, D., & Jipp, P. (1992). Economic returns from forest conversion in the Peruvian Amazon. *Ecological Economics, 6*(2), 163-173.

Pingali, P.L. (2012, July 31). Green Revolution: Impacts, limits, and the path ahead. *PNAS, 109*(31), 12302-12308. https://doi.org/10.1073/pnas.0912953109

Pitman, L. (2018, December). *History of Cooperatives in the United States*. Center for Cooperatives: University of Wisconsin-Madison.

Pizzorno, J. (2018, April 18). *Integrative Medicine*, 17(2): 8-11. https://www.ncbi.nlm.nih.gov/pmc/articles/PMC6396757/

Pletcher, K. (2020, February 5). *Opium Wars*. Encyclopædia Britannica. https://www.britannica.com/topic/Opium-Wars

Plume, K. (2022, March 14). *Plains drought to curb U.S. wheat harvest, adding to global supply worries*. Reuters. https://www.reuters.com/world/us/plains-drought-curb-us-wheat-harvest-adding-global-supply-worries-2022-03-14/

Polanyi, K. (2001). *The Great Transformation: The Political and Economic Origins of our Time* (2nd ed.). Beacon Press.

Pretty, J. (2008, February 12). Agricultural sustainability: Concepts, principles and evidence. *Philos Trans R Soc Lond B Biol Sci*, 363(1491): 447–465.

Prince, M., & Plank, W. (2012, December 6). A Short History of Apple's Manufacturing in the U.S. 6. https://www.wsj.com/articles/BL-DGB-25630

Pryor, S.C., Scavia, D., Downer, C., Gaden, M., Iverson, L, Nordstrom, R. ... Robertson, G.P. (2014). Ch. 18: Midwest. Climate Change Impacts in the United States: The Third National Climate Assessment, In J. M. Melillo, Terese (T.C.) Richmond, G. W. Yohe (Eds.), U.S. Global Change Research Program, 418-440. doi:10.7930/J0J1012N. https://nca2014.globalchange.gov/report/regions/midwest

Puno, R. (2017, April 17). *This world-renowned chef saved his town's economy with cheese and rice*. Upworthy. https://www.upworthy.com/this-world-renowned-chef-saved-his-towns-economy-with-cheese-and-rice

Randall, H.S. (2015). *The Life of Jefferson*, Volume 3. Bibliolife DBA of Bibilio Bazaar II LLC.

Ridley and Associates. (2008). *Are chain stores bad?* Cape Cod Commission Myth or Fact Series. https://archives.lib.state.ma.us/bitstream/handle/2452/202191/ocn827624022.pdf?sequence=1&isAllowed=y

Riedl, B. (2007). *How farm subsidies harm taxpayers, consumers, and farmers too*. The Heritage Foundation. https://www.heritage.org/agriculture/report/how-farm-subsidies-harm-taxpayers-consumers-and-farmers-too

Ritchie, H. & Roser, M. (2020). Renewable Energy. OurWorldInData.org. https://ourworldindata.org/energy

Roach, S. (2018, April 06). *US Needs China More Than China Needs the US*. Industry Week. https://www.industryweek.com/the-economy/article/22025438/us-needs-china-more-than-china-needs-the-us

Rock, K. (2020, May 26). *How Much of Iowa's Wind Power Stays in Iowa*. Sierra Club. https://www.sierraclub.org/iowa/blog/2020/03/how-much-iowa-s-wind-power-stays-iowa

Rodriquez, J.I. (2018). *Measuring Corruption in Mexico*. James A. Baker III Institute for Public Policy of Rice University. https://www.bakerinstitute.org/media/files/files/b190ca73/bi-pub-rodriguez-sanchezcorruption-121118.pdf

Romer, P.M. (1994). The Origins of Endogenous Growth. *The Journal of Economic Perspectives*, *8*(1), 3–22. doi:10.1257/jep.8.1.3. JSTOR 2138148

Roser, M., Ritchie, H., & Ortiz-Ospina, E. (2013). *World Population Growth*. OurWorldInData.org. https://ourworldindata.org/world-population-growth

Ross, J.F. (2018). *The Promise of the Grand Canyon: John Wesley Powell's Perilous Journey and His Vision for the American West*. Penguin Books.

Ross, M., & Edwards, C. (2012). In New Zealand, Farmers Don't Want Subsidies. This article appeared in *Huffington Post* on July 17, 2012. https://www.cato.org/publications/commentary/new-zealand-farmers-dont-want-subsidies

Saksa, P.C., Bales, R.C., Tague, C.L., Battles, J.J., Tobin, B.W., & Conklin, M.H. (2020, April). Fuels treatment and wildfire effects on runoff from Sierra Nevada mixed-conifer forests. *Ecohydrology*, (13)3. https://doi.org/10.1002/eco.2151

Sale, K. (1991). *Dwellers in the Land. A Bioregional Vision*. University of Georgia Press.

Salick, J., Mejia, A., & Anderson, T. (1995). Non-timber forest products integrated with natural forest management, Rio San Juan, Nicaragua. *Ecological Applications*, 5(4), 878-895.

Schauer, N.L. (1962). A history of Oakdale, Nebraska. *Student Work*. 545. https://digitalcommons.unomaha.edu/studentwork/545

Schilling, M. (2020, February 5). MIDWESTERN RAIN EVENTS AND CLIMATE CHANGE: HERE'S THE SPRING 2020 OUTLOOK. Successful Farming. https://www.agriculture.com/weather/future-conditions/midwestern-rain-events-and-climate-change

Schnepf, R. (2004). *Energy Use in Agriculture: Background and Issues*. The Library of Congress, Congressional Research Service, Resources, Science, and Industry Division. Order Code RL32677.

Schwandt, H., Currie, J., Bär, M., Banks, J., Bertoli, P., Bütikofer, A., … Wuppermann, A. (2021, September). *Inequality in Mortality between Black and White Americans by Age, Place, and Cause, and in Comparison to Europe, 1990-2018*. NBER Working Paper No. 29203. https://www.nber.org/system/files/working_papers/w29203/w29203.pdf

Schoenfeld, S. (2020). Americans Are Investing More in China—and They Don't Even Know It. January 14, 2020. *Foreign Policy Magazine*. https://foreignpolicy.com/2020/01/14/americans-investment-china-emerging-markets-united-states-trade-war/

Schumpeter, J. A. (1934). *The Theory of Economic Development: An Inquiry into Profits, Capital, Credit, Interest, and the Business Cycle*. Harvard University Press.

Schumpeter, J. A. (1950). *Capitalism, Socialism, and Democracy* (3rd Ed.). Harper and Brothers.

Scott, R. (2012). *1922 Car Prices*. 1920-30.com. http://www.1920-30.com/automobiles/1922-car-prices.html

Semuels, A. (2019, November 27). "They're Trying to Wipe Us Off the Map." Small American Farmers Are Nearing Extinction. *Time*. https://time.com/5736789/small-american-farmers-debt-crisis-extinction/

Shannon, C.E., & Weaver, W. (1949). The mathematical theory of communication. The University of Illinois Press.

Schwartzberg, L. (2019). *Fantastic Fungi*. Lear, L.D., Schwartzberg, L., Stemp, E.L. https://fantasticfungi.com/

Simard, S.W. (2018). Mycorrhizal Networks Facilitate Tree Communication, Learning, and Memory. In: Baluska et al. (Eds.), *Memory and Learning in Plants, Signaling and Communication in Plants*. Springer International Publishing AG. https://doi.org/10.1007/978-3-319-75596-0_10

Slocum, A. (2017, November 30). Extraction of Uranium from Seawater: Design and Testing of a Symbiotic System. Massachusetts Institute of Technology. Project No: 14-6557. https://www.osti.gov/servlets/purl/1423067/

Smith, A. (2019). *The Wealth of Nations* (5th ed.). Ixia Press. (Original work published in 1776).

Smith, T., Jaesok, S., & Shapiro, B. (2015, April). *General Social Survey Final Report: Trends in Psychological Well-being, 1972 – 2014*. University of Chicago.

Solnit, R. (2010). *Infinite City: a San Francisco Atlas*. University of California Press.

Soons, M.B., Heftinga, M.M., Dorland, E., Lamers, L.P.M., Versteeg, C., & Bobbink, R. (2017). Nitrogen effects on plant species richness in herbaceous communities are more widespread and stronger than those of phosphorus. *Biological Conservation, 212*, 390–397 (2017).

Spash, C.L. (2017). *Routledge Handbook of Ecological Economics: Nature and Society*. Routledge.

Spufford, P. (2002). *Power and Profit: The Merchant in Medieval Europe*. Thames & Hudson, Inc.

Staats, B.R., & Gino, F. (2011, April 26). *Specialization and Variety in Repetitive Tasks: Evidence from a Japanese Bank*. Harvard Business School. Working Paper No. 11-015.

Stiglitz, J. (2002). *Globalization and its Discontents*. W.W. Norton & Company.

Stiglitz, J. (2015a, April 22). *Trickle down economics has failed: Stiglitz*. CNBC. https://www.cnbc.com/2015/04/22/trickle-down-economics-has-failed-stiglitz.html

Stiglitz, J. (2015b). *The Great Divide. Unequal Societies And What We Can Do About Them*. W.W. Norton and Company Inc.

Stiglitz, J. (2017). The Globalization of our Discontent. Project Syndicate. https://www.project-syndicate.org/commentary/globalization-of-discontent-by-joseph-e--stiglitz-2017-12?barrier=accesspaylog.

Sugrue, T. (2004). From Motor City to Motor Metropolis: How the Automobile Industry Reshaped Urban America. Automobile in American Life and Society. University of Michigan – Dearborn. http://www.autolife.umd.umich.edu/

Suzman, J. (2016). *Affluence without Abundance*. Bloomsbury USA.

Taghvaeian, S., Frazier, R.S., Livingston, D., and Fox, G. (2017, March). *The Ogallala Aquifer.* Oklahoma State University Extension. Id: BAE-1531

Taiz, L. (2013). Agriculture, plant physiology, and human population growth: past, present, and future. *Theor.* Exp. Plant Physiol, 25(3), 167-181. https://doi.org/10.1590/S2197-00252013000300001

Tang, J., Luyssaert, S., Richardson, A.D., Kutsch, W., & Janssens, I.A. (2014). Steeper declines in forest photosynthesis than respiration explain age-driven decreases in forest growth. *Proc Natl Acad Sci USA, 111*(24), 8856-8860. doi:10.1073/pnas.1320761111

Templet, P.H. (1999, August). Energy, diversity and development in economic systems; an empirical analysis. *Ecological Economics, 30*(2), 223-233.

Thaler, E.A., Larsena, I.J., & Yua, Q. (2021, February 15). The extent of soil loss across the US Corn Belt. *PNAS*, 118(8). https://www.pnas.org/content/118/8/e1922375118 doi:10.1073/pnas.1922375118/-/DCSupplemental

The Global Economy. (2020). *China: GDP Per Capita*, PPP. The Global Economy. https://www.theglobaleconomy.com/China/GDP_per_capita_PPP/

The World Bank. (2020, May 28). *World Development Indicators. GDP Per Capita-United States.* The World Bank. https://data.worldbank.org/indicator/NY.GDP.PCAP.CD?locations=US

Thibedeau, J. (2019, November 1). *Innovative Technology Captures Energy from Waste Heat.* Power. https://www.powermag.com/innovative-technology-captures-energy-from-waste-heat/

Tilman, G.D. (1985). The resource-ratio hypothesis of plant succession. *American Naturalist, 125*(6), 827-852.

Tilman, G.D., Knops, J., Wedin, D., Reich, P., Ritchie, M., & Siemann, E. (1997). The influence of functional diversity and composition on ecosystem processes. *Science*, 277, 5330, 1300–1302.

Toffler, A. (1970). *Future Shock.* Random House.

Trading Economics. (2020). China GDP Per Capita. Trading Economics. https://tradingeconomics.com/china/gdp-per-capita

Tran, H.P.D. (2011). *Industrial Diversity and Economic Performance: A Spatial Analysis.* Dissertations, Theses, and Student Research from the College of Business. University of Nebraska, Lincoln. https://digitalcommons.unl.edu/businessdiss/19

Trefis Team. (2020, March 13). *Market Crashes Compared: -28% Coronavirus Crash Vs. 4 Historic Market Crashes.* Forbes. https://www.forbes.com/sites/greatspeculations/2020/03/13/market-crashes-compared28-coronavirus-crash-vs-4-historic-market-crashes/?sh=64b3f8ca4ee8

Treu, H., Nordborg, M., Cederberg, C., Heuer, T., Claupein, E., Hoffmann, H., & Berndes, G. (2017, September). Carbon footprints and land use of conventional and organic diets in Germany. *Journal of Cleaner Production*, 161(10), 127-142.

Tuser, C. (2019, December 11). New Belgium Brewery. Water and Wastes Digest. https://www.wwdmag.com/wastewater-treatment/new-belgium-brewery

Twenge, J.M., Cooper, A.B., Joiner, T.E., & Binau, S.G. (2019). Age, Period, and Cohort Trends in Mood Disorder Indicators and Suicide-Related Outcomes in a Nationally Representative Dataset, 2005–2017. *Journal of Abnormal Psychology, 128*(3), 185–199.

Twitty, E. (2003, August). *Silver Wedge: The Sugar Beet Industry in Fort Collins.* Produced by SWCA consultants for the City of Fort Collins, CO, Advance Planning Department. https://www.fcgov.com/historicpreservation/pdf/sugar-beet-industry-doc.pdf

United Nations. (1987). *Our Common Future.* Oxford University Press, 1987.

Urban, D.L., R.V. O'Neill, & Shugart Jr., H.H. (1987, February). A hierarchical perspective can help scientists understand spatial patterns. *BioScience, 37*(2), 119-127.

US Census Bureau. 2018. FT900: U.S. International Trade in Goods and Services. https://www.census.gov/foreign-trade/Press-Release/ft900_index.html

US Census Bureau. (2020, September 8). *Table P-1. CPS Population and Per Capita Money Income, All People: 1967 to 2019.* US Census Bureau. https://www.census.gov/data/tables/time-series/demo/income-poverty/historical-income-households.html

US Congressional Research Service. (2019, June 25). *China's Economic Rise: History, Trends, Challenges, and Implications for the United States.* CRS Reports, RL33534. *https://crsreports. congress.gov/product/pdf/RL/RL33534*

US Congressional Research Service. (2020). *Real Wage Trends, 1979 to 2019.* CRS Reports, R45090. https://crsreports.congress.gov

USDA. (2010). *Food Waste FAQs.* USDA. https://www.usda.gov/foodwaste/faqs

USDA. (2020a, February). *Ag and Food Statistics: Charting the Essentials.* USDA, Economic Research Service. Administrative Publication Number 083. https://www.ers.usda.gov/data-products/ag-and-food-statistics-charting-the-essentials/

USDA. (2020b). *USDA to Provide Additional Direct Assistance to Farmers and Ranchers Impacted by the Coronavirus.* Press Release No. 0378.20. https://www.usda.gov/media/press-releases/2020/09/18/usda-provide-additional-direct-assistance-farmers-and-ranchers

USDA. (2021). *Agriculture in a Changing Climate.* USDA climate hubs. https://www.climatehubs.usda.gov/agriculture-changing-climate

US Department of Energy. (2020). *Hydrogen production: Electrolysis.* USDOE. https://www.energy.gov/eere/fuelcells/hydrogen-production-electrolysis

US Department of Energy. (2020). *2020 U.S. Energy and Employment Report.* US Department of Energy. https://www.energy.gov/sites/prod/files/2017/01/f34/2017%20US%20Energy%20and%20Jobs%20Report_0.pdf

US Economic Development Administration. (2019, March). *Economic Development Districts.* USEDA. https://eda.gov/edd/

USGS. (2020, March 6). *Watershed boundaries for study sites of the U.S.* Geological Survey Surface Water Trends project. https://catalog.data.gov/dataset?tags=basin+boundaries

van der Werf, H.M.G., Knudsen, M.T., & Cederberg, C. (2020). Towards better representation of organic agriculture in life cycle assessment. *Nat Sustain, 3,* 419–425 (2020). https://doi.org/10.1038/s41893-020-0489-6

van Elven, M. (2018, August 16). *People do not wear 50 percent of their wardrobe, says study.* FashionUnited. https://fashionunited.com/news/fashion/people-do-not-wear-at-least-50-percent-of-their-wardrobes-according-to-study/2018081622868

Vosoughi, S., Roy, D., & Aral, S. (2018, March 9). The spread of true and false news online. *Science, 359*(380), 1146-1151.

Weiner, J. (1994). *The Beak of the Finch*. Vintage Books.

Wessel, D. (2007, January 11). Why Economists are Still Grasping to Cure Global Poverty. *The Wall Street Journal*. Section A7. https://www.wsj.com/articles/SB116845440351672808

Wilson, E.O. (1992). *The Diversity of Life*. W W Norton & Co Inc.

Wisconsin Historical Society. (2020). Paper Industry in Wisconsin. Wisconsin Historical Society. https://www.wisconsinhistory.org/Records/Article/CS2055

WEDC. (2019, August 5). *An Assessment of the Economic Contribution of Pulp, Paper and Converting to the State of Wisconsin*. Prepared for the Wisconsin Economic Development Corporation by the Wisconsin Institute for Sustainable Technology, University of Wisconsin.

Woodruff, J. (2019, March 19). *Bakery Industry Analysis*. Chron.com (the newspaper website of the Houston Chronical). https://smallbusiness.chron.com/bakery-industry-analysis-64831.html

Woolf, S., & Schoomaker, H. (2019). Life Expectancy and Mortality Rates in the United States, 1959-2017. *JAMA, 322*(20), 1996–2016. doi:10.1001/jama.2019.16932

World Bank. (2019). *GDP per unit of energy use (constant 2011 PPP $ per kg of oil equivalent)*. World Bank. https://data.worldbank.org/indicator/eg.gdp.puse.ko.pp.kd

World Population Review. (2021). *Healthiest Countries 2021*. World Population Review. https://worldpopulationreview.com/country-rankings/healthiest-countries

Yang, D.T., Chen, V.W., & Monarch, R. (2010). Rising Wages: Has China lost its global labor advantage? *Pacific Economic Review*, 15(4), 482–504.

Yarrow, K. (2014). *Decoding the New Consumer Mind: How and Why We Shop and Buy*. San Francisco, CA: Jossey-Bass, A Wiley Brand.

Yglesias, M. (2020). *One Billion Americans: The Case for Thinking Bigger*. Portfolio/Penguin.

Zero Energy Project. (2020). *Leading the Way: Cities on the Path to Zero*. Zero Energy Project https://zeroenergyproject.org/advocate/cities-on-a-path-to-zero/

Zuppinger-Dingley, D., Schmid, B., Petermann, J.S., Yadav, V., De Deyn, G.B., & Flynn, D.F.B. (2014). Selection for niche differentiation in plant communities increases biodiversity effects. *Nature, 15*, 108-111 (2014). doi: 10.1038/nature13869